lonely planet

HAWAIʻI

Meghan Miner Murray,
Jackie Oshiro, Sarah Sekula

SEAN STEININGER/SHUTTERSTOCK

Meet Our Writers

Meghan Miner Murray

@meghanminermurray

Meghan's favorite experience is exploring the night ocean (p214). 'It's more calming than creepy, and fills with a different cast of characters.' She moved from the DC area in 2014, and is an avid ocean swimmer, freediver and certified divemaster. Meghan wrote the Kaua'i and Hawai'i Island (The Big Island) chapters.

Jackie Oshiro

𝕏 @jackie_grows

Jackie was born and raised in Honolulu. She loves visiting the new art exhibits and galleries in Chinatown (p74) and will jump at any chance to drive visiting friends around the Ka Iwi Coast (p98). Jackie wrote the O'ahu, planning and Practicalities chapters.

Sarah Sekula

@sarahsomewhere

Sekula loves nothing more than being underwater (p186), especially during whale season when you can clearly hear the behemoths serenading each other. 'They are miles away, but as I'm snorkeling it's so loud, it feels like they are right there with me.' Sarah wrote the Maui, Lāna'i and Moloka'i chapters.

Contributing Writers

Amy C Balfour

@amycbalfour

Amy writes about travel and outdoor adventure across the US. She has contributed to more than 75 guidebooks for Lonely Planet. Amy updated the Maui, Lāna'i and Moloka'i chapters.

Sarah Etinas

sarahetinas.com

Sarah is an O'ahu local, travel writer and author of the Hawai'i travel website, Borders & Bucket Lists. Sarah updated the Kaua'i and O'ahu chapters.

0 30 km
0 15 miles
PACIFIC OCEAN
Nāpali Coast
Hā'ena
Hanalei
Kīlauea
Mt Wai'ale'ale
Kapa'a
Kaua'i 112
Līhu'e
Waimea
Hanapēpē
Kōloa
Po'ipū
Kaulakahi Channel
Ki'i Landing
Pu'uwai
Pani'au
Ni'ihau
Ka'ie'ie Waho Channel
0 30 km
0 15 miles
Kaua'i Channel
Waimea Bay
Waimea
Kahuku
Lā'ie
Windward Coast
PACIFIC OCEAN
Hale'iwa
Waialua
O'ahu
'Ewa Forest Reserve
Mt Ka'ala
Kualoa
Mākaha
Wahiawā
Kāne'ohe Bay
Wai'anae
Beyond Honolulu, O'ahu 80
North Shore 1hr
Wai'anae (Leeward) Coast
Pearl City
Kailua
Līhu'e, Kaua'i 40min
Pearl Harbor
Waimānalo Bay
Waimānalo
Kapolei
Honolulu, O'ahu 44
Waikīkī
Kona, Hawai'i Island 45min
Ka'iwi Channel
0 30 km
0 15 miles
Kalaupapa National Historical Park
Ho'olehua
Kalawao
Maunaloa
Kaunakakai
Kamakou
Waialua
Moloka'i 176
Kamalō
Puko'o
Pailolo Channel
Kapalua
Kahakuloa
Kahului Bay
Kā'anapali
Lahaina
Wailuku
Kahului
Lāna'i 172
Ke'anae
Lāna'i City
Mānele Harbor, Lāna'i 45min
Maui 142
'Au'au Channel
Lāna'ihale
Kihei
Mānele Harbor
Mā'alaea Bay
Kula
Haleakalā National Park
Hāna
Wailea
PACIFIC OCEAN
Pu'u'ula'ula
Mākena
Kaupō
Kealaikahiki Channel
'Alalākeiki Channel
'Alenuihāhā Channel
Kaho'olawe

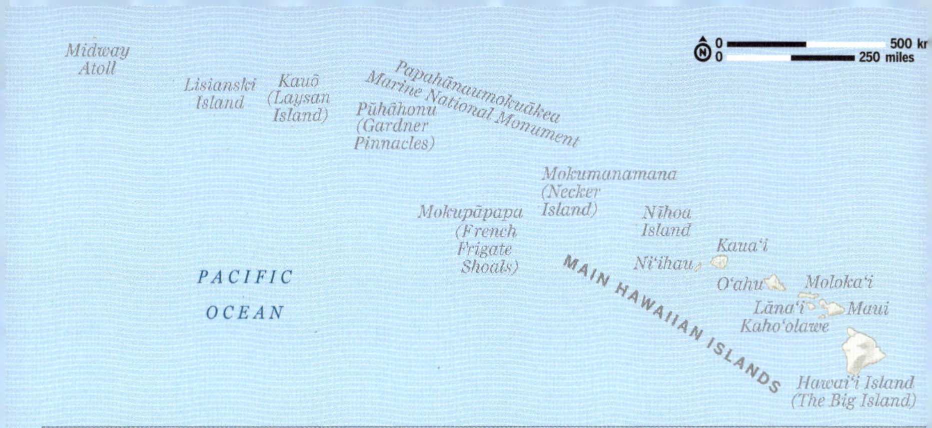
0 500 km
0 250 miles
Midway Atoll
Lisianski Island
Kauō (Laysan Island)
Papahānaumokuākea Marine National Monument
Pūhāhonu (Gardner Pinnacles)
Mokumanamana (Necker Island)
Mokupāpapa (French Frigate Shoals)
Nīhoa Island
PACIFIC OCEAN
MAIN HAWAIIAN ISLANDS
Kaua'i
Ni'ihau
O'ahu
Moloka'i
Lāna'i
Maui
Kaho'olawe
Hawai'i Island (The Big Island)

0 30 km
0 15 miles
Hāwī
Kohala Forest Reserve
Hāmākua Coast
Honoka'a
Kawaihae
Waimea (Kamuela)
Kohala Coast
Waikōloa Village
Mauna Kea Forest Reserve
Hawai'i Island (The Big Island)
Maunakea
Hilo Bay
Hilo Forest Reserve
Hilo
Hawai'i Volcanoes National Park 45min
Hawai'i Island (The Big Island) 200
Kailua-Kona
Kailua Bay
Keauhou
Kea'au
Mauna Loa Forest Reserve
Mountain View
Kealakekua
Captain Cook
Maunaloa
Pāhoa
Volcano
Puna Forest Reserve
Ho'okena
Hawai'i Volcanoes National Park
Hawai'i Volcanoes National Park
South Kona Coast
Pahala
Miloli'i
Punalu'u
Nā'ālehu
PACIFIC OCEAN

Walk through royal halls and learn about little-known histories. Meander amid vast collections of art. Trek through Earth's most diverse ecologies and search for the planet's rarest animals. Witness the natural world after dark. Roll up your sleeves and give back to the land. Dig into flavors from around the Pacific and delight in the tang of freshly picked tropical fruit. Discover new ways to explore the outdoors. Swim among reefs bursting with life or learn how to surf in the birthplace of the sport.

This is Hawai'i.

TURN THE PAGE AND START PLANNING YOUR NEXT BEST TRIP →

Above Humpback whales, Maui (p158)

Land Acknowledgement

Lonely Planet acknowledges the state of Hawai'i rests on the unceded lands of the Kānaka Maoli (Native Hawaiians). We honor their sovereignty and connection to their lands and waters, as well as their enduring commitment to a sustainable future for Hawai'i. Lonely Planet encourages you to learn more about the history of the Kānaka Maoli, and support their continued efforts to preserve the state's fragile ecosystems for future generations by being a mindful visitor. We also encourage you to consider volunteering and connecting with a local organization during your stay. For more information, see gohawaii.com/malama.

Previous spread Kīlauea, Hawai'i Volcanoes National Park (p206)
YVONNE BAUR/SHUTTERSTOCK

Contents

Best Experiences 6
Calendar 22
Trip Builders 30
7 Things to Know
About Hawai'i 40
Read, Listen,
Watch & Follow................ 42

Honolulu, O'ahu **44**

Hawaiian Foundations 50
Build Your Own Lū'au....... 54
Local Lifestyle 58
Modern Pulse 60
Reimagine Pearl Harbor ... 62
Take a Hike 64
Royal Waikīkī.................... 68
A New Look at Lē'ahi 70
Art in the Heart
of Honolulu 74
Listings 78

Beyond Honolulu, O'ahu **80**

A Day on
Kāne'ohe Bay 84
Nature by Night................ 86
The Wai'anae Coast 90
Sunrise & Breakfast......... 92
Plantation Legacy 94
Scenic Ko'olau 98
North Shore All Year........102
Aloha 'Āina 106
Listings 110

Kaua'i **112**

Into Nāpali 118
Adventure Buddy 120
Sugar Chutes
& Shacks.........................122
West Side Wander 124
Jurassic Jaunts 130
Bird's the Word...............132
Taro Trail 136
Listings 140

Maui **142**

Upcountry Magic 148
Peaks & Panoramas........152
Farm Fresh......................154
Paddle Out......................156
Whale Central.................158
Stellar Sights..................162
Heavenly Hāna 164
Small Town, Big Art.........166
Listings 170

A Weekend on Lāna'i **172**

Moloka'i **176**

Hike in Hālawa................182
Farm Frolics....................184
Fringe Benefits 186
No Coastal Crowds 188
Pedal Power................... 190
Listings 198

Hawai'i Island (The Big Island) **200**

Lava Lands 206
Brew Thru 212
Kona's Dark Sea 214
Hawaiian Heritage...........216
Surf's Turf 218
Hāmākua Coasting 220
Mālama Hawai'i.............. 222
Local Treats 224
Listings 234

Canoe inside a *hale* (traditional house; p231)

Practicalities 236

Arriving 238
Getting Around 240
Safe Travel 242
Money 243
Responsible Travel 244
Accommodations 246
Essentials 248

ESSAYS

The True Meaning of Aloha 56
Place Names 72
Ahupua'a 100
Nearly to Ni'ihau 128
Wild Chickens 134
Monster Waves 168
Catch of the Day 196
Inland Ocean Tastes & Tours 228
Conflict on the Mauna 232

VISUAL GUIDES

Hawaiian Monarchs 66
Familiar Flora 88
Local Comfort Foods 96
Common Reef Fish 138
Made on Maui 150
Maui Gone Wild 160
Shell Yeah! 194
Hawai'i Island's Varied Terrain 210
(Some) Features of a Hawaiian Landscape 230

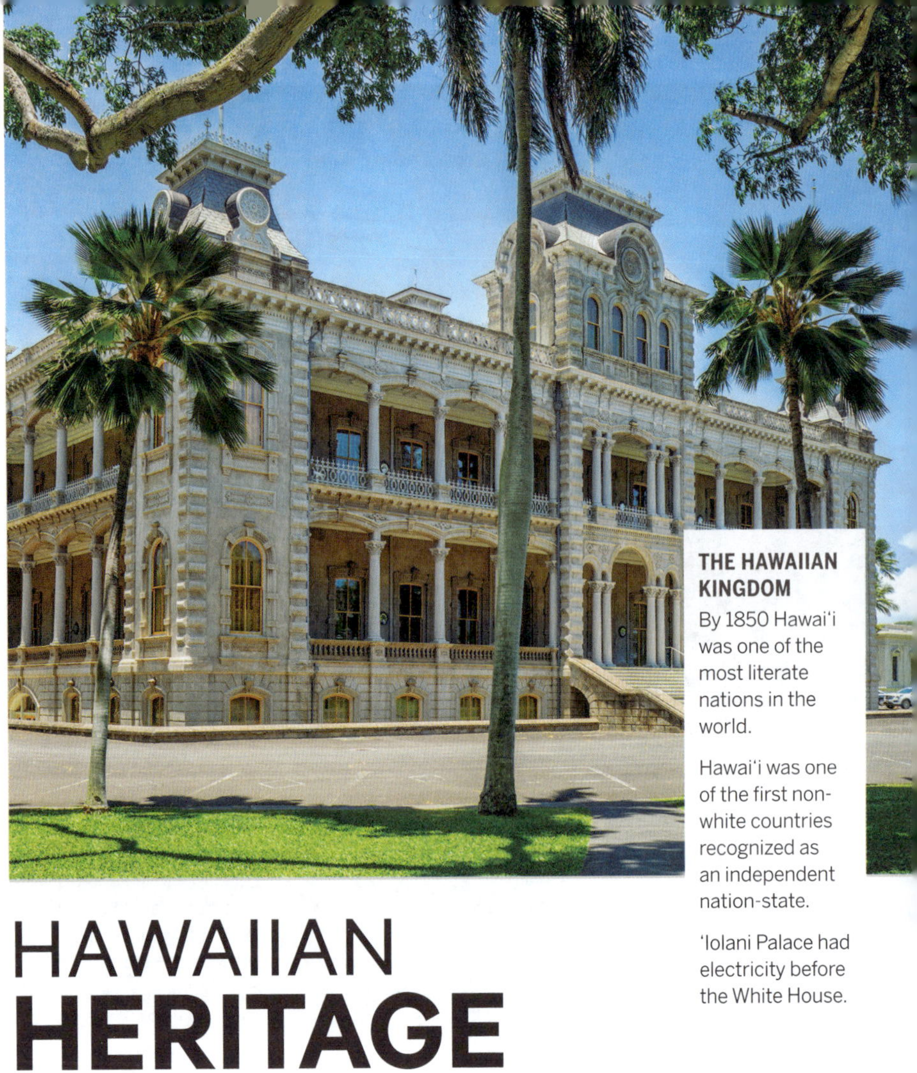

THE HAWAIIAN KINGDOM

By 1850 Hawai'i was one of the most literate nations in the world.

Hawai'i was one of the first non-white countries recognized as an independent nation-state.

'Iolani Palace had electricity before the White House.

HAWAIIAN **HERITAGE**

Long before Western contact, the Hawaiians built a thriving, complex civilization. And long before Hawai'i became a US state, it was a sovereign nation. This history is the backdrop for every part of modern Hawai'i. Find deeper meaning in your time in the islands by getting to know Hawai'i as it was for a thousand years – and Kanaka Maoli (Native Hawaiian) culture as it is today.

Left 'Iolani Palace (p76) **Right** Protest at 'Iolani Palace **Below** Hula dancers

→ THE SOVEREIGNTY MOVEMENT

Hawai'i was annexed in 1898 by the US without a treaty and many continue to oppose the illegal military and political occupation of the islands.

CRAIG ELLENWOOD/ALAMY

'ŌLELO HAWAI'I

'Ōlelo Hawai'i, the Hawaiian language, almost died out after it was outlawed in schools following the overthrow in 1893. Today, the number of speakers is rapidly increasing.

RIGHT: EMILY RIDDELL/ALAMY, LEFT: RICHIE CHAN/SHUTTERSTOCK

↑ HAWAIIAN RENAISSANCE

The 1970s saw a resurgence in Hawaiian cultural practices and political activism that is now called the Hawaiian Renaissance.

Best Hawaiian Heritage Experiences

- **Peruse the halls of Bishop Museum for a primer on Hawaiian history.** (p51)
- **Take a class in lei making, hula or traditional handcrafts.** (p55)
- **Pay respects at ancient sites and sacred ruins along the Kona Coast.** (p216)
- **Walk in the footsteps of royals amid the bustle of Waikīkī.** (p69)

Kalalau Trail

Challenging trail, beautiful beach

A steep, grueling, dangerous trek down 11 miles of switchbacks, this multiday adventure along the Nāpali Coast is incredibly rewarding and leads to one of the most beautiful beaches in the world.

25min from Hanalei

▶ p118

Waimea Canyon

Waterfalls & panoramas

A moderate hike to the top of the breathtaking 800ft Waipo'o Falls in Kōke'e, this 3.4-mile trail snakes along the edge of Waimea Canyon offering varied views of the waterfalls.

1hr from Līhu'e

▶ p127

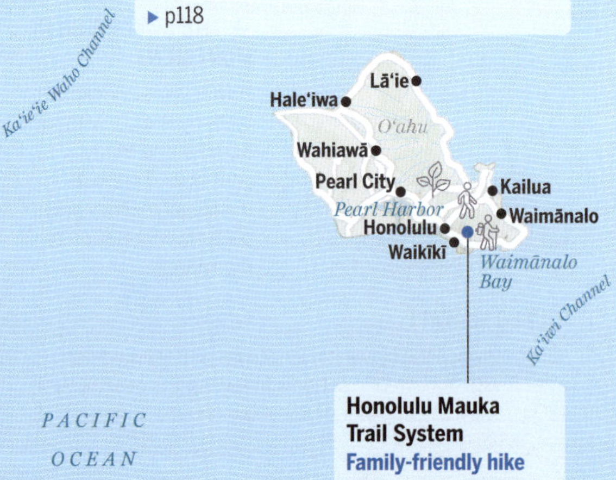

Honolulu Mauka Trail System

Family-friendly hike

Hike through lush rain-forest a short drive from Waikīkī. You can mix and match the crisscrossing Honolulu Mauka Trail System to customize your hiking experience.

25min from Waikīkī

▶ p64

IMMERSED IN **NATURE**

The small, isolated islands of Hawai'i have 10 of the world's 14 climate zones, making it one of the most ecologically diverse places on Earth. Trek through shaded rainforest, across barren lava fields or along the knife's edge of steep cliffs. But always stay on the trail – Hawai'i's rare ecologies are also very delicate and ask us to tread lightly.

FROM LEFT: NOBLIGE/GETTY IMAGES, LILLIAN K/SHUTTERSTOCK, PHOTO RESOURCE HAWAII/ALAMY, BOB POOL/SHUTTERSTOCK

Hālawa Valley

Private guided trek

Join a local guide on a lush – often muddy! – tropical hike that ribbons past numerous cultural sites before a dramatic finale: the 250ft Moa'ula and Hipuapua Falls, which cascade down the back of the lush Hālawa Valley. Take a swim in the gorgeous pools.

1½hr from Kaunakakai

▶ p182

Keonehe'ehe'e Trail

Into a volcanic crater

Commonly called 'Sliding Sands,' this tough, 11-mile trail takes you down into the crater of Haleakalā. Trek through dynamic alpine landscapes, at the edge of sheer cliffs and above the clouds. Not for the faint of heart or the ill-prepared.

1hr from Kahului

▶ p152

Hawai'i Volcanoes National Park

Across new earth

Walk some of the newest land on Earth and witness the creative power of lava. HVNP's extensive network of trails are suitable for every level of hiker, and some are wheelchair accessible.

45min from Hilo

▶ p206

MĀLAMA ʻĀINA FACTS

In 2021 Hawaiʻi banned sunscreens containing chemicals harmful to reefs.

Strict fishing regulations protect nearshore fish populations.

Some attractions limit access to mitigate over-stressing the environment.

MĀLAMA ʻĀINA

Mālama ʻāina means 'to care for the land' and is a core part of local culture. After all, when you live on a small island chain 2000 miles from the nearest landmass, you tend to realize it's important to care for the land you have. Take some time to show these beautiful islands that you care by getting your hands dirty and giving back while learning about Hawaiʻi's unique ecologies.

RAPHAEL RIVEST/SHUTTERSTOCK

Left *Mālama 'āina* sign **Right** Hiking, Kalalau Trail (p118), Nāpali Coast **Below** Map of *ahupua'a*

→ EASY WAYS TO MĀLAMA

Mālama 'āina in all that you do by staying on the trail, obeying posted signs and leaving rocks, sand and shells in place.

'ĀINA IS MORE THAN 'LAND'

Translating to 'that which feeds,' the word *'āina* encapsulates reverence for the life-giving nature of the Earth.

RIGHT: JUAN WILSON/ISLANDBREATH.ORG2016. LEFT: WILLIAM HAGER/SHUTTERSTOCK

↑ AHUPUA'A

Land divisions called *ahupua'a* spanned from ridgetop to the shore and were key to traditional land management.

▶ Learn more about *ahupua'a* on p100.

Best Mālama 'Āina Experiences

▶ **Learn about sustainable traditional land practices at Paepae o He'eia.** (p107)

▶ **Plant saplings to help conserve rare native forest at the Keau'ohana Forest Reserve.** (p223)

▶ **Help restore the degraded wetlands of Pu'uloa (Pearl Harbor).** (p63)

↘ STAR MAP
In 1976 the voyaging canoe *Hōkūle'a* sailed 2500 miles from Maui to Tahiti employing only traditional Polynesian navigating techniques grounded in using the night sky as a map.

NIGHTTIME **WONDERS**

When the sun goes down, a world of opportunity awakens. Experience a side of nature you don't often encounter in urban life. See the stars like you've never seen them before, swim with gentle giants, or fall asleep in the forest wrapped in the comfort of Hawai'i's warm island air.

Best Nighttime Experiences

- **Learn to read the stars like the Polynesian navigators at the summit of Haleakalā.** (p162)
- **Snorkel with massive mantas or scuba in a cloud of bioluminescence off the Kona Coast.** (p214)
- **Pitch a tent and fall asleep to the gentle sound of waves lapping at the shore on O'ahu's eastern coast.** (p86)

KELSIE DIPERNA/SHUTTERSTOCK

PLANTATION **ROOTS**

Hawai'i's diverse modern culture is a by-product of the days when American sugar plantations dominated the local economy, importing laborers from around the Pacific to work the fields. The influence of this era continues to be seen today in architectural styles, food culture and fashion designs, as well as the islands' multicultural residents.

TOP: DAVID FLEETHAM/ALAMY, BOTTOM: BRANDON COLBERT PHOTOGRAPHY/GETTY IMAGES

→ SHAKAS UP

Supposedly, the iconic *shaka* was created by rascal kids teasing a plantation worker who had lost his three middle fingers in a machinery accident.

Plantation History

- **Go tubing down irrigation ditches at old plantations in Līhu'e.** (p123)
- **Stay in an updated plantation-era bungalow on the secluded Waimea Coast on Kaua'i.** (p123)
- **Walk through a replica plantation village in Central O'ahu.** (p94)
- **Talk story with historians at the Lāna'i Culture & Heritage Center.** (p174)

FOODIE CULTURE

Hawai'i's eclectic mix of peoples has birthed a unique food culture. Learn more about the dishes you won't find anywhere else (p96).

Top Lāna'i Culture & Heritage Center **Bottom** *Shaka*

ENDANGERED SPECIES STATS

More than 30% of the US's listed endangered species are from Hawai'i.

Eight birds and one plant were formally declared extinct in Hawai'i in 2023.

One of the largest threats to native birds is the mosquito, which was only introduced in 1826.

ENDANGERED WILDLIFE

Hawai'i's isolation and geography make it one of the most biodiverse places on Earth, as well as the 'extinction capital of the world.' While habitat loss and introduced predators have besieged native species, it's still possible to witness wildlife you won't see elsewhere – just do so from a distance.

SHANE MYERS PHOTOGRAPHY/SHUTTERSTOCK

Left Nēnē geese **Right** Green sea turtle **Below** Trail sign, Haleakalā National Park (p152)

→ SEA TURTLES

Despite their endangered status, *honu* (Hawaiian green sea turtles) are often encountered along shores across the archipelago.

PROTECTION LAWS

Both state and federal laws prohibit touching any endangered animal, and there are guidelines for how close you can get.

▶ For details, see p41.

RIGHT: VINCENT K HO/SHUTTERSTOCK, LEFT: STEVEOEHLENSCHLAGER/GETTY IMAGES

↑ NOT JUST ANIMALS

Many of Hawai'i's native plants are also threatened with extinction. Over 200 species have fewer than 50 individuals left in the wild.

Best Endangered Wildlife Experiences

- **Search for some of Earth's rarest birds in the native forests of Kalalau Valley.** (p133)
- **Spot humpback whales as they migrate from Alaska to breed in the waters off Maui.** (p158)
- **Witness the mating dance of the Laysan albatross *(mōlī)* at Kīlauea.** (p133)
- **Join wildlife ecologists to track turtles, dolphins and whales off the Wai'anae Coast.** (p91)

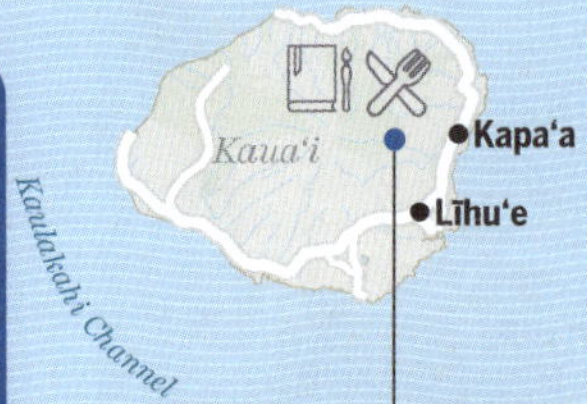

Lydgate Farms

Cheers to chocolate

Take an engaging three-hour tour of this award-winning chocolate farm. Along the way, sample tropical fruits, including sugarloaf pineapples, papayas and the cacao fruit itself (pictured), before finishing off the tour with a 10-course chocolate tasting that'll make you feel like a cacao sommelier.

15min from Kapa'a

▶ p140

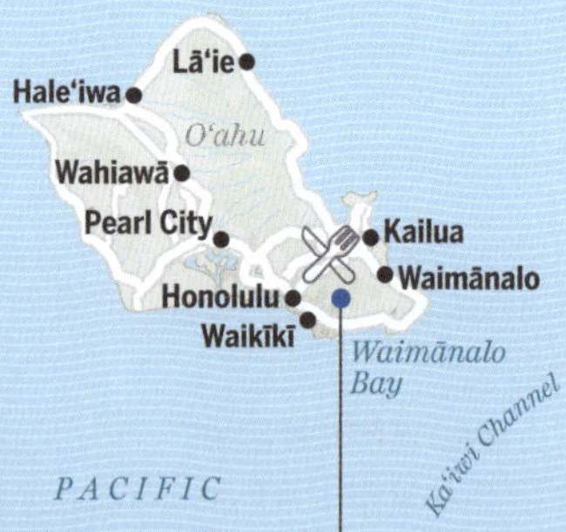

Mud Hen Water

Farm to table

Combining locally grown ingredients with flavors from around the Pacific, Hawai'i Regional Cuisine (Hawai'i's homegrown cuisine, a mix of different cultural influences) puts an upscale spin on local home cooking. Visit Mud Hen Water for some of the best.

10min from Waikīkī

▶ p59

FARM FRESH

Hawai'i's abundant rain and rich volcanic soil make for some of the best growing conditions in the world. From the expected crops like coffee and tropical fruits to surprising finds like cacao and lavender, explore the state's bountiful farms for exceptionally fresh food and unique souvenirs.

0 100 km
0 50 miles

FROM LEFT: KINGSAKAI/SHUTTERSTOCK, MUD HEN WATER, BLAZETUZ01/SHUTTERSTOCK, KANU HAWA/FLICKR/CC BY 2.0

Purdy's Macadamia Nut Farm

90-year-old orchard

Sample fresh macadamia nuts under a mac nut tree or take some home to toast them. The first trees in the orchard were planted in the 1920s.

15min from Kaunakakai

▶ p185

Upcountry Farmers Market

Locally grown delights

Find fresh produce, handmade crafts, delicious dishes and cut flowers at Maui's largest farmers market. Visit in summer for fresh seasonal fruits.

10min from Makawao

▶ p155

Ali'i Kula Lavender

Fragrant fields

Walk among fragrant rows of over 55,000 lavender plants or have a garden-fresh picnic on the lānai – complete with a homemade lavender-infused dessert.

30min from Pā'ia

▶ p149

Kona Coffee Cultural Festival

Coffee extravaganza

Kona has some of the best coffee-growing conditions in the world. Celebrate in November at Hawai'i's oldest food festival.

▶ p212

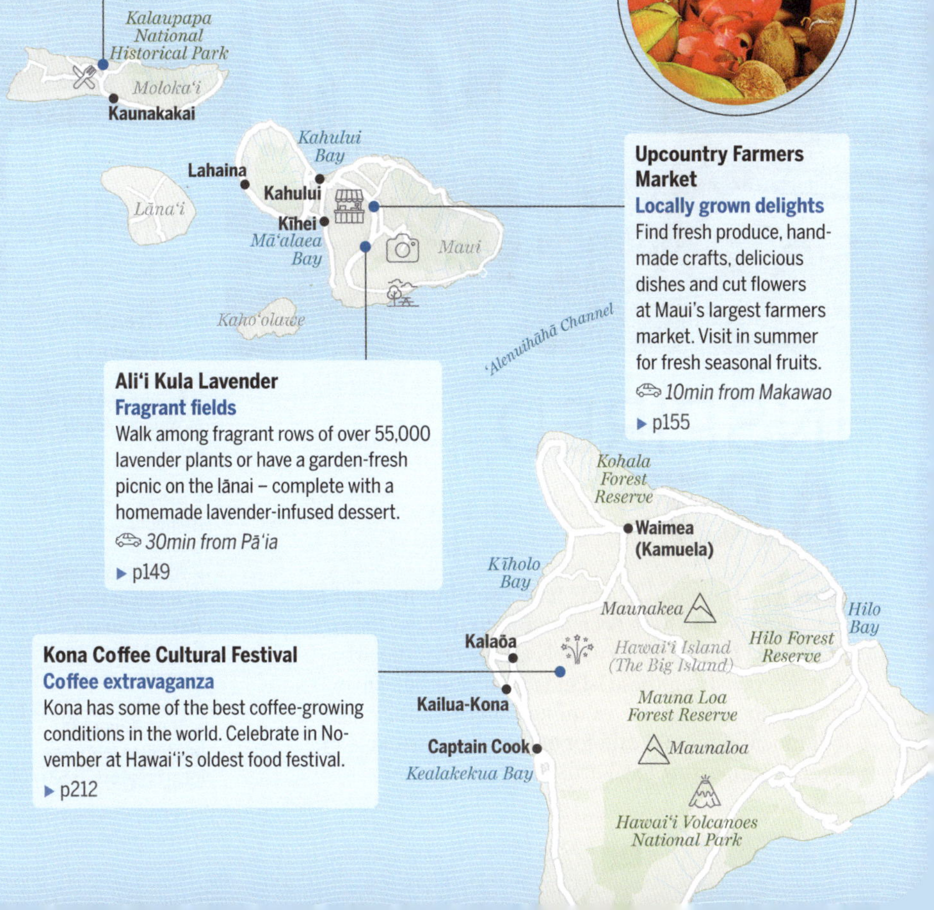

↘ SURF MURAL A 2021 Honolulu mural pays homage to the Hawaiian sport of surfing and two Native Hawaiians who brought it to the world stage – legendary waterman Duke Kahanamoku and Carissa Moore, surfing's first Olympic gold medalist.

REDEFINED MEDIA

INSPIRED ART

The Hawaiian Islands have been inspiring art for as long as people have been around to witness them. From song and dance to pastels and poetry, the art that emerges from these islands is substantial. Dive into the local art scene: examine gallery exhibits, ogle monumental murals, and forgo the plastic trinkets in favor of supporting local artisans.

Creative Hawai'i

- **Admire the murals of Wailuku, Maui.** (p166)
- **Browse galleries in Honolulu.** (p74)
- **Watch muralists in action at Hawai'i Walls or explore Kaka'ako's evolving art walls.** (p61)
- **Shop Kaimukī's boutiques featuring local creators.** (p58)

OFF THE BEATEN PATH

Hawai'i's unique settings ask to be admired unconventionally. Look for opportunities to engage with the islands in ways you might not normally sightsee – by air, horseback, bicycle or boat. With Hawai'i's dense forests, steep cliffs and jagged lava fields, roads can only take you so far – to see the rest you'll have to get creative.

★ STICK TO PUBLIC PATHS

No matter how you choose to get around, always be mindful of posted signs and private property.

Best Sightseeing Adventures

- **Soar over verdant valleys on a helicopter tour of Kaua'i.** (p131)
- **Mountain bike along Moloka'i's long stretches of empty roads.** (p190)
- **Four-wheel it to some of the most remote places on Lāna'i.** (p174)
- **Rev up an ATV and ramble across O'ahu's steep ridges and unique ecologies.** (p105)

← TAKE A TOUR

Guides can provide essential background for a deeper experience than you'd get on your own.

Top View of Kaua'i from helicopter (p131) **Bottom** Off-roading, Lāna'i (p174)

North Shore

Watch the pros

Watch from the shore as pro surfers take to the water to ride winter waves topping 30ft.

1hr from Honolulu

▸ p103

Nāpali Coast

Valley views from below

Rent a kayak and admire the majestic cliffs of Nāpali. Expect to see dolphins, monk seals and sea caves. Sign up for a day tour or reserve a permit to camp on the shore.

1¼hr from Līhuʻe

▸ p119

Waikīkī

Surf Waikīkī

Take a lesson to learn the right etiquette and technique then rent a board and take your pick of the beach's multiple breaks.

20min from Honolulu Airport

▸ p68

PACIFIC OCEAN

OCEAN ACTION

Hawaiʻi's aquatic landscape is just as diverse as its terrestrial sphere. With deep open ocean, barrier reefs, shallow sandbars and some of the most consistently surfable waves in the world, Hawaiian waters are an open canvas for adventure. But respect the ocean and be realistic about your own comfort in the water – the ocean is powerful even on calm days.

FROM LEFT: YI-CHEN CHIANG/SHUTTERSTOCK, THEODORE TRIMMER/SHUTTERSTOCK, LYNN FRIEDMAN/SHUTTERSTOCK, JEFF MILISEN/ALAMY

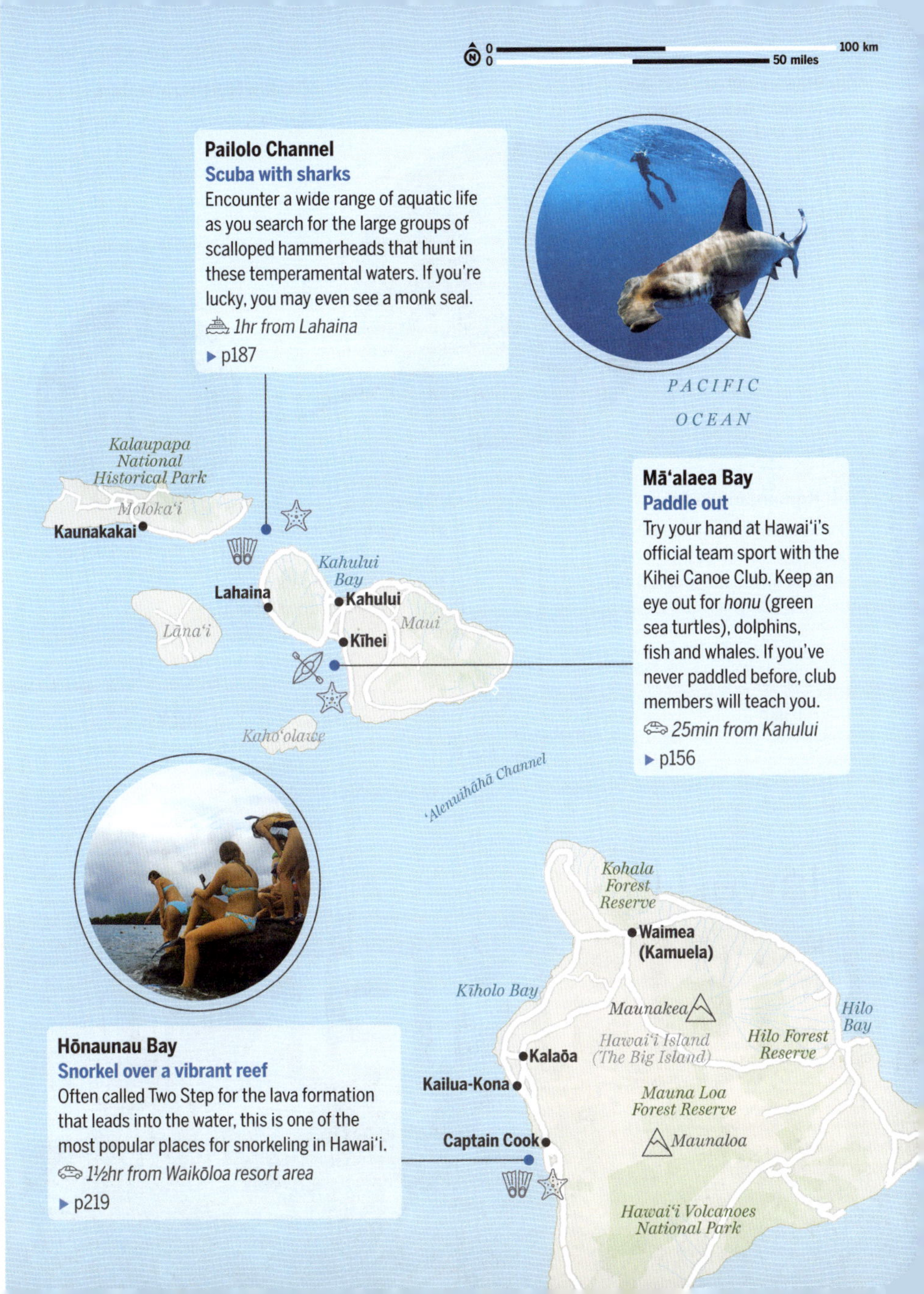

Pailolo Channel

Scuba with sharks

Encounter a wide range of aquatic life as you search for the large groups of scalloped hammerheads that hunt in these temperamental waters. If you're lucky, you may even see a monk seal.

1hr from Lahaina

▸ p187

Mā'alaea Bay

Paddle out

Try your hand at Hawai'i's official team sport with the Kihei Canoe Club. Keep an eye out for *honu* (green sea turtles), dolphins, fish and whales. If you've never paddled before, club members will teach you.

25min from Kahului

▸ p156

Hōnaunau Bay

Snorkel over a vibrant reef

Often called Two Step for the lava formation that leads into the water, this is one of the most popular places for snorkeling in Hawai'i.

1½hr from Waikōloa resort area

▸ p219

Summer is high season, and you'll find that accommodations and rentals tend to be more expensive. View tours and overnight adventures in advance at lonelyplanet.com.

↙ Calm Northern Waters

Serene summer waters along northern coasts make for great snorkeling and kayaking.

North Shore

▶ p102

↓ Kamehameha Day

Hawai'i celebrates Kamehameha Day on June 11 with a huge parade and elaborate festival.

→ Obon

Bon dance festivals are held from mid-July through August at the dozens of Japanese Buddhist temples throughout the state.

JUNE

Average daytime max: 85°F (29°C)
Humid days: 21

JULY

Hawai'i in SUMMER

FROM LEFT: UNIVERSAL IMAGES GROUP NORTH AMERICA LLC/ALAMY, YI-CHEN CHIANG/SHUTTERSTOCK, JASON MCCARTNEY/SHUTTERSTOCK, BOBBUSHPHOTO/GETTY IMAGES, BACKGROUND: GORDON FAHEY/SHUTTERSTOCK

↓ Hurricane Season

Hurricane season runs from July to November. Approaching storms can cause several days of rain, high winds and dirty nearshore waters.

↖ Kōloa Plantation Days

Ten-day festival celebrating Kaua'i's plantation heritage with cultural demonstrations, talks and food.

▸ koloaplantationdays.com

AUGUST

Average daytime max: 86°F (30°C)
Humid days: 26

Average daytime max: 87°F (31°C)
Humid days: 28

Packing Notes

A rash guard for long days in the water and shorts for everywhere else.

September and October can have some of the hottest and most humid days. Keep hydrated and reapply your sunscreen!

↗ **Aloha Festivals**

Celebrate Hawaiian culture with four weeks of festivals showcasing Hawai'i's rich heritage.

▸ alohafestivals.com

↘ **Eo e Emalani Festival**

Queen Emma's 1871 visit is commemorated at Kōke'e State Park with hula, cultural performances and crafts.

Kōke'e State Park

▸ kokee.org

↓ **Moloka'i Hoe**

Every October, the best canoe paddlers in the world gather to race across the 38-mile Ka'iwi Channel between Moloka'i and O'ahu.

▸ molokaihoe.com

SEPTEMBER

Average daytime max: 87°F (31°C)
Humid days: 28

OCTOBER

Hawai'i in AUTUMN

FROM LEFT: YI-CHEN CHIANG/SHUTTERSTOCK, LISA T SNOW/SHUTTERSTOCK, KANU HAWA/FLICKR/CC BY 2.0, STEPH COUVRETTE/SHUTTERSTOCK, OPERATION 2021/ALAMY, BACKGROUND: IMAGE SOURCE LIMITED/ALAMY

↓ Hawai'i Food & Wine Festival

Sample the islands' finest flavors across Maui, Hawai'i and O'ahu.

▸ hawaiifoodandwinefestival.com

↙ Makahiki

Mid-November marks the start of the Hawaiian year. Look out for events with traditional Hawaiian games.

← Kona Coffee Cultural Festival

Coffee connoisseurs delight in this multiday celebration of the strong island brew.

Kona Coffee Belt

▸ p212

▸ konacoffeefest.com

Average daytime max: 85°F (29°C)
Humid days: 27

NOVEMBER

Average daytime max: 83°F (28°C)
Humid days: 21

Packing Notes

Be prepared for hot, humid days and cool, breezy nights.

While the rest of the state gets wetter, Kona on Hawai'i Island gets drier during the winter.

↖ New Year Fireworks

Hawai'i takes its New Year celebrations very seriously. Expect large fireworks everywhere and smoky air throughout the 31st and 1st.

↖ Honolulu Marathon

Held on the second Sunday of December, the Honolulu Marathon draws over 30,000 runners to the capital.

▸ honolulumarathon.org

DECEMBER

Average daytime max: 80°F (27°C)
Humid days: 16

JANUARY

Hawai'i in WINTER

FROM LEFT: PHILLIP B. ESPINASSE/SHUTTERSTOCK, PANDORA PICTURES/SHUTTERSTOCK, JJM PHOTOGRAPHY/SHUTTERSTOCK, YOSHI CANOPUS/WIKIMEDIA/CC BY-SA 4.0, BACKGROUND: ABBY BOGGS/SHUTTERSTOCK

↘ Northern Swells

Winter brings epic waves to Hawai'i's northern shores, along with some of the biggest international surf competitions.

North Shore

▶ p102

↓ Waimea Cherry Blossom Heritage Festival

Pretty pink cherry tree blooms are the backdrop to this Japanese-focused fest in the cooler ranchlands of Kamuela.

Hawai'i Island

▶ facebook.com/p/Waimea-Cherry-Blossom-Heritage-Festival-100064661262713/

↓ Humpback Whale Season

Humpback whales flock to Hawai'i to give birth during the winter, often preferring Maui's shallow waters.

Maui

▶ p158

FEBRUARY

Average daytime max: 79°F (26°C)
Humid days: 12

Average daytime max: 79°F (26°C)
Humid days: 9

Packing Notes

A rain jacket for outdoor activities; if you're planning to be at high elevation, you'll want a proper coat as temperatures can drop to the 40s (4°C to 9°C).

The first week of May is often busy as visitors from Japan take advantage of their Golden Week holidays to travel.

↗ World Whale Day

Maui celebrates the migratory humpback whales with films, volunteering opportunities and a parade.

↘ Merrie Monarch Festival

A week-long cultural event and hula competition held in Hilo each spring.

▸ merriemonarch.com

MARCH

Average daytime max: 80°F (27°C)
Humid days: 9

APRIL

Hawai'i in SPRING

FROM LEFT: JEREMY L FOSTER/SHUTTERSTOCK, THOMAS TUNSCH/HULA DANCERS/WIKIMEDIA/CC BY-SA 4.0, YI-CHEN CHIANG/SHUTTERSTOCK, MADMARV00/FLICKR/CC BY 2.0, BACKGROUND: CHRISTOPHERMYA/SHUTTERSTOCK

← May Day is Lei Day

May 1 is dedicated to the celebration of flowers and lei. Festivities are held statewide with the largest in Honolulu.

← Waikīkī Spam Jam

Hawai'i loves its Spam so much that there's an entire festival dedicated to the canned meat every April.

▸ spamjamhawaii.com

↓ Lantern Floating

Observe the Memorial Day tradition of lighting lanterns on the water to honor lost loved ones at Ala Moana Regional Park.

▸ lanternfloatinghawaii.com

MAY

Average daytime max: 81°F (27°C)
Humid days: 10

Average daytime max: 83°F (28°C)
Humid days: 11

Packing Notes

T-shirt, shorts and rubbah slippahs (flip-flops) – spring often sees perfect tropical weather.

CITY & COUNTRY
Trip Builder

TAKE YOUR PICK OF MUST-SEES AND HIDDEN GEMS

From the urban jungle of Honolulu to the tropical jungles of Kaua'i, explore the dichotomy between Hawai'i's capital city and its greenest main island.

Trip Notes

Hub towns Līhu'e, Honolulu

How long 2 weeks

Getting around A car is a must on Kaua'i and a good-to-have on O'ahu.

Tips Kaua'i is home to the wettest place on Earth, so be aware that your trip could be a wet one. Try a summer visit for the best chances of sunshine.

FROM LEFT: MARIDAV/SHUTTERSTOCK, JA-IMAGES/SHUTTERSTOCK, JEANNE PROVOST/SHUTTERSTOCK

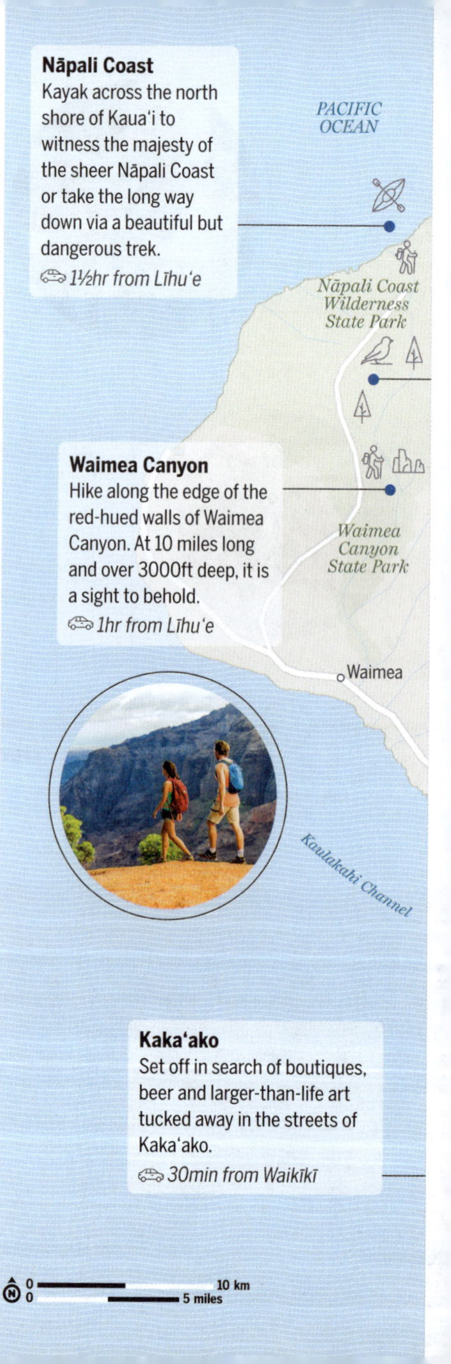

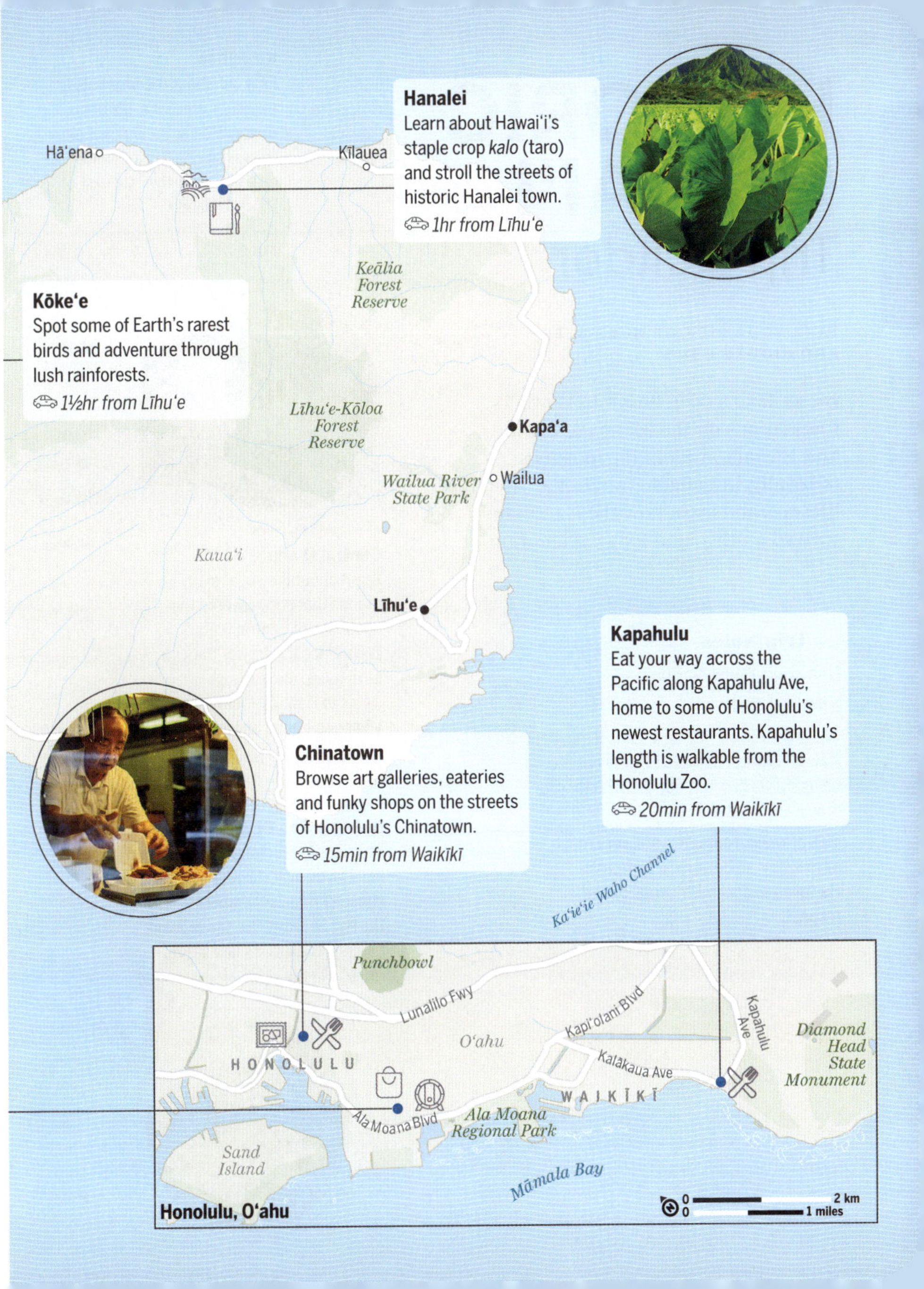

Hanalei
Learn about Hawai'i's staple crop *kalo* (taro) and stroll the streets of historic Hanalei town.
1hr from Līhu'e

Kōke'e
Spot some of Earth's rarest birds and adventure through lush rainforests.
1½hr from Līhu'e

Chinatown
Browse art galleries, eateries and funky shops on the streets of Honolulu's Chinatown.
15min from Waikīkī

Kapahulu
Eat your way across the Pacific along Kapahulu Ave, home to some of Honolulu's newest restaurants. Kapahulu's length is walkable from the Honolulu Zoo.
20min from Waikīkī

HISTORIC HAWAI'I
Trip Builder

TAKE YOUR PICK OF MUST-SEES AND HIDDEN GEMS

Take a deep dive into Hawai'i's foundations on the islands of O'ahu and Hawai'i. Walk in the footsteps of royalty, investigate traditional lifeways and learn how the Hawaiians thrived on this land for a millennium.

Trip Notes

Hub areas Honolulu, Kona

How long 10 days

Getting around Having a car is a must on Hawai'i Island. Honolulu is fairly easy to navigate via bus, but outside the city you may want to have a car.

Tips Hawaiian culture is still very much alive today, so be sure to approach Hawaiian history with curiosity and respect.

FROM LEFT: DLABAJDESIGN/SHUTTERSTOCK, PHILLIP B. ESPINASSE/SHUTTERSTOCK, GEORGE BURBA/SHUTTERSTOCK

Kawaihae
Find out about the final battles to unify the islands. It's commemorated at the Pu'ukoholā Heiau National Historic Site on the arid northwest coast of Hawai'i Island.
45min from Kona

Central O'ahu
Learn about the sugar plantations that once covered the flat plains of Central O'ahu. Experience this legacy through farm tours, rum tastings or a visit to Hawaii's Plantation Village (pictured above).
30min from Waikīkī

Nu'uanu Pali Dr
Stop along this historic path-turned-highway to visit Hānaiakamalama (Queen Emma's Summer Palace) and the Pali Lookout, the site of Kamehameha the Great's last battle.
10min from Downtown Honolulu

Keāhole

Tour the aquaculture endeavors around Hawaiʻi Island's westernmost point. The Kona Coast was once home to numerous fishponds that fed thousands. Present-day ventures aim to continue this legacy.

40min from Kona

Hōnaunau

Visit Puʻuhonua o Hōnaunau, a sacred place of refuge protected by Lono, the god of life. Today it's Hawaiʻi's last preserved place of refuge and a National Historical Park.

40min from Kona

He'eia

Lend a hand at the *ahupuaʻa* (land division) of Heʻeia, home to multiple organizations working to restore the traditional agricultural practices that sustained the Hawaiians for a thousand years.

40min from Waikīkī

Downtown Honolulu

Stroll Downtown Honolulu, the seat of Hawaiʻi's government since the monarchy. Take a tour of the grand ʻIolani Palace to see where it all started.

15min from Waikīkī

Waikīkī

Surf the favorite waves of the royals and search for historic landmarks amid the urban sprawl.

15min from Downtown Honolulu

O'AHU
Trip Builder

TAKE YOUR PICK OF MUST-SEES AND HIDDEN GEMS

Urban life, Hawaiian culture, crystal-clear waters and lush rainforests – sample it all on O'ahu. Hawai'i's most populous island is also the best place for an overview of modern life in the islands.

Trip Notes

Hub towns Honolulu, Kailua, Hale'iwa

How long 2 weeks

Getting around A car is almost a necessity if you're moving between areas, though TheBus does cover the whole island.

Tips Besides Waikīkī, there's heavy overlap between visitor and local spaces – be respectful of residential neighborhoods and peoples' daily lives, and remember that parking lots can fill fast for popular events like watching big-wave surfing during winter.

FROM LEFT: STEVE HEAP/SHUTTERSTOCK, BRESTER IRINA/ SHUTTERSTOCK, VIKTOR FUCHS/SHUTTERSTOCK

Kahuku

Chill out all day on the beach on the quieter side of the North Shore.

1hr from Honolulu

Windward Coast

Give back to the land, explore lush rainforest and snorkel in shallow waters.

30min from Waikīkī

Downtown Honolulu & Chinatown

Meander the halls of royal 'Iolani Palace or peruse galleries large and small. Art and culture overflow in these two neighboring areas.

20min from Waikīkī

Kaimukī

Eat your way through the hole-in-the-wall gems of Kaimukī.

10min from Waikīkī

Waikīkī

Relax among the calm beaches, good weather and restaurants and hotels that make this Hawai'i's tourist center. It's the best place to find a cultural lesson or learn to surf.

10min from Downtown Honolulu

Lē'ahi

Climb to the peak of this extinct cinder cone or peer down at the surfers below. Also known as Diamond Head.

10min from Waikīkī

MAUI NUI
Trip Builder

TAKE YOUR PICK OF MUST-SEES AND HIDDEN GEMS

Once one large island called Maui Nui, the islands of Maui, Moloka'i and Lāna'i are now quite separate with distinct personalities. Experience vibrant town life, secluded beaches, outdoor adventure and rural living all within Maui Nui.

Trip Notes

Hub towns Kīhei, Kahului

How long 10 days

Getting around Each island requires you to have a rental car. Take a passenger ferry between Maui and Lāna'i, but you'll have to fly to Moloka'i.

Tips If you plan to visit Haleakalā or the Upcountry areas, be sure to pack layers – it can get unexpectedly cold at altitude.

FROM LEFT: STARR ENVIRONMENTAL/FLICKR/CC BY 2.0, ALEKSEI POTOV/ SHUTTERSTOCK, ARKANTO/SHUTTERSTOCK

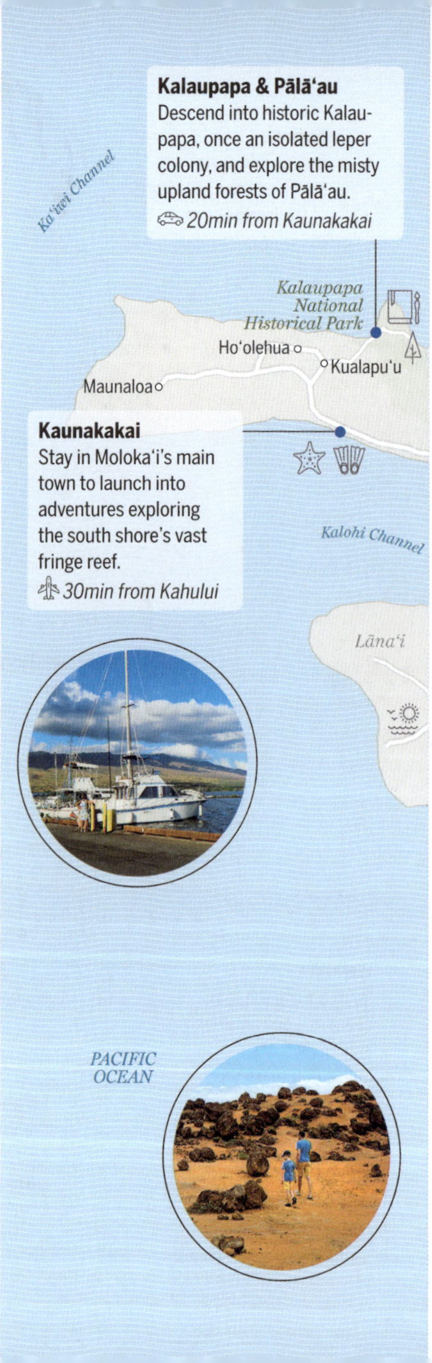

Kalaupapa & Pālā'au
Descend into historic Kalaupapa, once an isolated leper colony, and explore the misty upland forests of Pālā'au.
20min from Kaunakakai

Kaunakakai
Stay in Moloka'i's main town to launch into adventures exploring the south shore's vast fringe reef.
30min from Kahului

Hāna Coast
Ride along the breathtaking Hāna Hwy and spend the day relaxing in nature in secluded Hāna Town. Take a tour so you can sit back and enjoy the views.
2hr from Kahului

Kā'anapali
Lounge on a world-famous white-sand beach or sign up for an ocean adventure with one of the luxury resorts or an outfitter.
45min from Kīhei

Wailuku
Take a self-guided walking tour past the historic and and architecturally significant buildings and admire the murals showcasing city history.
10min from Kahului

Lāna'i
Explore secluded shores. Home to just 3000 people, Lāna'i is the smallest of Hawai'i's main islands.
1hr 10min from Mā'alaea

Upcountry
Tour some of Hawai'i's most fertile farms on the slopes of Haleakalā, tasting everything from fresh fruit to goat cheese.
15min from Kahului

Haleakalā
Watch the sunrise from the top of the largest dormant volcano on Earth, or hike down into its otherworldly caldera.
1hr from Kahului

NATURAL WONDERS
Trip Builder

TAKE YOUR PICK OF MUST-SEES AND HIDDEN GEMS

The world's tallest mountain, most active volcano, densest biodiversity and quietest place – the islands of Hawai'i and Maui are home to some of Earth's most dramatic natural wonders.

Trip Notes

Hub towns Kona, Hilo, Kā'anapali

How long 10 days

Getting around Unless you're planning to take tours the whole time, you'll need a car (though there are great tours to all the best places).

Tips If you plan to visit the national parks or volcano summits, bring warm layers. Be sure to clean your shoes after every hike to prevent spreading ROD (Rapid 'Ōhi'a Death, a fungus).

FROM LEFT: CAVAN IMAGES/GETTY IMAGES, MNSTUDIO/SHUTTERSTOCK, ALEX RATSON/GETTY IMAGES

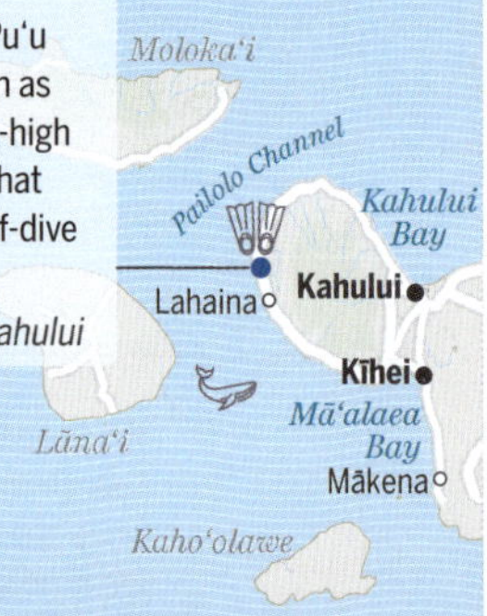

Kā'anapali
Snorkel beneath Pu'u Keka'a, also known as Black Rock, a 20ft-high lava promontory that hosts a sunset cliff-dive ceremony nightly.
40min from Kahului

North Kohala
Sneak around the desert slopes of Kawaihae and watch the Earth come to life on the northwest coast of Hawai'i, which is speckled with small towns and dramatic beaches.
1½hr from Kona

Kona
Swim among vibrant coral ecosystems along the arid coast, or sip coffee during a farm tour on the slopes of misty Hualālai.
1½hr from Hilo

Haleakalā National Park

Spend your days hiking through rainforest and cinder. At night, crystal-clear air and pitch-dark sky offer fantastic stargazing at the summit.

1½hr from Kahului

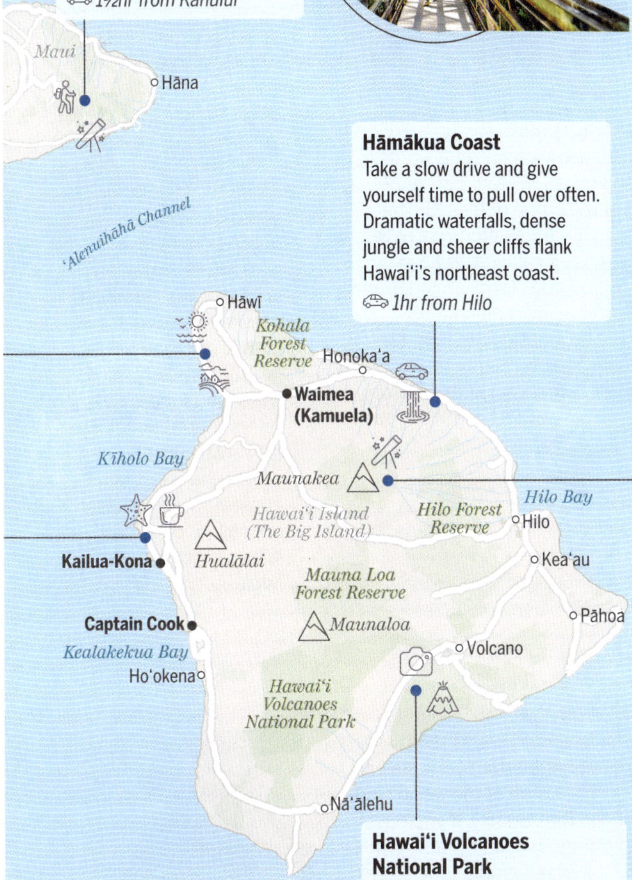

Hāmākua Coast

Take a slow drive and give yourself time to pull over often. Dramatic waterfalls, dense jungle and sheer cliffs flank Hawaiʻi's northeast coast.

1hr from Hilo

Maunakea

Admire Maunakea – measured from its base below the sea to its summit, it's the tallest mountain on Earth and revered as a sacred space in Hawaiian culture.

1½hr from Kona

Hawaiʻi Volcanoes National Park

Hike across lava flows and through native forest and witness the birth of new earth. The park is about the size of Oʻahu.

45min from Hilo

7 Things to Know About HAWAIʻI

INSIDER TIPS TO HIT THE GROUND RUNNING

1 A Kingdom, Occupied

Prior to becoming a US state, Hawaiʻi was a sovereign nation recognized by the international community. In 1893 a group of white businessmen and US military personnel staged a coup, seizing power in the name of the US. The annexation was never legally recognized by the Hawaiian Kingdom, and many people continue to fight for sovereignty today. Being mindful of this history will add depth to your experience.

2 'Hawaiian' as an Adjective

When referring to people, only those with Native Hawaiian ancestry are 'Hawaiian.' All other residents simply call themselves 'locals.' Similarly, 'Hawaiian food' only refers to traditional Hawaiian cuisine while other common contemporary cuisines are called 'local food.' When in doubt, use 'local.'

3 The Lahaina Wildfire

On August 8, 2023, one of the deadliest wildfires in US history tore through Lahaina, killing more than 100 people, destroying the historic downtown and displacing thousands. Much of downtown remains closed as the city rebuilds. Remain respectful and kind while traveling and refrain from asking locals too many questions about the fire.

4 Account for Traffic

With lower speed limits, fewer lanes and seemingly constant roadwork, Hawaiʻi has some of the worst traffic in the country. If you have time-sensitive plans, give yourself ample time to get there.

▶ Find more transportation info on p240

FROM LEFT: GARUMNA/SHUTTERSTOCK, VECTOR TRADITION/SHUTTERSTOCK, IMAGE SOURCE LIMITED/ALAMY, SOFYA_IVA/SHUTTERSTOCK, JULIA AUGUST/SHUTTERSTOCK

5 Directional Words

Instead of cardinal directions, you'll often hear these terms:

mauka – toward the mountains

makai – toward the ocean

windward – the east side of each island

leeward – the west side of each island.

In Honolulu, directions are often given in relation to Diamond Head (east) and 'Ewa (west). On O'ahu, Honolulu is usually referred to as 'town.'

▶ Learn about Hawai'i's place names on p72

6 Laws Protecting Nature

Due to its biodiversity and isolation, Hawai'i has the unfortunate distinction of 'extinction capital of the world,' and there are several laws in place to protect its endangered species.

Turtles and seals Although it's fairly common to see *honu* (Hawaiian green sea turtles) and *'īlioholoikauaua* (Hawaiian monk seals) both on the beach and in the water, it's important to keep your distance. Stay at least 10ft away from turtles and 50ft away from monk seals. It's a state felony to touch or feed endangered species, and violations can result in fines up to $15,000.

Sunscreen Hawai'i has banned sunscreens containing oxybenzone and octinoxate, which are proven to harm coral. While other chemicals are still allowed, look for a sunscreen with only zinc oxide or titanium dioxide to ensure it's reef-safe.

Plastic bag ban You can buy a paper bag at the register, but it's helpful to carry a reusable bag of your own.

▶ For more ways to have a positive impact when you travel, see p244

7 Microclimates

It can be raining where you're standing but sunny just down the street, and just because it's raining now, doesn't mean it will be in 10 minutes. Hawai'i's weather changes quickly and often, so try to be flexible with your plans and expectations. Generally, the windward and *mauka* areas of each island are more likely to see rain and cloud cover.

▶ Discover some of Hawai'i's terrains and microclimates on p210

Read, Listen, Watch & Follow

READ

Kuleana (Sara Kehaulani Goo; 2025) A memoir and exploration of ancestral land ownership in Hawai'i.

Sharks in the Time of Saviors (Kawai Strong Washburn; 2020) Haunting yet hopeful exploration of modern Hawaiian identity.

The Food of Paradise (Rachel Lauden; 1996) Part cookbook, part history primer.

Hawaii's Story by Hawaii's Queen (Queen Lili'uokalani; 1898) Political history of Hawai'i before and after the overthrow.

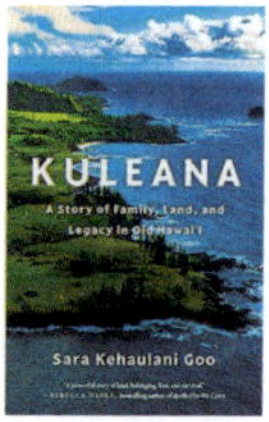

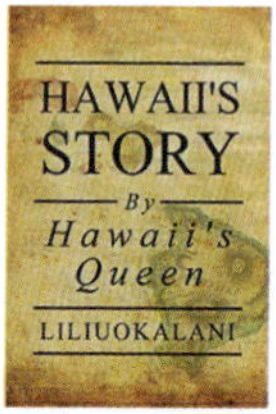

LISTEN

The Music of George Helm – A True Hawaiian (1977) Retro exemplar of the classic Hawaiian falsetto. Posthumously released album from Hawaiian Renaissance leader George Helm.

Keep It Aloha (Kamaka Dias) Weekly Q&A podcast with influential residents on Hawai'i topics.

Facing Future (Israel Kamakawiwo'ole; 1993) Gentle vocals invoke a poignant nostalgia. Includes hit song 'Over the Rainbow.'

PAUL MORIGI/GETTY IMAGES

Rain on Sunday (Paula Fuga; 2021) Comfort-filled melodies from this singer-songwriter (pictured above). Like a warm blanket on a Hawaiian winter morning, delivered with clear, powerful vocals.

WATCH

Kapaemahu (2020; pictured top right) The *mo'olelo* (story) of a Waikīkī landmark captured in a beautifully animated short.

Island Earth (2016) Documenting the collision of tradition, industry and the future of food in Hawai'i.

Chief of War (2025) Historical dramatization of island unification.

I Was a Simple Man (2021) An honest glimpse of a fractured family over several decades.

Go for Broke (2017) Drama recounting the heroic actions of the 442nd Regimental Combat Team (pictured bottom right) during WWII.

FOLLOW

@ainamomona
Educational posts on modern Hawai'i.

@native_hawaiian_plants
Up-close captures of Hawai'i's unique ecology.

@tonybarnhill808
Colorized images from the Hawai'i of yesteryear.

@hisarahlee
Surf photographer chasing epic waves.

@fluxhawaii
Hawai'i's premier modern culture magazine.

HONOLULU, O'AHU

HISTORY | CULTURE | ART

RESEARCHED BY JACKIE OSHIRO; UPDATED BY SARAH ETINAS

- Trip Builder (p46)
- Practicalities (p48)
- Hawaiian Foundations (p50)
- Build Your Own Lū‘au (p54)
- The True Meaning of Aloha (p56)
- Local Lifestyle (p58)
- Modern Pulse (p60)
- Reimagine Pearl Harbor (p62)
- Take a Hike (p64)
- Hawaiian Monarchs (p66)
- Royal Waikīkī (p68)
- A New Look at Lē‘ahi (p70)
- Place Names (p72)
- Art in the Heart of Honolulu (p74)
- Listings (p78)

DAVE H. FINE/SHUTTERSTOCK

Dive deep into Hawaiian culture at the **Bishop Museum** (p51)
20min from Waikīkī

Peruse galleries during the day and dance all night in **Chinatown** (p74)
30min from Waikīkī

Admire the hundreds of murals dotting **Kaka'ako**, then drop into a brewery for an IPA (p61)
30min from Waikīkī

Learn to surf on the favorite waves of royalty in **Waikīkī** (p68)
30min from Downtown Honolulu

HONOLULU
Trip Builder

Historic capital and modern metropolis, Honolulu proudly displays its rich heritage and storied past. Immerse yourself in the legacy of the Hawaiian Kingdom and explore the movements and cultures that have made Hawai'i what it is today.

FROM LEFT: THEODORE TRIMMER/SHUTTERSTOCK, JEFF WHYTE/SHUTTERSTOCK, KEVIN LEBRE/GETTY IMAGES, STRUCTURED VISION/SHUTTERSTOCK

Practicalities

OSUGI/SHUTTERSTOCK

ARRIVING

Daniel K Inouye International Airport (HNL) The airport is a short 15 minutes from Waikīkī, depending on the traffic. Take your pick from the 10 car-rental companies housed in the Consolidated Rent-A-Car (CONRAC) facility across from Terminal 2. Rideshares can cost $20 to $60 depending on the time of day. Public buses depart from the upper level and cost $3. The Skyline rail also costs $3 but, as of 2026, it can only take riders as far as Kalihi. Shuttles range from $20 for two to around $200 to book a private ride.

HOW MUCH FOR A

Iced coffee $6–7

Surfboard rental per day $40

Designer aloha shirt $148

WHEN TO GO

JAN–MAR
Highs around 80°F (27°C). Rainy season with more cloud cover.

APR–JUN
Highs around 84°F (29°C). Sunny and warm. First week of May can be crowded.

JUL–SEP
Highs around 88°F (31°C). High season. Sunny and hot.

OCT–DEC
Highs around 84°F (29°C). Hot through October. December gets crowded.

GETTING AROUND

Car The most convenient way to get around, but gas can be expensive and Honolulu has bad traffic. Rideshare services are available or check out Hui Car Share to rent a car for a few hours.

Bus Extensive and reasonably punctual coverage, but travel times can be long. Pick up a HOLO Card if you plan to take the bus more than a couple of times.

Skyline As of 2026, O'ahu's new rail system features 13 stations connecting Kapolei to Kalihi, including a stop at the airport. You'll need a HOLO Card to ride.

Bicycle Biki bike-share stations are found throughout urban Honolulu and are a great way to see the city. Download the app to locate stations and purchase a pass.

EATING & DRINKING

There's no place better to sample the flavors of the Pacific: find quality Japanese, Chinese, Filipino, Korean, Thai and Vietnamese food.

Hawai'i Regional Cuisine Hawai'i's homegrown cuisine combines fresh local ingredients with flavors and techniques from around the Pacific for a high-end take on classic Hawai'i home cooking. Look for ingredients such as *'ulu* (breadfruit; pictured top), *kalo* (taro), *limu* (seaweed) and *'uala* (sweet potato).

Hawaiian food Not to be confused with local food, traditional Hawaiian food centers around *kalo*, pork, coconut and fish (for example, poke; pictured bottom).

Best Hawaiian food for beginners Highway Inn (p55)

TOP: MARIDAV/SHUTTERSTOCK
BOTTOM: ALEXANDER PROKOPENKO/SHUTTERSTOCK

CONNECT & FIND YOUR WAY

Connectivity Cell-phone data is reliable throughout the city except around Tantalus (p64). You'll find wi-fi at most cafes, shopping centers and hotels.

Navigation Downtown and Waikīkī have a lot of one-way streets, so if you're driving it's a good idea to use a navigation app. Download offline access ahead of time if you don't have data coverage.

RESERVATIONS

If there's a restaurant you want to visit, be sure to make a reservation or you may face an hours-long wait.

WHERE TO STAY

Because of O'ahu's zoning laws, accommodations are limited to three main areas – Waikīkī, Ko'olina and the North Shore – though there are a few hotels and B&Bs scattered elsewhere. Short-term vacation rentals are also largely limited to these areas, due to county permitting laws.

Location	Pros/Cons
Waikīkī, 'Ewa side	Closer to the action of Honolulu. Very crowded.
Waikīkī, Diamond Head side	Also quite crowded. Better beach access; close to restaurants on Kapahulu Ave.
Kāhala	Quiet; serene. Just one expensive resort.
Elsewhere (Mānoa, Ala Moana, Downtown)	Removed from Waikīkī and very few options.

MONEY

Honolulu is expensive – there's no getting around it. Expect to pay 10% to 15% more than elsewhere. Save by using public transportation and buying groceries to avoid eating out for every meal.

01 HAWAIIAN Foundations

CULTURE | NATURE | HISTORY

Hawai'i boasts a rich, thousand years of human history that is often misrepresented in guidebooks and pop culture. Start your visit by learning about traditional and modern Hawaiian culture for a deeper appreciation of your time in the islands.

PHILLIP B. ESPINASSE/SHUTTERSTOCK

How to

When to go By kicking off your stay with a visit to Bishop Museum, not only will you get a chance to appreciate Hawai'i from a Hawaiian perspective, but you'll also have time to schedule another visit in case you run out of time – there's a lot to see.

Make the most Try to prioritize taking guided tours where they're offered. You'll often hear personal anecdotes and local stories not found in brochures.

CLEANFOTOS/SHUTTERSTOCK

FUZHEADO/WIKIMEDIA/CC0

Start Here

If you're looking for a meaningful experience, start with a day at the **Bishop Museum**. Established in honor of Bernice Pauahi Bishop, the last royal descendant of the Kamehameha line, the museum is a captivating display of Hawaiian history and culture. Learn about the geology of the Hawaiian archipelago, the rise and fall of the Hawaiian Kingdom, and how the Hawaiians built a thriving society that worked in harmony with the islands' unique ecologies. Understanding Hawai'i's rich history is key to appreciating Hawai'i today.

Kuleana & Mālama

Kuleana (responsibility and privilege) and *mālama* (to care for) are values integral to life in Hawai'i. Guided by the understanding that the privilege of experiencing Hawai'i's natural

No Geotagging

Location tagging on social media has led to excess numbers of people in places that don't have the capacity to support them, causing erosion and environmental degradation. Feel free to tag businesses and restaurants, but *mālama* Hawai'i's beaches, trails and other natural areas by keeping location sites intentionally broad (for example, 'Kona Coast, Hawai'i').

Top left Bishop Museum interior **Bottom left** Kūka'ō'ō Heiau, Mānoa Heritage Center (p52) **Top right** Bishop Museum

beauty comes hand-in-hand with the responsibility to care for it, locals tend to be very conscientious about protecting the environment and invite visitors to do the same. **808 Cleanups** (808cleanups.org) hosts multiple restoration and cleanup service opportunities every week at various places around the island. Participating in one of its events is a great way to meet locals, learn about the history and cultural significance of a particular place, and give back to the land.

Sacred Spaces

Heiau There are dozens of these ancient stone temples around the islands. Because heiau hold such cultural importance, it's best to go with a guide who can offer context. Visit the **Mānoa Heritage Center** to take a tour of **Kūka'ō'ō Heiau**, a reconstructed heiau on O'ahu and the only one in the Waikīkī *ahupua'a* (land division). Note that some heiau, particularly on the neighbor islands, are not marked, and any ruins should be treated with respect.

Kuleana

There is no Hawai'i without Native Hawaiians. The history of these islands spans centuries before they were annexed to the United States and is woven into every aspect of modern Hawai'i. In learning about our history, you understand a new perspective, and you gain a greater appreciation for the *'āina* (land) that has welcomed you and the people that live here. We are not relics or tourist attractions – we belong to a living, breathing culture, and as a guest, you have a *kuleana* (responsibility) to respect our home.

Contributed by Nikki Oka, *Native Hawaiian and Special Assistant, White House Initiative on Asian Americans, Native Hawaiians, and Pacific Islanders (WHIAANHPI)*

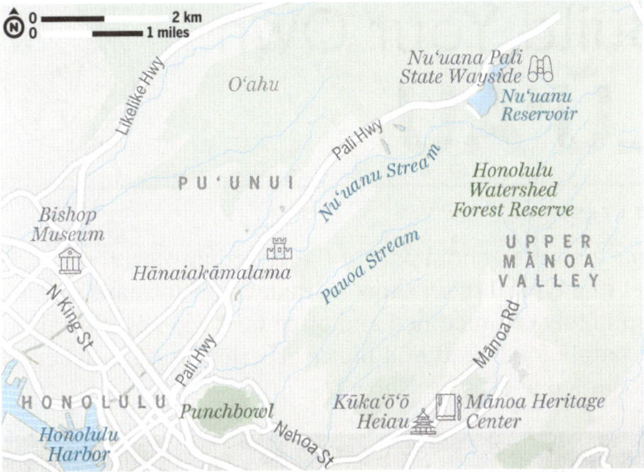

Left View from the Nu'uanu Pali State Wayside (Lookout)
Below Hānaiakāmalama

Royal relics Overthrown in 1893, the Hawaiian Kingdom is still quite close to the present day, and many royal buildings and landmarks are open to the public. Visit the serene **Hānaiakāmalama**, Queen Emma's summer palace, in the lush Nu'uanu Valley to learn about the life and legacy of one of Hawai'i's most beloved monarchs. Just up the street, stare down onto the Windward Coast from the **Nu'uanu Pali State Wayside** (also called the Pali Lookout), the site of King Kamehameha's infamous final battle to unify the Hawaiian Islands.

Lei Culture

One traditional Hawaiian custom that's been adopted into modern local culture is the practice of giving lei. Garlands of fresh flowers and other natural materials (and sometimes candy and origami money) are regularly given as congratulations, in celebration, to convey gratitude and as a greeting or farewell. To buy a lei as a gift or to wear to dinner, pop into Chinatown to browse the dozen or so lei stands in the area or swing by your nearest grocery store. A few tips: avoid the purple orchid lei made with imported flowers, pick a twisted rope of *maile* or *ti* as a masculine option, and look for an open lei (or be prepared to snip it in half yourself) if the recipient is pregnant.

02 Build Your Own LŪ'AU

HAWAIIAN CULTURE | FOOD | FESTIVAL

The *lū'au* has become a quintessential part of the Hawaiian vacation but much of what you'll get in a typical *lū'au* show – dramatic performances and a huge feast – has been highly commodified and often isn't a good cultural representation. Seek out separate food, craft and music experiences for a richer understanding you can't get at a one-off *lū'au* show.

VIDAHAWAII/SHUTTERSTOCK

How to

Talk story The best way to learn is through what locals call 'talking story' – chatting. If you're curious about anything you're seeing or eating, just ask! Locals appreciate it when visitors express genuine interest and are usually happy to help.

Ordering food For Hawaiian food first-timers, some classic dishes to try include poi, *laulau* (meat and fish steamed in taro leaves), *haupia* (coconut pudding), *kālua* pig and *lomi lomi* salmon. If you're feeling a little adventurous, try the squid *lū'au* or *'opihi* (edible limpet).

GORDON FAHEY/SHUTTERSTOCK

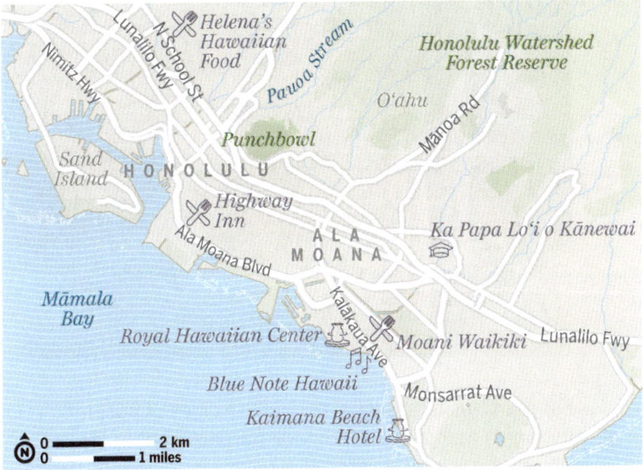

Hawaiian food Traditional Hawaiian food is simple, hearty and healthy. Some of the main ingredients you'll see are *kalo* (taro), pork, coconut and fresh fish. Visit **Highway Inn** for all-in-one plates to try a little bit of everything. If you already know what you like, head to **Helena's Hawaiian Food** for family-style eating.

Cultural practices The best way to experience Hawaiian culture is to learn from a cultural practitioner and try it yourself. The **Royal Hawaiian Center** (royalhawaiiancenter.com/events) offers small classes in *'ukulele,* hula, *lauhala* weaving and lei making. Many hotels, such as the **Kaimana Beach Hotel**, offer in-house cultural programming as well. At the intersection of food and culture is **Ka Papa Lo'i o Kānewai**, a traditional *lo'i kalo* (taro field) run by the University of Hawai'i at Mānoa. On community workdays volunteers get to hear *mo'olelo* (stories), learn a little Hawaiian and get some hands-on experience in traditional agriculture.

Music and hospitality Big family parties and *kanikapila* (impromptu music playing) are at the heart of celebrations in Hawai'i. Find this lively atmosphere at **Moani Waikiki**, a restaurant owned by the family behind reggae band the Green. The restaurant features family recipes and a daily rotation of local musicians across all genres. For a more music-focused atmosphere, check the lineup of international and local artists at **Blue Note Hawaii**.

Top left Outdoor performance at the Royal Hawaiian Center
Bottom left Kamehameha Day Festival parade

Hawaiian Culture Festivals

Prince Kūhiō Festival Held in late March to honor Hawaiian royal and territorial delegate to the US Congress, Jonah Kūhiō Kalaniana'ole (1871–1922). The festival includes a parade as well as local food and craft vendors and performances.

May Day is Lei Day On May 1, Hawai'i celebrates its rich floral culture with a day of lei making, hula performances, cultural demonstrations and food.

Kamehameha Day Festival Held on June 11, this festival celebrates the legacy of King Kamehameha and the Hawaiian monarchy with a parade rich in Hawaiian culture and symbolism, along with food, demos and performances.

With insights from Dr Trisha Kehaulani Watson
Trisha is a Kanaka Maoli (Native Hawaiian) born and raised on O'ahu.

The True Meaning of Aloha

TLENSCH/SHUTTERSTOCK

ALOHA IS A TWO-WAY STREET

Perhaps the most universally known Hawaiian word is 'aloha.' Most people will rightfully explain that it means 'hello,' 'goodbye' or 'love.' While these are all true, aloha is not so simple.

For many visitors, 'aloha' conjures images of hospitality, warm welcome and tranquil paradise. These ideas, however, are incomplete, used by the tourism industry to sell plane tickets, hotel rooms and tours. Scholar Mary Kawena Pukui writes, 'Eating, drinking, singing and talking together, the ties of man to fellow man are strengthened in the mutual regard and love summed up as aloha.' Aloha, in the traditional sense, is a two-way connection. To experience aloha is to give as much as it is to receive. Unfortunately, popular understandings of aloha have created a situation where millions of visitors come to Hawai'i expecting to receive aloha without realizing that they must also reciprocate by giving their aloha back to Hawai'i. As a result, the land and its people are becoming worn down and increasingly less able to support this one-way relationship.

In 2019, prior to the COVID-19 pandemic, over 10 million tourists were coming to Hawai'i every year. Many of these tourists sought out 'hidden sites,' resulting in residential neighborhoods being overrun by thrill-seeking visitors with little regard for the privacy or private properties of local communities. Local ire against visitors began to grow, as the state showed little concern about the massive number of tourists coming to the island and even less concern for the adverse impacts these influxes had on local communities.

Over the years, many disreputable publications have revealed and promoted sites that are both illegal to visit (being on private property) and dangerous. Hawai'i residents are frustrated with visitors who have little regard

Left Aloha written on a tree **Middle** People playing 'ukulele and singing **Right** Face-to-face embrace

LEE FOSTER/ALAMY

LEE FOSTER/ALAMY

for how they disrupt locals and fail to understand the true meaning of 'aloha,' which is defined by an attitude of respect.

Legendary chef, and former friend of the islands, Anthony Bourdain is credited for telling others to 'be a traveler, not a tourist.' This is the best advice for how to enjoy the islands. Come with a sense of wonder, reverence and respect. Be humble and open to learning. Walk softly, wherever you may go. You paid for an opportunity to visit and experience these islands, but that does not entitle you to behave however you wish or go wherever you please. If you come to Hawai'i expecting its people to serve you and your every whim, please just do not come.

Come with a sense of wonder, reverence and respect. Be humble and open to learning. Walk softly, wherever you may go.

Aloha is an act of reciprocity. You will get as much of it as you give. The attitude you project is the attitude you will receive. Those who unlock Hawai'i's magic do so by leaving their urgency and expectations behind. They come with an open heart and open mind. They come with a genuine aloha for the people who make Hawai'i extraordinary. These are the people that Hawai'i shares herself with; these are the people who truly feel her aloha.

Aloha, Defined

Some will say the word aloha comes from two separate and important Hawaiian words, '*alo*' and '*hā*.' *Alo* means 'to face,' and it is considered proper and respectful to engage face to face. *Hā* means to breathe or exhale, and this breath is considered almost a life force. As such, those raised in the Hawaiian culture were taught to greet their *kūpuna* (elders) with 'aloha,' which includes a face-to-face embrace, inhaling and exhaling deeply during this exchange.

To show aloha is to show love, respect and reverence for others and for Hawai'i. It is critical that anyone who visits comes with respect for these extraordinary islands and those who call them home.

03 Local LIFESTYLE

FOOD | LIFESTYLE | SHOPPING

The bustling neighborhood of Kaimukī is where locals go to play. Take a break from sightseeing and adventuring with an afternoon spent along bustling Wai'alae Ave. Sample creations from Hawai'i's top chefs, kick up your feet for a spa pedicure or treat yourself to a gourmet gelato made with local ingredients. If you want to do as the locals do, then head over to Kaimukī.

VIBBILY/ALAMY

How to

Getting here Kaimukī is walkable from Waikīkī, though the way there is pretty hilly, so it's best to get a rideshare or drive. If you're driving, there's a large municipal parking lot on 12th Ave.

When to go With brunch spots open from 7am and ice cream spots not closing until at least 10pm, there's no wrong time to hit Wai'alae Ave.

Top tip @keepitkaimuki on Instagram is the definitive source on all things Kaimukī. Check it out as you plan your day.

ERIC BRODER VAN DYKE/GETTY IMAGES

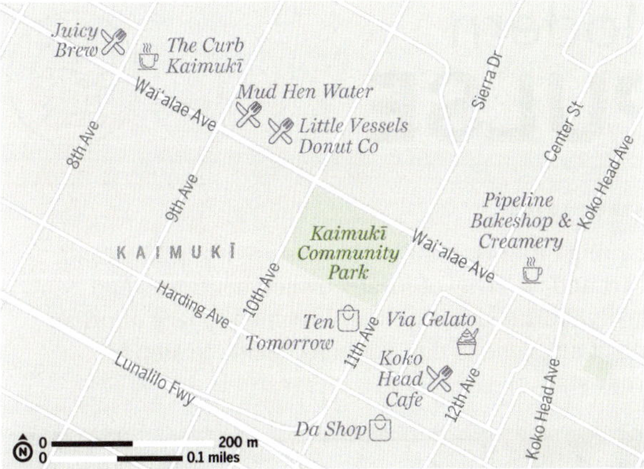

Top left Kaimukī Crack Seed Store
Bottom left Kaimukī Christmas Tree

Taste Hawai'i Regional Cuisine Combining local ingredients with flavors and techniques from around the Pacific, Hawai'i Regional Cuisine (HRC) is a modern, upscale interpretation of classic local home cooking. **Mud Hen Water** is run by HRC pioneer Ed Kenney and offers a seasonal menu in a laid-back atmosphere. If you come as a group for dinner, order family style to try as many dishes as possible. Down the street, try **Koko Head Cafe** for a flavorful brunch, or **Juicy Brew** (Thursday to Sunday only) for a vegan spin on HRC.

Let off some steam If you're looking for a change of pace, Kaimukī offers all sorts of opportunities to slow down. Savor an expertly made matcha or espresso from **The Curb Kaimukī** (thecurbkaimuki.com), drop in for a class with **Yoga Room Hawaii** (yogaroomhawaii.com) or stop in at one of the many nail salons clustered around Wai'alae and 12th Aves.

Treat yourself Head up to 12th Ave when it's time for something sweet. **Pipeline Bakeshop & Creamery** features made-from-scratch pastries, including beloved *malasadas* (Portuguese-style donuts). **Little Vessels Donut Co** serves up delicious vegan donuts in innovative, seasonal flavors. Or round out your evening with a locally inspired scoop from **Via Gelato**.

Get some retail therapy Whether you're looking to buy for yourself or bring home a gift, shopping at Kaimukī's boutiques will ensure you're supporting local. Visit bookstore **Da Shop** for a selection of local favorites and international best sellers or **Ten Tomorrow** for island-inspired women's wear.

Best of Kaimukī

Nana Ai Katsu Premium katsu shop with friendly staff and delicious local Japanese flavors.

The Public Pet Local pet-supply store with pet treats, food, toys and accessories made in Hawai'i. Unique pet-friendly space with an urban vibe.

Pu'u o Kaimukī Mini Park Enjoy panoramic views of East Honolulu from this park space, also the site for Kaimukī's annual Christmas-tree lighting.

Kaimukī Crack Seed Store Choose from popular varieties of local snacks and crack seed.

Jordan Lee, *founder of Keep it Kaimuki @keepitkaimuki*

04 Modern PULSE

STREET ART | BOUTIQUES | BREWERIES

If there's something going on in Honolulu, chances are it's in Kakaʻako. Dotted with vibrant street art and an array of locally owned boutiques and eateries, this funky, young neighborhood has quickly become the face of urban Honolulu. With things to do at any time of day, you may decide to stop by several times throughout your stay.

TONY WEBSTER/WIKIMEDIA/CC BY 2.0

How to

Getting around Kakaʻako is flat and walkable, and the best way to see all of its fun details is by foot. Biking is also a great option as there are Biki stations aplenty. Launch from the Ward area where there's ample parking.

When to go Kakaʻako often sees some intense midday sun. Morning or late afternoon/early evening are the most comfortable times to be walking around.

RUTHIE ARORA/SHUTTERSTOCK

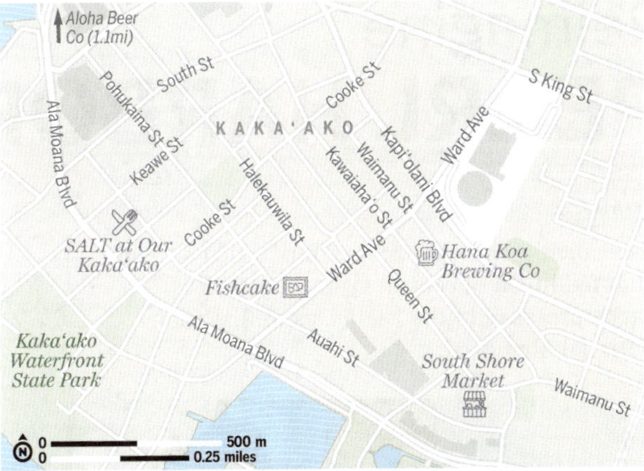

Top left SALT at Our Kaka'ako
Bottom left South Shore Market

An urban art movement The mural arts festival **Hawai'i Walls** (formerly POW! WOW! Hawai'i; worldwidewalls.com/hawaii) got its start in Kaka'ako in 2010, with local and international artists flocking to the neighborhood to paint their large-scale masterpieces. In recent years, the event has expanded to other Honolulu neighborhoods such as Kalihi and Palama, but Kaka'ako remains the most mural-bedecked of them all. Stroll around to admire the dozens of stunning murals, and when the sun gets a little too hot, pop over to the shops at **SALT at Our Kaka'ako** for a quick bite or a cold brew.

Breweries abound Whether you're looking for a place to lunch or winding down a day of adventure, one of Kaka'ako's breweries and craft beer specialists will probably fit the bill. Stop in at **Hana Koa Brewing Co** for its seasonal brews and stay for a meal packed with local ingredients. Or, with an atmosphere reminiscent of a classic local family party, **Aloha Beer Co** invites you to enjoy the evening air in its large outdoor space. If you can't seem to find the happy-hour menu, try asking about the *pau hana* (end of work) specials instead.

Local makers and creators Skip the kitsch and shop local at **South Shore Market**, which features products from dozens of local artists, including stationery, homewares and apparel. If you're looking for something bigger, stop by **Fishcake** (fishcake.us), a design showroom and multi-hyphenate art space.

Kaka'ako's Small Businesses

My shop, **Keiko Jewelry**, has lots of local, handmade jewelry, and we carry a lot of activewear, like Active by Teal. We also have a jewelry bar that's really popular. **Yireh** and **Mahina Made** just opened near us, and I love going there for their lei tees and their print dresses. And the **Jules & Gem** next door opened not too long ago either. I really love its perfumes and lotions, and really everything that is has. I also really like **Dis-and-Bark** for my dogs. It has a lot of cute dog toys and dog treats, and their staff is really friendly and knowledgeable.

Kristi Hayashida, *owner of Keiko Jewelry @keiko_jewelry*

05 Reimagine PEARL HARBOR

NATURE | HISTORY | HAWAIIAN CULTURE

Pu'uloa, the area also called Pearl Harbor, was once a rich agricultural food basket that fed much of central O'ahu. Today, it is the center of the US military's presence in the Pacific, as well as the site of the Pearl Harbor National Memorial.

DENNIS MACDONALD/SHUTTERSTOCK

How to

Getting around The H-1 between Downtown and Pearl Harbor has some of the worst rush-hour traffic. Plan accordingly.

When to go Any time of year is great, but you'll want to visit the Pearl Harbor National Memorial as close to the 7am opening as possible to avoid the crowds.

Quick facts The full traditional name of Pearl Harbor is Ke Awa Lau O Pu'uloa, the many bays of the long hill, referencing the once abundant fishponds.

PHOTO RESOURCE HAWAII/ALAMY

SVETLANASF/SHUTTERSTOCK

World War II In the face of Japanese internment during WWII, the 442nd Regimental Combat Team, made up mostly of second-generation Japanese immigrants from Hawai'i, became the most decorated regiment in US military history. Visit the **Japanese Cultural Center of Hawai'i** to grasp the legacy of Hawai'i's Japanese immigrants as well as the nearly forgotten Honouliuli Internment Camp.

Pearl Harbor National Memorial The site of the Japanese attack on Pearl Harbor that prompted the US's involvement in WWII, this memorial now commemorates those who died during the 1941 event and the following war effort. Visit the USS *Arizona* Memorial, the Battleship *Missouri* Memorial, the Pacific Fleet Submarine Museum and the Pearl Harbor Aviation Museum for the full experience.

Rebuilding Pu'uloa Despite the US military's continued presence, several initiatives have emerged to restore the now-contaminated wetlands of Pu'uloa. **Hui O Ho'ohonua** (hoh808.org) teaches visitors and locals alike about Hawai'i's unique wetland ecologies through community workdays to help restore the West Loch of the larger Pearl Harbor waterway. Check its website for information about volunteer opportunities.

Above USS *Arizona* Memorial
Top left Battleship *Missouri* Memorial
Below left Japanese Cultural Center of Hawai'i

Hawaiian Renaissance

A political, cultural and artistic movement in the 1970s, the Hawaiian Renaissance was driven, in part, by protests against the US military's use of Kaho'olawe for bombing practice after WWII.

06 Take a HIKE

HIKING | NATURE | SCENIC VIEWS

Get lost under the canopy of a tropical rainforest just minutes from urban Waikīkī. The Honolulu Mauka Trail System features a network of 18 trails that crisscrosses over three extinct cinder cones – Puʻu ʻŌhiʻa, Puʻuʻualakaʻa and Puʻu Kākea – collectively referred to as **Tantalus**. Hike for an hour, or mix and match trails to create an all-day adventure.

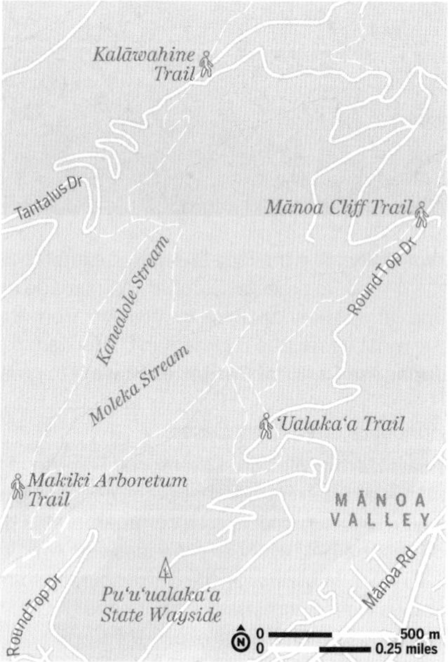

How to

Getting here The drive up Round Top Dr and Tantalus Rd is narrow, winding and dotted with potholes. Be aware of cars and bikes that may pop out from around the bends.

Load your maps Phone reception is spotty, so be sure to pre-load an offline map. You can also download PDF maps (tantalustrailway.org).

Gear up The tropical canopy locks in moisture, and trails can sometimes be quite muddy.

A quick jaunt Most of the trails are fairly short, making it easy to choose if you're short on time. The **Kalāwahine Trail** is a relaxing, well-rounded hike about 1.5 miles long. If you get to the end and don't feel like turning back yet, you can extend it to **Pauoa Flats** for some nice views.

All-day adventure You can easily stitch trails together to create a trek up to 10 miles long without worrying too much about getting lost – each junction has good signage, and though the trails never feel crowded, they are well traveled. If you're looking to maximize your route, the **Makiki Arboretum Trail** is the best place to start.

Top right Sunset view from the Tantalus in Puʻuʻualakaʻa State Wayside
Bottom right Kalāwahine Trail

JOHN D. IVANKO/ALAMY

ERIC BRODER VAN DYKE/GETTY IMAGES

Nā Ala Hele

Nā Ala Hele is the state trail program, which oversees some of the most stunning hikes on O'ahu. All Nā Ala Hele trails are public and well maintained. Trail information is available online (hawaii trails.ehawaii.gov).

Scenery stops There are several lookout points along Round Top Dr, but **Pu'u'ualaka'a State Wayside** offers one of the best bird's-eye views of Honolulu. Pause for a picnic or go exploring down the **'Ualaka'a Trail** while you're there.

Native restoration Most of the plants you'll see are non-native, invasive species that took over when the native forest was cleared for ranching in the early 1900s. While it's generally difficult to find native forest on O'ahu, a portion of the **Mānoa Cliff Trail** offers a rare glimpse of how the island's mountains once looked. Step into the gated restoration area and see if you can tell the difference.

Hawaiian
MONARCHS

03

02

01

05

04

01 King Kamehameha the Great
Kamehameha I. United the Hawaiian Islands and founded the Kingdom of Hawai'i in 1810.

02 King Kamehameha II
Son of Kamehameha and also called Liholiho. Traveled with his wife to England, where they both died of measles.

03 Queen Ka'ahumanu
Favorite wife of Kamehameha I. Served as co-regent to Kamehameha II and III. Credited with abolishing the strict traditional *kapu* system of governance.

04 King Kamehameha IV
Nephew of Kamehameha III. Devoted to providing healthcare and education for Hawaiians. Died of asthma at 29.

05 King Kamehameha III
Younger brother of Kamehameha II. Under his reign, Hawai'i became one of the most educated nations in the world.

06 Queen Emma
Wife to Kamehameha IV. Founded the Queen's

06

08

07

09

11

10

Hospital and Hawai'i's first school for girls.

07 King Lunalilo
Elected by legislature. A proponent of democracy and popular among Hawaiians. Known as 'The People's King.' Died without an heir.

08 Princess Ka'iulani
The would-be heir to the Hawaiian Kingdom. Worked tirelessly to restore Hawaiian sovereignty. Died at 23.

09 King Kalākaua
Elected after Lunalilo's death. Called the 'Merrie Monarch' and encouraged traditional arts. Renovated 'Iolani Palace and circumnavigated the world.

10 King Kamehameha V
Also known as Prince Lot, the older brother to Kamehameha IV. Encouraged the revival of traditional practices. Last of the Kamehameha line.

11 Queen Lili'uokalani
Sister of Kalākaua. Worked to restore power to the Hawaiian people. Overthrown for American business interests. Hawai'i's last monarch.

01 S. GREG PANOSIAN/GETTY IMAGES, **02** THE HISTORY COLLECTION/ALAMY, **03** THE PICTURE ART COLLECTION/ALAMY, **04** HISTORIC IMAGES/ALAMY, **05** THEODORE TRIMMER/SHUTTERSTOCK, **06** THE HISTORY COLLECTION/ALAMY, **07** PHOTO 12/ALAMY, **08** ARCHIVE PL/ALAMY, **09** JEFF WHYTE/SHUTTERSTOCK, **10** CLASSIC IMAGE/ALAMY, **11** THEODORE TRIMMER/SHUTTERSTOCK, **PICTURE FRAMES** KITTIBOWORNPHATNON/SHUTTERSTOCK

07 Royal WAIKĪKĪ

HISTORY | BEACH | WALKING TOUR

Long before the first tourists arrived in Hawai'i, Waikīkī was the capital of O'ahu and a favorite place of Hawaiian chiefs and royals due to its rich wetlands and great surf. Today, glimpses of this royal past remain among the modern shops and hotels, offering a deeper experience to those who seek it.

BRAVE BEHIND THE LENZ/SHUTTERSTOCK

Trip Notes

Getting here If you're not staying in Waikīkī, driving in and parking can be difficult and expensive, and it may make more sense to take the bus. If you do plan to drive, the **Waikiki Shopping Plaza** has decent flat-rate parking.

When to go Waikīkī generally has great weather year-round, but you may find temperatures (and crowd sizes) are most comfortable for walking during the spring and fall.

Learn to Surf

Where better to learn to surf than on the waves surfed by royals? If you're a beginner, and even if you've surfed before, it's best to start with a lesson. Waikīkī's waves are surfed by visitors and locals alike, and learning the etiquette is key to staying safe.

01 'Āinahau was the home of Princess Ka'iulani and was once considered 'the most beautiful estate in the Hawaiian Islands.' Today, **'Āinahau Triangle Park** commemorates the princess and her home.

02 Helumoa was the name of a grove of 10,000 coconut trees and home to O'ahu's chiefs. Today, it hosts the vast gardens of the **Royal Hawaiian Center** (pictured left) and its **Helumoa Hale** cultural facility.

03 King Lunalilo gifted Queen Emma the land where the recently revitalized **International Market Place** now sits. Visit the shopping center for food, music and its lush gardens dedicated to the queen.

04 The **Duke Kahanamoku Statue** celebrates the legendary surfer and waterman. To learn to surf on the favorite waves of Hawaiian royalty, visit **Moniz Family Surf** right across the street.

05 Prince Kūhiō served as Hawai'i's delegate to Congress after the overthrow to fight for the rights of Hawaiians. **Prince Kūhiō Beach Park** sits on the site of his home.

FROM TOP: JEFF WHYTE/SHUTTERSTOCK
THEODORE TRIMMER/SHUTTERSTOCK

08 A New Look at LĒʻAHI

FOOD | SCENERY | ART

There is perhaps no more iconic view of Honolulu than of the white, sandy beaches of Waikīkī with the towering shape of Lēʻahi (pictured below) in the background. Commonly called Diamond Head, Lēʻahi is the remnant of a cinder cone whose dramatic slopes deserve to be seen from all angles. Take some time to admire majestic Lēʻahi from new perspectives.

PHILLIP B. ESPINASSE/SHUTTERSTOCK

Trip Notes

Getting around The area around Lēʻahi is hilly, and it's definitely easiest to drive. But if you're up to walking, the sidewalks are wide, and you'll have plenty to look at as you go.

Weather This area is generally clear, dry and hot. Bring good sun protection and water.

Shangri La Tickets to this estate are available one month in advance (shangrilahawaii.org/tickets) and sell out quickly.

Behind the Name

Lēʻahi means 'brow of the 'ahi' (yellowfin tuna), referring to its iconic shape, which resembles the dorsal fin of a tuna ('ahi). The name was given by the goddess Hiʻiaka. The nickname 'Diamond Head' came from British sailors who initially thought the calcite crystals embedded in Lēʻahi's slopes were diamonds.

01 On the far side of Lē'ahi, tour Doris Duke's estate, **Shangri La** (shangrilahawaii.org), which houses an impressive collection of Islamic art. The tour starts and ends at the Honolulu Museum of Art or Bishop Museum.

02 Watch the surfers from **Diamond Head Lookout**, or walk down to the beach below. Note that the beach is rocky and the waters can sometimes be rough.

03 **Monsarrat Avenue** at the base of Lē'ahi is lined with local favorite eateries – including several great spots for breakfast. Try ARS Cafe for a classy cup of coffee.

04 Pick up a fresh *poke* bowl or a plate of Hawaiian or Filipino comfort food from **Fort Ruger Market**, a local favorite tucked into the neighborhood of Kaimukī.

05 Head up to **Pu'u O Kaimukī Park** for a picnic and a captivating view of Lē'ahi from behind. This little park on a hill is a great place to watch the sunset.

FROM TOP: ERIC BRODER VAN DYKE/SHUTTERSTOCK
ERIC BRODER VAN DYKE/SHUTTERSTOCK

Place Names

KEEPING NATIVE PLACE NAMES ALIVE

Hawai'i's native place names hold invaluable knowledge about ecology, history and Hawaiian culture. Learning the Hawaiian names for the places you visit will add new perspectives to your travels.

GOLDDIAMONDPHOTOGRAPHY/SHUTTERSTOCK

Left Wāwāmalu (Sandy Beach) **Middle** Hūnānāniho **Right** Ironwood trees at Hūnānāniho

For many visitors, Hawai'i's native place names can be a challenge with their repeating syllables, similar sounds and abundance of vowels. It isn't hard to see why many have long preferred to use nicknames that make sense in their own language. After all, 'A-Bay' is much easier for English speakers to remember than 'Anaeho'omalu. But in changing a place's name, you also change its story.

More than a Name

Hawaiian place names are encoded with deep layers of history, culture and reverence. 'How many place names are there or were there in the Hawaiian Islands?' asks Samuel Elbert in the preface to the still-used 1976 edition of *Place Names of Hawaii*, a definitive reference. 'Even a rough estimate is impossible: a hundred thousand? a million?' There were names for individual *lo'i kalo* (Hawaiian wet taro fields), offshore anchoring points, forest clearings and even particular rocks and trees. Names described the topography, commemorated an event or referenced a myth or legend.

When these names are replaced, we lose valuable history, mythology and knowledge vital to understanding the islands and the culture that developed on them. Hawai'i's landscapes and the Hawaiian culture are the backbone of Hawai'i today, and it's important to honor their native place names.

Defining Places

Koko Head, whose steep face is climbed by thousands each day, is the nickname for Kohelepelepe, which recalls

F.NORMAN/CC BY 2.0

PPICTURES/SHUTTERSTOCK

a myth in which the goddess Pele is saved by her sister Kapo and explains the crater's shape.

The town of ʻAiea refers to the native ʻaiea tree, which tells us the tree was once abundant in the area, although it no longer grows there.

The East Honolulu valley of ʻĀina Haina may sound Hawaiian, but it's really a nickname referring to the land's Western owners, the Hind family (ʻĀina Haina means 'Hind's Land'). The valley's name is Wailupe, which means 'water kite,' telling us this was once a place where kites were flown.

> When these names are replaced, we lose valuable history, mythology and knowledge vital to understanding the islands and the culture.

The name Lanikai was invented in the 1920s by a developer who owned a large piece of coastal land in Kailua. Funnily, 'Lanikai,' which is supposed to mean 'heavenly ocean,' isn't even grammatically correct and should instead be Kailani. The Hawaiian name for this area is Kaʻōhao, which means 'the tying,' and commemorates a historic event where two women were beaten in a traditional board game and were tied together as punishment before being unexpectedly rewarded.

'Sandy Beach' is the topographically descriptive name for Wāwāmalu, which means 'shady valley,' in reference to the inland areas that once grew sweet potatoes in abundance. Without this name, it's hard to imagine any climate other than near-punishing sunshine along the Ka Iwi Coast.

Hawaiian Revival

Even locals are not immune to the nicknaming of places, and through the years many places were officially documented with these nicknames rather than their original names. Over the past several years, however, there has been an increase in awareness surrounding the importance of preserving Hawaiʻi's original place names, leading to the restoring of several place names. What was once Waimānalo Bay Beach Park, also called Sherwoods, now goes by its original name, Hūnānāniho. In Lāʻie, Pounders Beach, nicknamed for its shorebreaks, has been officially restored to Pahumoa Beach. In Kailua, Lanikai Elementary School now goes by Kaʻōhao School.

09 Art in the Heart of HONOLULU

ART | SHOPPING | NIGHTLIFE

World-class art collections and award-winning dishes, funky vintage shops and grungy dive bars – there's something to satiate every flavor of self-expression in the Downtown/Chinatown area. Let your afternoon melt into evening in Honolulu's historic business, nightlife and cultural center.

JEFF GREENBERG/GETTY IMAGES

JEFF WHYTE/SHUTTERSTOCK

Museums & Events

Downtown Honolulu is a hub for art on display. On the formal side of things, the **Capitol Modern: The Hawai'i State Art Museum** features an extensive collection of works by local artists and pieces inspired by the beauty of the islands. The museum regularly hosts hands-on workshops and after-hours live-music events. A bit down the road, the **Honolulu Museum of Art** has one of the most extensive collections of Asian and Pacific art in the United States.

The Capitol Modern also hosts the more laid-back **Art + Flea** market twice per month, on the first and third Saturdays. Operated by the nearby small business **MORI by Art + Flea**, this market features dozens of local artists, thrifters and more. Find everything from shell jewelry to screen-printed tees to stained glass trinkets at this gem of an event.

WESTEND61/GETTY IMAGES

ⓘ Common Sense

Downtown's homeless situation is very visible, and many of the homeless in this area are affected by mental illness/addiction. High foot traffic makes Downtown generally safe, but it's wise to pay attention to what's going on around you.

Top left Capitol Modern: The Hawai'i State Art Museum **Top right** Honolulu Museum of Art **Bottom left** Royal insignia on the gate of 'Iolani Palace

Historic Architecture

Downtown Honolulu has been the seat of Hawai'i's business and government since 1845, and many buildings reflect this history. From the English Gothic **Cathedral of St Andrew** to the Spanish colonial revival **King Kalākaua Building**, Downtown is dotted with stand-out sites. Let's not forget **'Iolani Palace**, an architectural marvel – complete with cast-iron filigree and koa wood interiors – which had electricity before the White House and was once the home of the Kingdom of Hawai'i's reigning monarchs. **AIA Honolulu** (aiahonolulu.org), a local architecture firm, offers a walking tour that invites you to see the area through the eyes of an architecture historian.

Buy or Browse

Chinatown's narrow storefronts offer the ideal space for several delightfully specific shops that make for great browsing. Stroll down **Maunakea Street** to peek into the little lei shops that have decorated Hawai'i's high-school graduates for generations. Equal parts vintage shop and museum, **Tin Can Mailman** is packed to the ceiling with old-school

Art on Your Sleeve

Roberta Oaks Namesake store of the modern aloha-wear designer known for her bright colors and playful prints.

Sig on Smith Open only on Fridays, this little space is the only O'ahu outpost of legendary Hawai'i Island designer Sig Zane.

Fighting Eel Started back in 2003, this island-inspired clothing store has quite the selection of floral wear for men, women and *keiki* (kids).

Old Ironside Tattoo Sailor Jerry's original tattoo shop, and the oldest tattoo parlor in Hawai'i. The shop upholds Jerry's legacy, specializing in his iconic style of sailor tattoos. The **Sailor Jerry Festival** is also held in Chinatown every June.

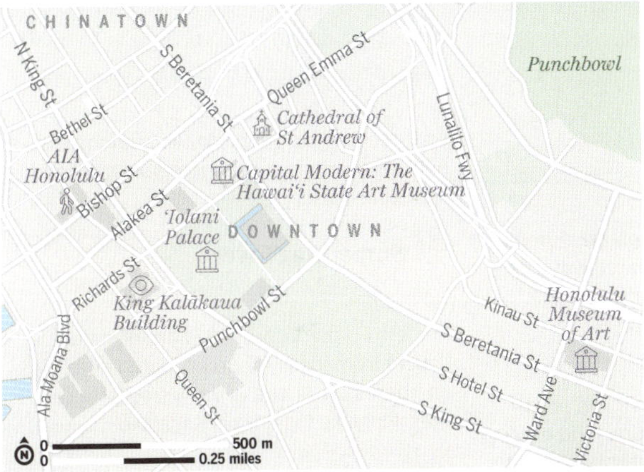

Left Sig Zane shirts
Below Cathedral of St Andrew

Hawaiiana that harkens back to the age of *Blue Hawaii*. Two blocks away, **Native Books Hawai'i** offers careful selections of art and design and Hawaiian publications and invites you to spend a while talking with their knowledgeable staff.

Artisanal Eats

For the epicurean traveler, Chinatown is home to an array of one-of-a-kind eateries that pay homage to the bright flavors and fresh ingredients of the islands. Head over to **Po'ai by Pono Potions** for a cup of coffee elevated by handcrafted, locally grown botanical elixirs. One-man-show **Wing Ice Cream** serves up an assortment of handmade ice creams in seasonally relevant and often off-the-wall flavor combos. Make a reservation at **Fête** for locally inspired, farm-to-table cuisine – in 2022 chef Robynne Maii was the first Native Hawaiian woman to win a James Beard Foundation Award.

Spirits with Spirit

Every bar in Chinatown has its own personality. Visit **Skull & Crown Trading Co** for a delightfully immersive, top-notch tiki-bar experience. **Smith's Union Bar** is a vibey dive bar with a rich history as the oldest bar in Honolulu – and it has karaoke. If you like to dance, get in line at **Scarlet Honolulu** for EDM, multiple dance floors and regular drag shows.

FAR LEFT: DPA PICTURE ALLIANCE/ALAMY
LEFT: NAGEL PHOTOGRAPHY/SHUTTERSTOCK

Listings

BEST OF THE REST

Creative Souvenirs

Local Motion

Lifestyle and surf shop with creative in-house designs on shirts, towels, insulated water bottles and more. Great for practical souvenirs that are cool enough to actually use.

House of Mana Up

This locally owned store only stocks products from Hawai'i entrepreneurs. Find everything from *liliko'i* (passion fruit) chocolate to glass lei.

Kealopiko

Locally designed modern island apparel featuring traditional prints and island motifs in gentle earth tones.

Kaka'ako Kasuals

A creative take on the unofficial footwear of Hawai'i – the rubber slipper. In stores statewide, find simple designs for wear while out and about as well as funky prints for around the house.

Good Food, Live Music

Nico's Pier 38 $$

Specializes in local favorites and fresh fish. Live music every night and occasionally in the afternoon as well. On Honolulu Harbor.

Restaurant 604 $$

Serves traditional American and a selection of local favorites with live music most evenings. Located on the water in Pu'uloa near the USS *Arizona* Memorial – a great sunset spot.

House Without a Key $$$

Set in the luxurious Halekulani resort, this waterfront venue paints the prettiest of pictures with sunset cocktails, seafood plates, hula performances and incredible local and Hawaiian music.

Something Sweet

Holey Grail $

Made-to-order taro-based donuts in unique flavors from locally sourced ingredients, plus an impressive lineup of dairy-free lattes and teas. Flagship location in Kaka'ako.

Ubae $

The place for all things *ube* dessert – cakes, tarts, cookies, pastries. If you're a fan of the bright purple yam, Ubae is a must. In the Kalihi neighborhood, a little over a mile from Bishop Museum.

Ululani's Hawaiian Shave Ice $

With two Honolulu locations, Ululani's has mastered the art of shave ice-making with its soft ice texture and flavorful natural fruit syrups.

Liliha Bakery $

Famous for its Coco Puffs: puff pastries filled with a chocolate pudding and topped with a

DOUGLAS PEEBLES PHOTOGRAPHY/ALAMY

Liliha Bakery

generous dollop of chantilly – a sweet, custardy, buttery frosting made this way only in Hawai'i.

Veranda $$$

On Saturdays, enjoy a full-course afternoon tea with an ocean view on the back porch of the Kahala Hotel.

High-End Sushi

Sushi Sasabune $$$

One of the first *omakase* (chef's choice) sushi experiences in Hawai'i – and still one of the best, with a well-rounded menu and large selection of sake. Located on King St behind an unassuming storefront.

Sushi Tokiwa $$$

Hidden inside the larger Restaurant Suntory, Sushi Tokiwa offers arguably the most high-end *omakase* experience in the city. The simple but impeccable nigiri is the star. Reservations are a must.

Sushi Sho $$$

Located in the Ritz Carlton, beneath dramatic vaulted ceilings. Sushi for the modern palate, incorporating ingredients from around the world, including locally sourced fish and flavorings.

Tane Vegan Izakaya $$$

Captures the essence of sushi without any fish, serving whole-food plant-based dishes with full-bodied flavors. Will likely be less expensive than your typical upscale sushi experience.

Trails for All Levels

Mānoa Falls

Easy 1.7-mile valley hike to a small waterfall. Trail is gravel-lined and well maintained, making it great for kids and beginners. Can get muddy and may be fairly crowded.

PHILLIP B. ESPINASSE/SHUTTERSTOCK

Mānoa Falls trail

Wa'ahila Ridge

Moderate 4.5-mile trail that travels along the ridge and offers stunning views of the valley and city below the entire way. Starts from a state park in a quiet neighborhood directly *mauka* (toward the mountains) of Waikīkī.

Kuli'ou'ou Ridge Trail

Strenuous 4.7-mile trail that isn't technically difficult but can be steep. Ends with a fantastic view of windward O'ahu. The trailhead is in a quiet neighborhood in East Honolulu, so be mindful of residents.

Lyon Arboretum

Run by the University of Hawai'i at Mānoa. Has multiple different sections with great signage and documentation for those interested in learning about tropical and native plant species.

Koko Crater Botanical Garden

Tucked into the far side of Koko Head, this garden is home to a collection of rare and native dryland species, offering a glimpse of an ecosystem not commonly seen.

Foster Botanical Garden

Right in the middle of Downtown Honolulu, this garden is an oasis of green amid the concrete. Hosts free tours through its collection of tropical trees.

BEYOND HONOLULU, O'AHU

NATURE | CULTURE | SCENIC VIEWS

RESEARCHED BY JACKIE OSHIRO; UPDATED BY SARAH ETINAS

- **Trip Builder** (p82)
- **Practicalities** (p83)
- **A Day on Kāne‘ohe Bay** (p84)
- **Nature by Night** (p86)
- **Familiar Flora** (p88)
- **The Wai‘anae Coast** (p90)
- **Sunrise & Breakfast** (p92)
- **Plantation Legacy** (p94)
- **Local Comfort Foods** (p96)
- **Scenic Ko‘olau** (p98)
- **Ahupua‘a** (p100)
- **North Shore All Year** (p102)
- **Aloha ‘Āina** (p106)
- **Listings** (p110)

MH ANDERSON PHOTOGRAPHY/SHUTTERSTOCK

Hike along the coast of **Ka'ena Point** to see rare wildlife (p91)
80min from Waikīkī

Go off-roading with **North Shore EcoTours** (p105)
50min from Waikīkī

Kayak to the **Kāne'ohe Bay Sandbar** (p85)
30min from Waikīkī

Sample rum made with native sugarcane at **Kō Hana Rum** (p94)
40min from Waikīkī

Get your hands dirty in a traditional *lo'i kalo* (taro field) at **Kāko'o 'Ōiwi** (p108)
30min from Waikīkī

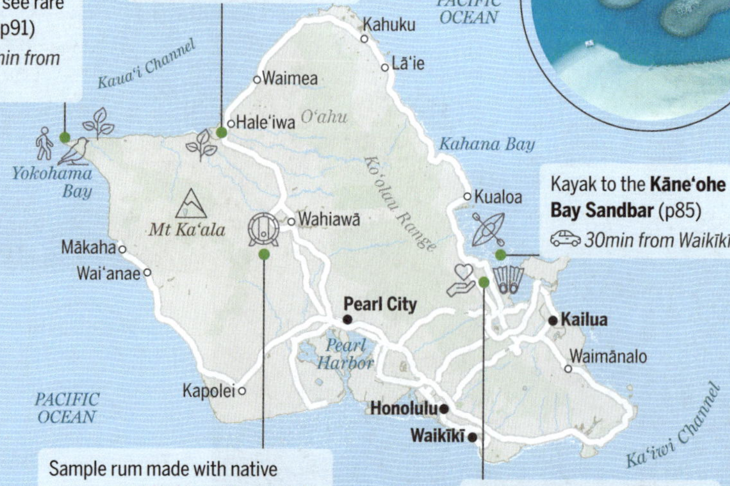

BEYOND HONOLULU, O'AHU

Trip Builder

Take a break from urban life and explore the varied landscapes and lifestyles of O'ahu. Drive along the lush Ko'olau mountain range, explore Hawai'i's multicultural heritage in Central O'ahu and be impressed by the power of the waves on the North Shore.

VIOLET-BLUE/GETTY IMAGES

Practicalities

ARRIVING

If you're not staying in Waikīkī, your best transportation options are a rental car or shuttle.

GETTING AROUND

Car Driving is the most convenient way to get around the island and go at your own pace.

Bus O'ahu's bus system services the whole island, but it's likely to make travel times very long in areas outside Honolulu unless your destination is nearby.

LOCATION LINGO

West Side The Wai'anae Coast past the end of the H-1 Fwy.

Country The area from Wahiawā to the North Shore.

Kona winds Hot, humid weather from the southwest (as opposed to the usual trade winds from the northeast).

ED FREEMAN/GETTY IMAGES

WHERE TO STAY

Due to O'ahu's zoning laws, accommodations are limited to designated resort areas – Waikīkī, Ko'olina, Turtle Bay/Lā'ie and Mākaha – though B&Bs can be found elsewhere.

Location	Pros/Cons
Waikīkī	In the middle of town; convenient; possible to not have a car. Crowded.
Ko'olina	Inclusive resorts; slower paced; calm swimming coves. Quite far from most activities.
Turtle Bay	Closer to nature; good for a relaxing vacation. Almost necessary to have a car.

HOW MUCH FOR A

Poke bowl $15

Snorkel gear hire $20

Helicopter tour $350

TOP: HAPA PHOTOGRAPHY/SHUTTERSTOCK
BOTTOM: JJAVA DESIGNS/SHUTTERSTOCK

EATING & DRINKING

Classic local foods are variations on the foods brought to the islands by plantation workers from around the Pacific and largely fall under the category of comfort foods. Find some of the island's best local eats throughout Central O'ahu and up the Windward Coast.

Best Spam musubi
7-Eleven (p110)

Must-try saimin noodles
Shige's Saimin Stand (p95)

CONNECT

Wi-fi access is available at most cafes, shopping centers and hotels.

10 A Day on KĀNE'OHE BAY

SNORKELING | DIVING | HAWAIIAN CULTURE

Once part of an ancient volcano caldera, Kāne'ohe Bay is now a popular snorkeling and boating spot due to its calm, clear waters and shallow offshore sandbar. Launch your adventures from the scenic He'eia State Park to immerse yourself in the island's rich history and ecology.

JAMES KIRKIKIS/SHUTTERSTOCK

How to

Getting here There are multiple routes you could take to Kāne'ohe, all of them very scenic. Be careful of contraflow lanes during morning and afternoon rush hours.

When to go The drier summer months make for better onshore and in-water conditions. During winter, waters can get murky.

Top tip Gear rentals are the way to go unless you're planning to take your Walmart fins back home as a souvenir.

CHRIS.RYCROFT/FLICKR/CC BY 2.0

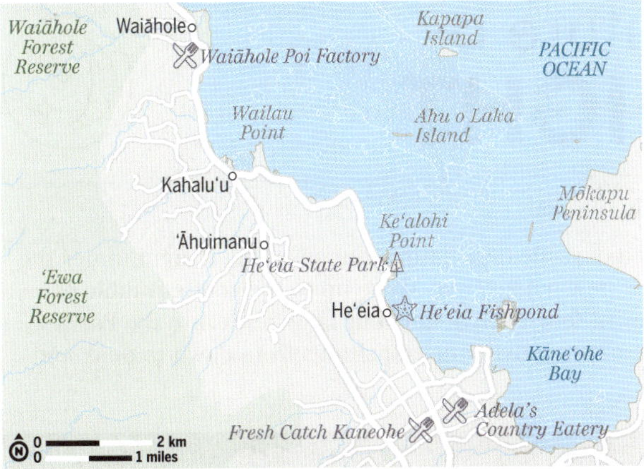

Explore the bay Kāne'ohe Bay is calm, shallow and home to O'ahu's healthiest coral reef – making it great for kids and beginner snorkelers. About a mile offshore is a vast sandbar that's only about a foot underwater at low tide, shallow enough to walk on and enjoy panoramic views of the Ko'olau Range. Paddle out to the sandbar to chase fish across the sandy seafloor, or venture out over the edge to explore the deeper areas bursting with life.

New rules prohibiting rentals within 1000ft of the shoreline mean you'll want to arrive prepared. For SUP, kayak and snorkel gear rentals, check out **Kailua Beach Adventures** (kailuabeachadventures.com) if you're staying in the Kailua area, or **KAI Adventures** if you're anywhere else – both will deliver to residences near their location. It takes about 30 minutes to kayak to the sandbar from shore. If you're hoping to catch the sandbar at its shallowest, be sure to check the tide forecast to pick the right time to go.

Discover a ancient history Once you're dry and back on land, take a guided walking tour of historic **He'eia State Park** (dlnr.hawaii.gov/dsp/parks/oahu/heeia-state-park). Learn about the ancient area's legends, indigenous plants and cultural significance, as well as the incredible efforts to restore He'eia Fishpond (p107).

Top left Paddleboarding, Kāne'ohe Bay **Bottom left** Waiāhole Poi Factory

Area Eats

Fresh Catch Kaneohe
Local favorite spot for fresh fish. Take your pick from around a dozen types of *poke* (cubed raw fish mixed with a variety of flavorings) scooped à la carte or served over hot rice. Or pick up a filling plate lunch – try the 'ahi katsu.

Waiāhole Poi Factory
Perhaps the best place on the windward side for Hawaiian food, serving fresh, hand-pounded *poi* (steamed, mashed taro) and simple traditional dishes. Try its *kūlolo,* a sticky sweet made with taro and coconut.

Adela's Country Eatery
Unique take-out noodle spot with house-made pastas using *kalo* (taro), *ube* (purple yam), avocado and *'ulu* (breadfruit).

11 Nature by NIGHT

OUTDOORS | CAMPING | ADVENTURE

Hawai'i is normally a daytime destination, but spending a night under the stars can offer a completely new perspective. Wake up to the gentle rumble of the ocean or to a symphony of forest birds. Let your body relax into the Earth's rhythms as you experience nature's dynamic transitions from dawn to dusk and beyond.

EVAN AUSTEN/SHUTTERSTOCK

How to

Camping permits All campgrounds on O'ahu require a permit. Book most sites through the state up to 30 days in advance (explore.ehawaii.gov) or the city up to seven days in advance (camping.honolulu.gov).

When to go Summer will give you the best chance of good weather.

Midweek closures Many city and county campsites are closed on Wednesday and Thursday nights.

BARRY WINIKER/GETTY IMAGES

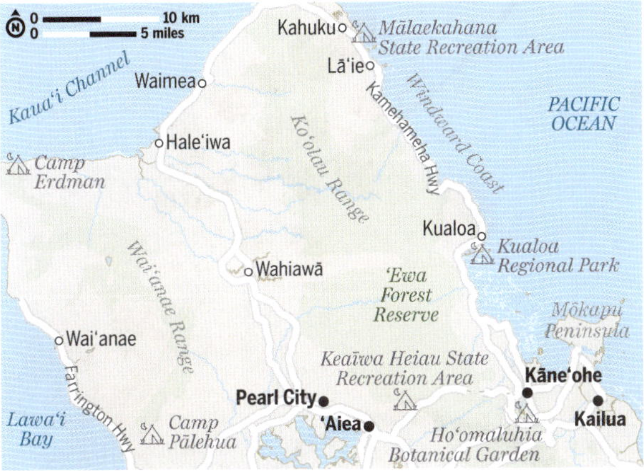

Top left Milky Way seen from O'ahu **Bottom left** Camping, Kualoa Regional Park

Camping for All Levels

Pitch a tent You don't get much closer to nature than when you're separated from it by just a thin piece of nylon. Most beachfront campgrounds are fairly near the road, and you'll likely be able to hear the sound of cars passing. The campgrounds at **Kualoa Regional Park** are further removed – ideal if you're looking for tranquility. For family-friendly camping, head to the mountains. The **Keaīwa Heiau State Recreation Area** is tucked into a quiet neighborhood west of Honolulu, and some of its campsites have covered pavilions with barbecue grills. The park is also home to the 4.8-mile, kid-friendly **'Aiea Loop Trail**. On the lush windward side, the **Ho'omaluhia Botanical Garden** has numerous campsites, clean bathrooms, beautiful scenery and a lake area to explore. It does get a fair amount of rain during the winter, however.

Book a cabin A couple of privately run campgrounds offer cabins and more comprehensive facilities. **Camp Pālehua** (camppalehua.org) is in a restricted area of the Wai'anae Mountains and has its own private trails and cultural programming. **Camp Erdman**, owned and operated by the YMCA of Honolulu, is nestled right on the North Shore and has both cabin and yurt options.

Be Prepared

Be sure to read up ahead of time so there are no unwelcome surprises during your camping trip. Most O'ahu campgrounds are pretty barebones – while some do have bathrooms and shower facilities, others do not. Some campgrounds are close to the road or near homeless encampments. Campgrounds with gates that lock overnight offer peace of mind but may limit your entrance and exit times. O'ahu is a small, densely populated island, and most public park facilities show obvious signs of wear and use.

The campgrounds we list here are likely your best bet for a predictable camping trip.

Familiar **FLORA**

02

01

03

04

05

06

07

01 Ti
Seen in shades of red and green with a wide range of sizes. Used commonly in cooking and lei making.

02 Rainbow shower trees
Canopies erupt in beautiful shades of pink, orange, white and yellow in early summer. Introduced species found widely on O'ahu.

03 Plumeria
Lightly fragrant lei flower most commonly seen in white and yellow, with pink and burgundy varieties as well.

04 Kukui
This tree's oily nut was burned to make candles; now used mostly in lei.

05 Naupaka
Native coastal bush with a dainty half flower described in legends as half of a pair of star-crossed lovers.

06 Haole koa
Fast-growing, highly invasive tree originally introduced by Westerners.

07 ʻŌhiʻa
Important native tree found in almost all native forests. Not widely seen on O'ahu

08

09

10

11

12

13

anymore. In danger due to fungal disease.

08 Hau
Shrubby tree found in coastal areas. Its bright yellow flowers denote its relation to the hibiscus.

09 Strawberry guava
Commonly seen on hiking trails. Highly invasive, so feel free to munch on its sweet red fruits as you go.

10 Ginger
Highly invasive and found throughout Hawai'i's wet forests. White and yellow varieties have a lovely fragrance.

11 Kiawe
Kiawe thorns often puncture slippers at the beach. Highly invasive, but its fragrant wood makes for great grilling.

12 Uluhe
Native fern found in mountain forests and seen commonly along most hiking trails. Grows densely and aids in erosion control.

13 Pā'u o Hi'iaka
Crawling coastal ground cover. Its name means 'skirt of Hi'iaka' and alludes to a traditional myth.

12 The Wai'anae COAST

COMMUNITY | WILDLIFE | OUTDOORS

Two words to remember when on the sunny Wai'anae Coast are community and complexity. Far removed from the density of Honolulu, the people of Wai'anae hold on to the community values that often get lost in the city. Yet this area has been historically underfunded and exploited by business and military interests. Enjoy Wai'anae with respect for its resilience.

PIKAPPA/GETTY IMAGES

How to

Getting here It's easy to speed on Farrington Hwy, so mind speed limits and watch out for the large speed humps as there are often pedestrians along the road.

When to go The Wai'anae Coast is reliably sunny year-round. Check the surf report during winter as waters can get rough.

Safety Be aware of petty crime. Use common sense and keep belongings out of sight when away from your car.

FERRANTRAITE/GETTY IMAGES

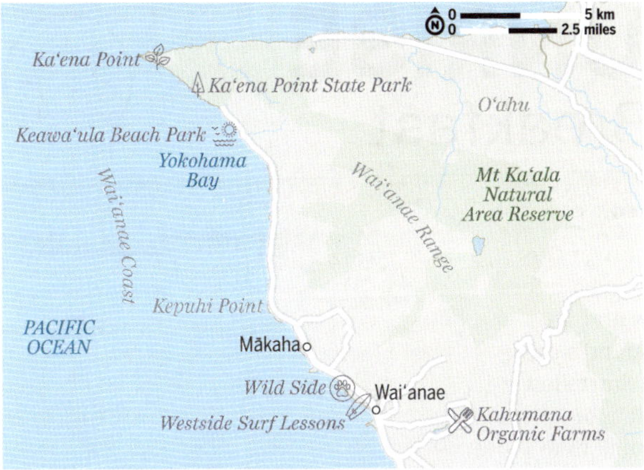

Community focus Wai'anae will often offer you a more personable experience than elsewhere on O'ahu, so long as you come with curiosity and respect. Skip the crowds of Waikīkī and learn to surf in a more intimate setting with **Westside Surf Lessons** (westsidesurflessons.com). Stop for lunch at **Kahumana Organic Farms** (kahumana.org) for a casual farm-to-table meal overlooking the working fields.

Pristine waters Because it's so dry, Wai'anae's waters are exceptionally clear and home to an abundance of marine animals. To get up close, join the ecologists and wildlife biologists at **Wild Side** (sailhawaii.com) for a tour to see dolphins, whales and turtles. If you'd prefer to lounge on the beach, check out **Keawa'ula Beach Park**, though note that waves can sometimes be dangerous.

Ka'ena Point The northwest tip of O'ahu is known as a leina-a-ka'uhane, or leaping place of the dead, where souls depart the land of the living to join the ancestors. It's also a nature reserve where albatross and shearwaters nest every year. From the parking lot in **Ka'ena Point State Park**, it's a scenic 2.5-mile hike along the rocky coast to the point. Don't forget to wear sunscreen and bring plenty of water. Ka'ena is also accessible from the north in Mokulē'ia, but the hike in from the west offers better views.

Top left Keawa'ula Beach
Bottom left Hiker, Ka'ena Point dunes

Visiting Respectfully

Nearly a century of chronic underinvestment, land and resource seizures, and economic undermining in favor of tourism have all but ensured the intergenerational poverty experienced throughout the Wai'anae Coast today. As a result, many of the area's residents are understandably skeptical of visitors. Be mindful of this history if you choose to visit – heed signs that say '*kapu*' or 'keep out,' even if they appear unofficial; support small businesses; try not to call attention to yourselves; and be polite in your interactions, even if responding to hostility.

13 SUNRISE & Breakfast

SCENIC VIEWS | FOOD | BEACH

Looking straight out over the Pacific Ocean, Oʻahu's east coast offers unparalleled sunrise views and an opportunity to savor the island's cool, calm and quiet mornings. Start slow with a stroll along the beach, or sprint into the new day with a quick hike before fueling up for your adventures ahead.

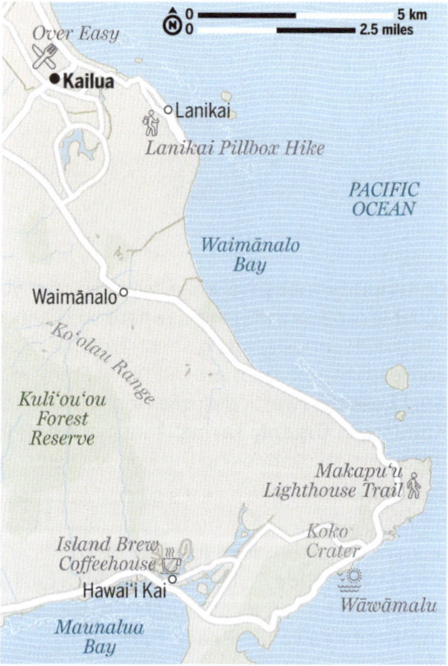

How to

When to go Depending on the time of year, sunrise can range from around 5:50am to 7:05am. Don't forget to check your breakfast restaurant's hours too.

Weather tip A few clouds on the horizon won't detract from the view, but there won't be much to see if there's rain or significant cloud cover. The east side can also be quite windy, so don't forget a jacket.

Sunrise on the beach

There's nothing quite like watching the sunrise to the sound of the ocean lapping at the sand. Most beaches along the Windward Coast have calm morning waters and are ideal for a stroll along the shore or an early-morning dip. If you want a more dynamic view, check out **Wāwāmalu**, also known as **Sandy Beach**. Wāwāmalu's waves break powerfully on the shore, offering an impressive, yet dangerous, display.

Early-morning exercise

For a better vantage point, altitude is key. The **Makapuʻu Lighthouse Trail** is fully paved and safe to do even in the dark. Give yourself about 30 minutes to reach

Top right Sunrise on the Lanikai Pillbox Hike trail
Bottom right Over Easy breakfast

PHILLIP B. ESPINASSE/SHUTTERSTOCK

HAPA PHOTOGRAPHY/SHUTTERSTOCK

Winter Weather

The windward side is reliably wet between November and April. For the best views during these months, pick a spot along the drier Ka Iwi Coast like **Makapu'u** or **Wāwāmalu**.

the top – though you'll have a great view almost the entire way up. If you're up for more of a challenge, the **Lanikai Pillbox Hike** (Ka'iwa Ridge Trail) has a stunning view of the sun coming up over Nā Mokulua, the two islets just offshore. This trail requires hiking experience and shoes with good traction. It's about 30 minutes up fairly steep, eroded terrain and not recommended during or after rain.

Where to eat Kailua and East Honolulu have breakfast options aplenty. To keep the good vibes going, **Island Brew Coffeehouse** in the Hawaii Kai Shopping Center has light breakfast fare and waterfront seating. Local favorite **Over Easy** in Kailua serves fresh takes on breakfast classics.

14 Plantation LEGACY

LOCAL CULTURE | FOOD | FESTIVALS

Beginning in the mid-1800s, laborers were imported from around the world by the American sugar plantations that dominated Hawai'i's economy. Workers faced harsh conditions and racial discrimination, but this dark history laid the foundations for the multiethnic melting pot that is Hawai'i today.

How to

Getting here Traffic to and from Central O'ahu can be bad around rush hour, so plan for a visit between midmorning and midafternoon.

The plantation era Roughly from 1850 to 1950. The industry was dominated by companies owned by the descendants of American missionaries and paved the way for the annexation of Hawai'i.

The workers Laborers came from China, Japan, Portugal, the Philippines, Korea and Puerto Rico.

Step back in time For a glimpse at the systems that brought all of these cultures together, head over to **Hawaii's Plantation Village** (hawaiiplantationvillage.org), an outdoor museum featuring fully furnished replicas of plantation buildings, including houses of the various ethnic groups and community buildings.

Sugar today While the plantations of old are long gone, sugar is still being grown in Central O'ahu by **Kō Hana Rum** (kohanarum.com). Visit its farm in Kunia for a tasting tour to sample its rum, made with native heirloom sugar-cane varietals.

Mix plate One of the most enjoyable products of the plantation era is Hawai'i's

Top right Hawaii's Plantation Village **Bottom right** Musicians at a bon dance festival

PHOTO RESOURCE HAWAII/ALAMY

YI-CHEN CHIANG/SHUTTERSTOCK

Hawaiian Pidgin

Hawaiian Pidgin developed as a way for the plantation workers from different cultures to communicate. It is now considered its own language and is widely spoken throughout the islands today.

unique culinary heritage. Order a hot bowl of saimin (noodle soup) at **Shige's Saimin Stand** or pick up a plate lunch from mom-and-pop shop **Forty Niner Restaurant**. If you know your Asian food, you'll notice things look familiar, with some notable differences. Craving *poke*? **Tanioka's Seafoods & Catering** has long been a local favorite with its extensive spread of options. Pick up a spam *musubi* while you're there too.

Cultural celebrations With a mix of cultures comes a mix of celebrations. **Chinese New Year** is celebrated throughout the islands, with the biggest events held in Honolulu's Chinatown. From mid-June to August, Japanese Buddhist temples host **bon dance festivals** to honor family members who've passed away. The **Korean Festival** is held in August and the **Okinawan Festival** is over Labor Day weekend.

Local Comfort **FOODS**

01

02

03

04

05

01 Spam musubi
The quintessential hand-held food. Sweet soy-glazed Spam on rice held together by a strip of nori (dried seaweed).

02 Saimin
Neither Chinese nor Japanese, saimin is a local creation. Soft egg noodles in a light shrimp-based broth with a few key garnishes.

03 Meat jun
Thinly sliced beef with an eggy coating. Hawai'i's version of the Korean *jeon*. A standard option at most plate lunch places.

04 Loco moco
A healthy serving of rice topped with a hamburger patty, a fried egg and a dousing of brown gravy. Born in Hilo.

05 Butter mochi
Sweet, buttery, springy baked mochi. Less sticky than traditional mochi. Bought by the tray.

06

07

08

09

10

06 Manapua
Steamed bun filled with pork. Essentially a large *char siu bao*. The name comes from *mea 'ono pua'a* (tasty pork thing).

07 Crack seed
Assorted Chinese preserved dried fruit often flavored with sour dried plum powder called *li hing mui*.

08 Pastele
The Puerto Rican *pastele* is similar to a tamale. Pronounced 'patele' in Hawai'i and often seen in *pastele* stew.

09 Mochiko chicken
Deep-fried, bite-sized pieces of chicken coated in *mochiko* (rice flour). Another classic plate lunch pick.

10 Malasada
Pillowy Portuguese-style fried donut. Often found in Hawai'i filled with custard, *haupia* (coconut pudding) or fruit jelly.

01 PHILIP KINSEY/SHUTTERSTOCK, **02** CHRISTOPHERMYA/SHUTTERSTOCK, **03** THE DANCING LIGHTS/SHUTTERSTOCK, **04** AO NORI/SHUTTERSTOCK, **05** LEIGH ANNE MEEKS/SHUTTERSTOCK, **06** CRYSTAL EYE STUDIO/SHUTTERSTOCK, **07** PHOTO RESOURCE HAWAII/ALAMY, **08** MIKE HERNA/SHUTTERSTOCK, **09** IMAGE PROFESSIONALS GMBH/GETTY IMAGES, **10** AXEL MEL/SHUTTERSTOCK

15 Scenic KO'OLAU

DRIVE | SEA CLIFFS | NATURE

Strap in, roll down your windows and get ready for one of the most scenic drives in the islands. From steep cliffs and crashing waves to verdant valleys and tropical rainforest, the dynamic drive along O'ahu's eastern shoreline is awe-inspiring to visitors and locals alike. Spend a day slowly meandering beside the steep cliffs of the Ko'olau mountain range.

SHAUN JEFFERS/SHUTTERSTOCK

Volcano Remnants

The Ko'olau Range (pictured) is the western flank of a once massive volcano. About a million years ago, the eastern half slid into the ocean, extending over 100 miles underwater in one of the largest landslides in Earth's history. Kāne'ohe Bay is what remains of the old summit caldera.

Trip Notes

Getting around This route is best started from town so you're driving in the outside lane closer to the shore. If it's still light out when you're done, try taking the scenic H-3 Hwy back to town.

When to go Summer offers the best conditions. Winter can be wet, making some outdoor activities hard. But if you're up for the adventure, Ko'olau is beautiful in the rain and you may spot waterfalls.

FROM TOP: JOHN D. IVANKO/ALAMY, DANIEL SHUMNY/SHUTTERSTOCK

05 Park at Turtle Bay and take a leisurely, 1-mile stroll along the beach to **Kalaeokauna'oa (Kahuku Point)** to catch the sunset amid the native coastal flora.

04 Take a horseback or UTV tour of idyllic **Gunstock Ranch**. Learn about the history of the area and become a part of the Hawaiian Legacy Reforestation Initiative.

03 Feed the koi at **Byodo-In Temple**, nestled up against Ko'olau's steep ridges. It's part of the Valley of the Temples memorial complex, so be mindful of those paying respects.

02 Pop into **ChadLou's Coffee Roasters** (chadlouscoffeeroasters.com) for farm-to-cup coffee and fresh banana bread. Or savor the moment by booking a coffee-tasting experience.

01 Take in the deep blue waters and sheer cliffs of the Ka Iwi Coast at **Hālona Blowhole**. But mind the guardrails – the wind, spray and ocean currents make for a dangerous combo.

Ahupua'a

TRADITIONAL LAND DIVISIONS

Traditional land divisions called *ahupua'a* were key to the Hawaiians' incredibly successful agricultural systems. Although most are no longer used in the way they once were, *ahupua'a* live on in different ways today.

Left O'ahu landscape **Middle** Map of O'ahu *ahupua'a* **Right** *Ahupua'a* boundary marker

HOWARD KINGSNORTH/GETTY IMAGES

A thousand years ago, the first Polynesian voyagers arrived in the Hawaiian Islands carrying with them the plants, animals, tools and technologies to sustain life. Weaving their knowledge and culture together with the elements and natural processes unique to these islands, the Hawaiians developed a stable, thriving civilization.

Key to their success was a highly sophisticated system of resource management, which rested on land divisions called *ahupua'a*. Spanning from ridgetop down to the reef, each *ahupua'a* contained the food and resources needed to support its inhabitants. Crops were grown upland in *lo'i* (flooded fields) or *māla* (dryland fields), *loko i'a* (fishponds) were constructed at the shore, and sources of water were managed and maintained so that all had access to clean freshwater.

Wealth, Redefined

So what happened? When the first Westerners arrived in 1778, they brought with them a host of diseases the Hawaiians had no immunity against. As a result, it's estimated that by 1840 the Native Hawaiian population had declined by as much as 84%. This steep population loss meant that there were fewer people to maintain the various systems within the *ahupua'a* and that Hawaiians were more susceptible to pressures from outside powers. Subsequently, in 1850, a legal redefining of land ownership stripped most Hawaiians of their land and subsistence.

Losing the *ahupua'a* system went beyond simply upsetting systems of agriculture – it also signaled a shift in values. Traditionally, there was no such thing as land

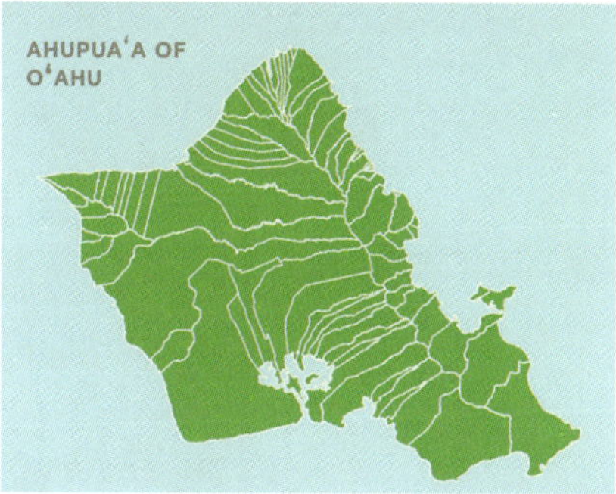

FERGAL CONDON/LONELY PLANET

EEKIM/FLICKR/CC BY 2.0

ownership. In fact, the land was not something that could be owned, but rather it was understood that if people took care of the land, the land would take care of people, and thus wealth equated to communal abundance.

Shifting to a system of privatized land and removing Hawaiians from their ancestral ways of life created new meanings of wealth and severed the important cultural connection between Hawaiians and the land.

It was understood that if people took care of the land, the land would take care of people, and thus wealth equated to communal abundance.

Ahupua'a Today

Today there are initiatives across the islands working to restore connection to the land, revive Hawaiian agricultural systems and sustainably feed the people of Hawai'i. On O'ahu, the *ahupua'a* of He'eia is the best example of a working *ahupua'a* with both the fishpond and croplands currently being restored.

Aside from agricultural uses, many *ahupua'a* are still recognized areas, and you may be familiar with the names of some traditional *ahupua'a* like Waikīkī, Honolulu and Kailua – although these names are now used for slightly different geographic areas. But that doesn't mean the traditional places have been lost. In fact, there's been a push in recent years to use traditional names and boundaries more often.

Sign of Past Times

As you drive along O'ahu's coastal roads, you may notice brown signs punctuating the landscape – they're particularly unmissable along Kamehameha Hwy on the Windward Coast. Each of these signs marks the boundary of a traditional *ahupua'a,* reminding all who pass of the ingenuity of the Hawaiians. If you look closely, the image printed on the signs is a mound of rocks topped with a pig's head. Rock mounds called *ahu* were used as boundary markers, and tributes such as pigs – *pua'a* – were placed on *ahu* as a tax to the chief. This is where the name *ahupua'a* comes from.

16 NORTH SHORE All Year

BEACH | SURF | COUNTRY

With massive waves in the winter and calm shores during the summer, O'ahu's North Shore offers very different experiences throughout the year. But no matter when you visit, there's always plenty to do – in and out of the water.

PHILLIP B. ESPINASSE/SHUTTERSTOCK

SEAN DAVEY/GETTY IMAGES

Winter Wave Watching

The swell shifts north around November, bringing waves that can top 40ft. Waves this size attract professional surfers from around the world and make for an incredible show. One of the best places to watch is **'Ehukai Beach Park**, also known as **Banzai Pipeline**. If an especially big swell comes in, the North Shore can get crowded with folks trying to catch a glimpse of the pros. Arrive in the area before 8am, and don't move your car until you're ready to leave – you won't find parking again.

Even on days that look calm, the current can be very strong during the winter. Pay attention to any signs posted on the beach, and never turn your back on the water. The waves may pick up suddenly, and many beaches on the North Shore have dangerous shorebreak.

CASSIO WIEHE/SHUTTERSTOCK

Skip Turtle Beach

Tourists trying to spot *honu* (green sea turtle) at **Laniākea Beach** (Turtle Beach) cause major traffic on the only road to the North Shore. It's best to skip this overpopulated spot – *honu* can be seen along the entire coast. And when you do see one, remember to stay at least 10ft away.

Top left Surfer riding the Banzai Pipeline
Bottom left Surf photographers
Top right *Honu* (green sea turtle)

For fun in the water during the winter, try stand-up paddleboarding (SUP) or kayaking down the mellow **'Anahulu River** in Hale'i-wa. Pick up a rental from one of the many rental shops nearby or take a SUP tour from **Blue Planet Adventure Co** (blueplanet adventure.com).

Snorkel All Summer

During the summer, the North Shore's waters are placid and glassy – the ideal snorkeling conditions. Pūpūkea Beach Park offers two options. **Shark's Cove** is one of the best dive spots on O'ahu and is great for those with some snorkeling and diving experience, as it's rocky and has a fairly steep drop-off. Just to the south, **Three Tables** is sandy with a more gradual slope, making it an excellent spot for beginners. Both locations are very popular, so it's best to arrive by 9am in order to secure parking. Stop by **Surf N Sea** (surfnsea.com) in Hale'iwa to

Hale'iwa Eats

Having grown up on the North Shore I have seen a lot of food places come and go, but my favorites have been around since I was a kid. Lunch is a teri chicken sandwich at **Kua 'Aina**. Dinner is heavy *pūpū* (appetizers) – like sashimi, *kalbi* Korean ribs and popcorn shrimp – and Moe'ritas at an outside table at **Haleiwa Joe's**.

Recommended by Liz House, *co-founder of Guava Shop in Hale'iwa @guavashop*

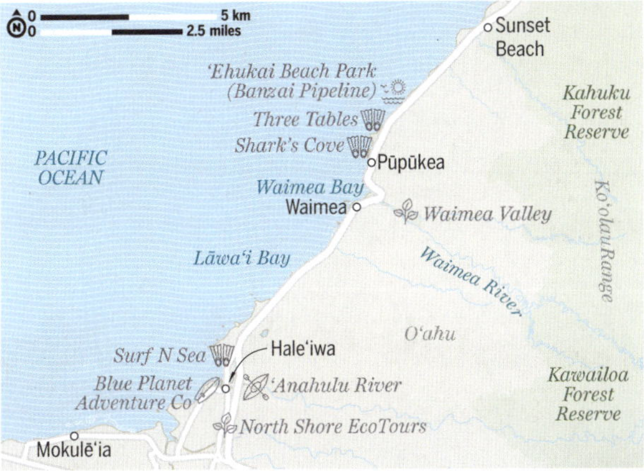

Left Waimea Valley waterfall
Below Shark's Cove seabed

rent all the gear you'll need for just $15 per day. Prescription mask rentals are available here.

Waimea Valley

The lush Waimea Valley is home to a botanical garden, cultural activities and an easy hike that leads you to a waterfall with a swimming hole. Sign up for the daily Kipahele Tour to learn about Waimea's rich history and visit the *kauhale,* a traditional living site. When you're done for the day, keep your car parked there and hop across the street to sandy Waimea Bay.

Go Off-Roading

Join **North Shore EcoTours** (northshoreeco tours.com) for an off-road ATV adventure through private lands led by Native Hawaiian guides. Climb steep ridges and slosh through muddy trails as you learn about O'ahu's unique environment – think of it as a hiking tour on wheels. For those who actually want to hike, the operator also offers guided hiking tours to scenic vistas or a pristine mountain swimming hole.

FAR LEFT: CHRISTIAN MUELLER/SHUTTERSTOCK
LEFT: BENNY MARTY/SHUTTERSTOCK

17

Aloha 'ĀINA

ENVIRONMENT | CULTURE | NATURE

Aloha 'āina – love of land – is a guiding tenet of Hawaiian culture and represents reverence for the mutual relationship between humans and nature. Look into joining community workdays to learn about Hawaiian philosophies, meet locals and help give back to the land.

PHOTO RESOURCE HAWAII/ALAMY

FUNBOXPHOTO/SHUTTERSTOCK

He'eia Fishpond

Loko i'a, Hawaiian fishponds, are a form of aquaculture found nowhere else on Earth and demonstrate exceptional understanding of the environment's natural processes. While there are several types of fishpond, the main type involves building a retaining wall around brackish waters where freshwater streams or springs meet the ocean offering ideal conditions for growing algae. Baby fish swim into the walled section to feed on algae, and once they grow large enough they can no longer swim out and are thus stuck within the fishpond.

Paepae o He'eia (paepaeoheeia.org) is working to restore He'eia Fishpond on the Windward Coast of O'ahu, which encloses 88 acres and is estimated to be as much as 800 years old. To learn about *loko i'a* and see

PHOTO RESOURCE HAWAII/ALAMY

Beyond 'Land'

'Āina is the word used for 'land,' but a more accurate translation is 'that which feeds,' which acknowledges the life-giving nature of the Earth. Unlike the connotations of 'land,' *'āina* is not something that can be owned and used but is instead treated as a relative to care for and receive care from.

Top and bottom left He'eia Fishpond
Top right Hawaiian tile

He'eia Fishpond for yourself, you can sign up for a tour, or check out its website for more info on community workdays.

Kāko'o 'Ōiwi

Just inland from He'eia Fishpond in the same *ahupua'a* is a 400-acre wetland restoration project run by nonprofit **Kāko'o 'Ōiwi** (kakoooiwi.org). According to old photographs and oral histories, the He'eia Wetlands were home to extensive fields of wetland taro, the main Hawaiian staple crop. For almost a hundred years before Kāko'o 'Ōiwi was granted use in 2010, the land went largely untouched, allowing invasive species to take over. Since then, 6 acres of *lo'i kalo* (taro fields) have been restored to full working order and 20 more have been cleared for dryland farming. Kāko'o 'Ōiwi offers opportunities to volunteer and learn more about Hawai'i's traditional staple crop as well as its sophisticated water-management practices. If you're looking to

Why Aloha 'Āina?

He Ali'i ka 'āina; He kauwā ke kanaka. The land is Chief; man is the servant.

We must always recognize our place in the natural world. By doing so, we ensure it remains in perpetuity for generations to come. We are laying the foundations for what they will inherit, and we must get it right. Your visit should include a layer of recognition, honoring the host culture. Give yourself the privilege to do as the locals do, hands to the land, as servants to it, guided by Aloha.

Contributed by Kimeona Kane, *director of Community Outreach at 808 Cleanups @808cleanups*

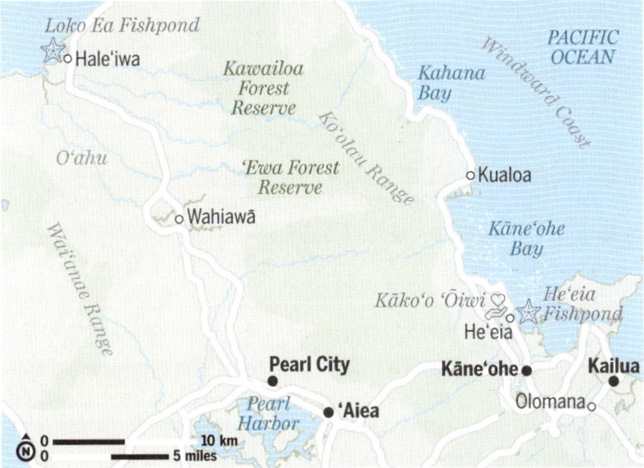

Left Kāko'o 'Ōiwi
Below Loko Ea Fishpond

get a little muddy, there are two types of community workdays: *lo'i* workdays to help plant, weed and harvest the *lo'i kalo;* and wetland workdays to remove invasive species, out-plant native species and clear out waterways.

Loko Ea

Up on the North Shore, **Mālama Loko Ea** (lokoea.org) is working to improve the environment around and restore ecosystem balance to the historic **Loko Ea Fishpond**. Although the fishpond has been continuously in use since before Western contact, previous stewards failed to maintain the surrounding ecosystem and introduced invasive species like tilapia. Mālama Loko Ea is working to restore the fishpond to sustainably and abundantly feed the North Shore community. It also offers a hands-on tour where visitors can learn about the area's cultural history, hear traditional *mo'olelo* (stories) and help with various restoration activities.

FAR LEFT: DOUGLAS PEEBLES PHOTOGRAPHY/ALAMY
LEFT: DOUGLAS PEEBLES PHOTOGRAPHY/ALAMY

Listings

BEST OF THE REST

Quick Bites

Seven Brothers $

Big, delicious burgers and sides at locations across the North Shore: Kahuku, Lā'ie Hale'iwa and Shark's Cove.

Kalapawai Market $

Pick up sandwiches, wraps or baked goods to go before jetting off for a long day at the beach. Locations in Kailua, Waimānalo and Kapolei.

7-Eleven $

Hawai'i's 7-Elevens are on another level. Pick up a Spam *musubi,* hand-roll sushi or a hot plate of *pancit* (noodles) to take with you on your adventures.

Zippy's $

Stop by this beloved local diner chain for a meal on the run. Most locations have a dedicated takeout window with a curated menu of to-go plates. Try its famous chili and rice or a Zip Pac bento.

Foodland $

This local grocery-store chain has a large selection of *poke,* prepared foods and self-branded snacks, as well as standard self-catering items. *Poke* bowls are a great deal at around $10.

Foodie Tours

Mānoa Chocolate

Learn about the bean-to-bar process and sample flavors with Mānoa Chocolate's team of chocolate sommeliers on a tour of its factory in Kailua.

21 Degrees Estate

Delve a little deeper into the chocolate-making process on an in-depth tour of the 21 Degrees Estate farm in Kāne'ohe. Rest assured, a chocolate tasting is included as part of the tour.

Kahuku Farms

Take a tractor ride through commercial fruit and veggie fields and try a few freshly picked fruits. Once you're done, stop by the farm cafe for perhaps the freshest meal you've ever had.

Lokoea Farms

Explore tropical fruit orchards, feed chickens and learn to husk a coconut on a tour through Lokoea Farms in Hale'iwa. If you like what you see, it's possible to book a farm stay (lokoeafarms.com).

Sweet Land Farm

Drop by Sweet Land Farm in Waialua to feed the goats. While you're there, pick up some artisan goat cheese or treat yourself to a goat-milk gelato.

KARA KNIGHT/SHUTTERSTOCK

Kalapawai Market

Veggie Friendly

Raised by the Waves $

Fully plant-based and proudly plastic free, this aesthetic little eatery in Kahuku offers a healthy post-beach refuel away from the crowds of Hale'iwa.

Down to Earth Organic & Natural $

This locally owned health-food store has locations in Honolulu, Kailua, Kaka'ako, Pearlridge and Kapolei. Build your plate from its hot bar, order a smoothie or sandwich from the counter or pick up a pre-made tofu *musubi*. The entire store is vegetarian or vegan, so stock up on snacks for the road.

Adela's Country Eatery $$

Unique take-out noodle spot with house-made pastas using *kalo* (taro), *ube* (purple yam), avocado and *'ulu* (breadfruit). For the easiest vegetarian experience, you'll want to build your noodle plate, rather than picking one of the predetermined combinations. All of the noodles themselves are vegan, but the toppings may not be.

Noods Ramen Bar $$

To-go ramen shop in Kāne'ohe (with two additional locations in Honolulu). Known for black garlic miso ramen and a wide array of vegan options.

Beaches for the Family

Ko Olina Lagoons

The four protected coves at Ko Olina were engineered for calm, clean waters great for even the smallest kids. And you don't have to stay at the resorts – the beach is open to the public.

ED FREEMAN/GETTY IMAGES

Surfers, Waimea Bay

Lanikai Beach

Set against the backdrop of the Mokulua islets, Lanikai Beach in Kailua has pillowy soft sand and gentle turquoise waters. Pay attention to any signs about parking in the neighborhood.

Waimea Bay

This North Shore beach is fantastic for swimming, snorkeling and cliff jumping in the summer, then hosts epic surf competitions in the winter.

Kuilima Cove

Wide beach, calm waters and abundant marine life. Located in the Turtle Bay Resort complex. Park in the public spaces on the right side of the lot and walk straight to the water.

Waimānalo Bay Beach Park

This large beach is rarely busy. While the waters are often calm, there are still some days when the waves can be a touch too big for comfort. Hang out near the lifeguard towers.

KAUA'I

NATURE | ADVENTURE | RELAXATION

RESEARCHED BY MEGHAN MINER MURRAY; UPDATED BY SARAH ETINAS

- **Trip Builder** (p114)
- **Practicalities** (p116)
- **Into Nāpali** (p118)
- **Adventure Buddy** (p120)
- **Sugar Chutes & Shacks** (p122)
- **West Side Wander** (p124)
- **Nearly to Ni'ihau** (p128)
- **Jurassic Jaunts** (p130)
- **Bird's the Word** (p132)
- **Wild Chickens** (p134)
- **Taro Trail** (p136)
- **Common Reef Fish** (p138)
- **Listings** (p140)

LUDO KOOS/SHUTTERSTOCK

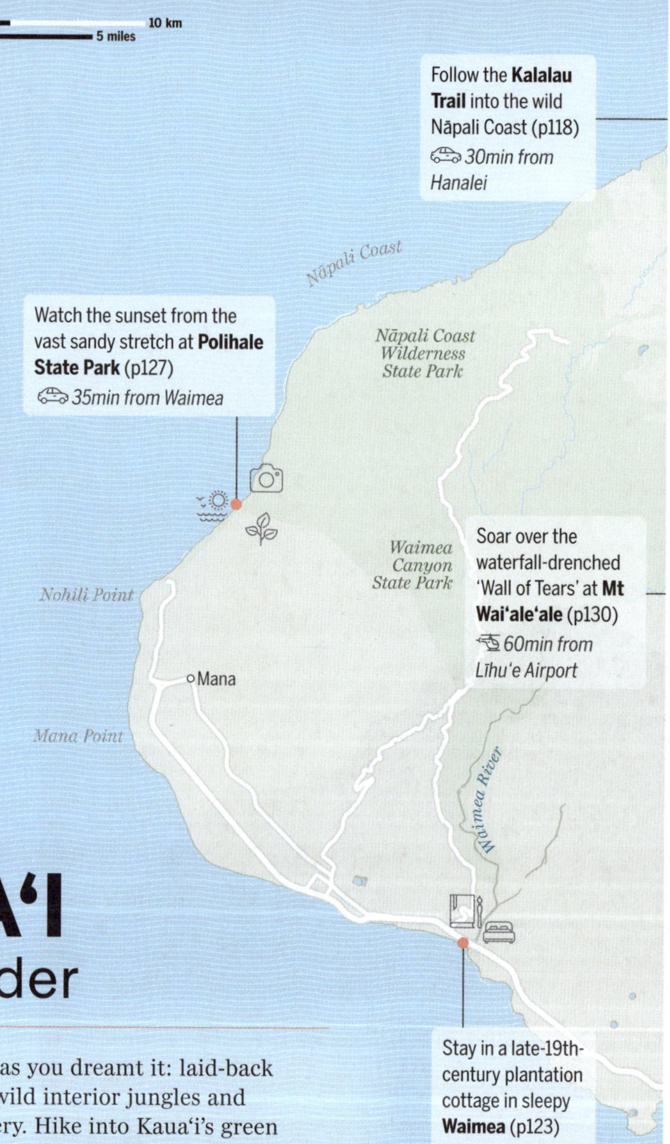

KAUA'I
Trip Builder

This is Hawai'i as you dreamt it: laid-back beach towns ringing wild interior jungles and no-filter-needed scenery. Hike into Kaua'i's green mountain curves, kayak to a hidden waterfall and immerse yourself in its recent sugar-plantation history with sleepy, rum-soaked nights.

CLOCKWISE FROM TOP LEFT: PJV/SHUTTERSTOCK, STEVE JOHNSON/GETTY IMAGES, STEVE BLY/ALAMY, MICHAEL BARAJAS/SHUTTERSTOCK

Practicalities

HARALD L. VAAGAN/SHUTTERSTOCK

ARRIVING

Līhu'e Airport (LIH) On the southeastern side, Līhu'e (pronounced *lee*-hoo-ay) is Kaua'i's only point of entry, unless arriving by cruise ship. Most interisland flights route through Honolulu.

Hotel shuttles, taxis, rideshares (Lyft, Uber, Holoholo), car rentals and the **Kaua'i Bus** (thekauaibus.com; $5 day pass to points island-wide) service the airport. Car rentals can sell out during busy times, so book in advance.

HOW MUCH FOR A

Shave ice $7

Surf lesson $75+

Helicopter tour $350

WHEN TO GO

DEC–JAN
Busy season. North American winter/festive holidays.

FEB–JUN
Shoulder season. Good weather and warming ocean waters.

JUL–SEP
Calmest offshore and best time for Ni'ihau charters.

OCT–NOV
Start of whale season.

GETTING AROUND

Rental car Great for freedom of movement. Check discount hawaiicarrental.com to compare rates or **Turo** (turo.com) to rent cars from locals. Many hotels and resorts charge extra for parking.

Kaua'i Bus A regular and reliable but slower way to travel. Over a dozen routes offer service from Kekaha to Hanalei beginning at either 5am or 6am and ending between 9pm and 10pm depending on route. Due to staffing shortages, there is no Sunday service.

North Shore shuttle To ease North Shore traffic congestion, a **shuttle service** (gohaena.com) runs from Princeville or Waipā Park and Ride to Hā'ena State Park stopping at several beaches.

EATING & DRINKING

TOP: STANLEY WAI/GETTY IMAGES
BOTTOM: WOLFGANG KAEHLER/ALAMY

While shave ice (pictured top) – a fluffy ice dessert doused in fruit juices, condensed milk and sometimes served atop ice cream – and sweet taro products like *kūlolo* and mochi cake can be had throughout Hawai'i, Kaua'i has some of the best of both. Check out stellar examples at **Wailua Shave Ice** (wailuashaveice.com) in Kapa'a and **Hanalei Taro & Juice Co** (hanaleitaro.com).

Best Japanese
AMA Restaurant (pictured bottom; p141)

Must-try ice cream
Pink's Creamery (p141)

WHERE TO STAY

Most visitors opt to stay in the southerly resort area of Po'ipū, but outside of downtown Līhu'e, most locations will meet tropical-vacation expectations.

Location	Pros/Cons
Po'ipū	Good beaches and a variety of shopping and dining options. Mostly visitor/vacation area.
Līhu'e	Closest to airport and town amenities. Industrial feel and away from best beaches and attractions.
Wailua/Kapa'a	Centrally located with easy access to many attractions; close to airport. Fewer great beaches.
Princeville	Scenic, private and pricier accommodations nearest to Kīlauea Point Lighthouse.
Hanalei	Fun island town with good shopping and dining; closest to northern beaches. Few hotels; mostly vacation rentals.
Waimea	Close to Waimea Canyon and west-side beaches. Remote; few nearby dining options.

CONNECT & FIND YOUR WAY

Connectivity Reliable wi-fi is widely accessible in major towns and resort areas. In the interior and remote areas on the island's west side, cell reception may be spotty.

Navigation Major roads ring the island (except for a 19-mile gap along the Nāpali Coast) providing access to population centers, almost all of which are coastal.

ABOUT THE RAIN...

Expect rain. Except for the interior (one of Earth's rainiest locales) showers are typically short-lived and followed by sunshine.

MONEY

Check out permitted vacation rentals – many are in the same area as resorts, some have swimming pools, and self-catering meals is a great way to save money.

18 Into NĀPALI

KAYAKING | ADVENTURE | HIKING

Kaua'i's crowning gem is the 17-mile-long undulating green Nāpali Coast. Sure, you can take a dinner cruise for sunset views, but fully immersing in its majesty under your own steam is far more rewarding. Whether you opt to kayak or to hike the grueling Kalalau Trail, you'll make memories that will last a lifetime.

How to

Getting around Trailhead and longer kayak departures are from Hā'ena State Park; overnight parking is included with camping permits.

When to go Kayaking only May to September, which is also the best season to hike.

Permits & reservations Kalalau Valley camping permits are required for all overnighters and serve as landing permits for kayakers. Reserve up to 30 days in advance (camping.ehawaii.gov, kalalautrail.com).

Hiking

Reserve two to five nights for the adventurous 22-mile expedition into the **Kalalau Valley** and back (you'll want extra days to bask in the remote splendor). The first stretch traverses Hanakāpī'ai Valley, where a detour leads to a cascade emptying into a **swimmable pool**. The trail then climbs out of the valley, through subsequent valleys, and past ancient taro terraces – a reminder that this route has been followed since antiquity. Another waterfall awaits before the final descent to **Kalalau Beach**, where you can camp under leafy canopies or in protected sea caves beyond its white stretch. With your extra days, lounge on the

Top right Hikers, Kalalau Valley
Bottom right Aerial view of Nāpali Coast

JUERGEN_WALLSTABE/SHUTTERSTOCK

MARIDAV/SHUTTERSTOCK

Fountain of Youth

Before departing Hā'ena, take a peek into **Waikapala'e** sea cave. Its blue maw moonlighted as the mythical pool in the 2011 film *Pirates of the Caribbean: On Stranger Tides.*

beach, swim in stream-fed pools, explore the verdant valley and be lulled to sleep by crashing waves under a vast canopy of stars.

Kayaking

The shortest out-and-back kayak trips traverse 12 miles of open water, so find your rhythm and enjoy the ride. You'll feel dwarfed by the 4000ft-high Nāpali cliffs edging inland in waves of green. If conditions are right, tuck into the protective nooks of surging sea caves and coast beneath the refreshing cascades of seaside waterfalls. Paddle alongside spinner dolphins, endangered monk seals and turtles. Tackle the entire coastline and you'll be rewarded with more valleys, hidden shores and the beach-spanning **Honopū Arch**. Bonus: expect calmer conditions on the protected last leg. Most excursions are guided.

19 Adventure BUDDY

HIKING | DOGS | DAY TRIP

What could be better than hiking Kaua'i's scenic mountain trails followed by a dip in the sea and a refreshing shave-ice snack? Doing it all with a furry friend by your side. Kaua'i was one of the first places in the country to offer a program that pairs well-socialized and adoptable shelter dogs with hiking companions for field trips.

BRIGITTE THERIAULT/GETTY IMAGES

How to

Getting here Get your dog from the Kaua'i Humane Society building off Kaumuali'i Hwy south of Līhu'e.

Hours Pickups are pre-scheduled and fall between 10am and noon; drop-offs are same-day by 5pm.

Cost $75 for the day; a $100 fee is charged if a dog is not returned on time.

Good to know You must be 18 years old or over. You cannot transport dogs in open-topped vehicles (truck bed or convertibles).

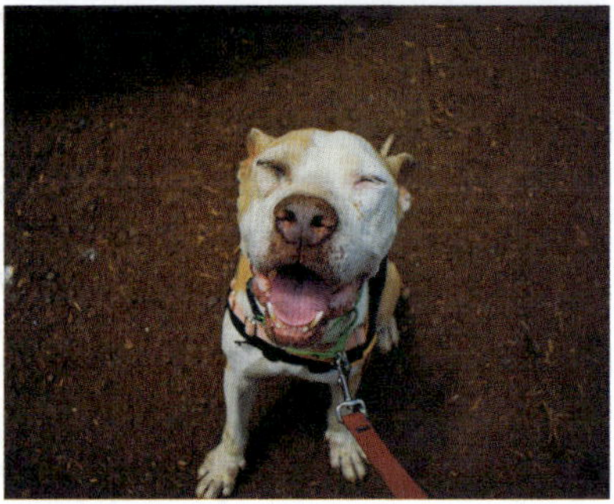

VANESSA S HUNTER/SHUTTERSTOCK

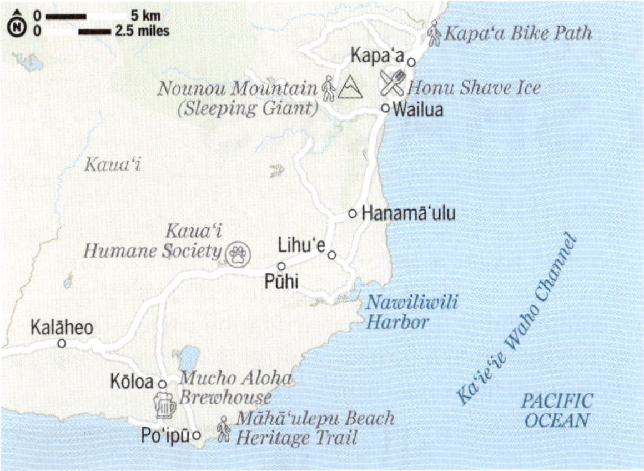

Kaua'i is well known for its abundant nature, jungle trails and scenic lookouts. For many visitors, there's just one thing missing: a furry hiking companion, something the tiny island has in spades. The **Kaua'i Humane Society's** (kauaihumane.org) shelter-dog field-trip program pairs well-adjusted and adoptable pups with human explorers for this reason.

Over 1400 dogs pass through the Kaua'i Humane Society's doors each year, most of which are adoptable animals, found abandoned or stray. Nearly all shelter dogs are of mixed-breed varieties, the result of raising dogs to track and hunt another island animal – the wild boar.

Field-tripping dogs reap several obvious benefits – the chance to escape the kennels, stretch their legs in the great outdoors, and romp and socialize with humans. There's also the possibility that the exposure will help these dogs find homes – all are outfitted with collar, leash and 'adopt me' vests before their excursions. The society estimates around 10% of outings result in adoption.

Because of the dearth of adoptive homes on Kaua'i, hundreds of adoptable animals are flown to partner shelters on the US West Coast each year, where Hawai'i's unique mixed breeds are highly prized pets. The society makes it easy to sponsor your field-trip friend (or any other shelter animal) to find a home off-island, especially if you fall in love and that home is yours.

Top left Beauceron shepherd dog on a Kaua'i trail **Bottom left** Post-hike pitbull

Where to Go

The **Māhā'ulepū Beach Heritage Trail** is a gorgeous, easy hike on the South Shore and a great place from which to spot sea turtles and whales (in winter). Afterwards, stop by **Mucho Aloha Brewhouse** in Kōloa for lunch and dog-friendly outdoor seating. The two **Nounou Mountain** (Sleeping Giant) hikes on the East Side are more physically challenging options with sniff-worthy wildflowers and panoramic ocean and interior mountain views. For something more relaxing, stroll down the **Kapa'a Bike Path** then head to **Honu Shave Ice**, where dogs get their own beef-broth-flavored shave ice treat.

Recommended by Kaua'i Humane Society
@kauaihumanesociety

20 Sugar Chutes & SHACKS

HISTORIC SITES | SUGAR HISTORY | RUM TASTING

Though the last large crop of Kaua'i sugar was harvested in 2009, after more than a century in cultivation, evidence of its storied history persists in overgrown buildings, rusted equipment and hard-won irrigation canals. Dive directly into sugar history by tubing through former plantation ditches, sipping a mai tai, then ending your day in a seaside sugar-worker's bungalow.

HOLGER LEUE/GETTY IMAGES

Sugar History

Hawaiians cultivated sugarcane before Western contact, but Kōloa on Kaua'i saw the first successful large-scale commercial sugar enterprise. The industry boomed, and the volume and diversity of international laborers hired to work the fields and factories continues to reverberate in the diverse culture of modern Hawai'i.

Trip Notes

Afternoon refresh Tubing tours are most refreshing noon to late afternoon.

Winter high season November to early January and mid-February to March, visitors should book tours and accommodations more than a month out.

Be prepared Bring post-tubing clothes and insect repellant.

Drive safe Rum tasting then dinner (or lunch) is a smarter combo; even better, designate a driver.

03 At **Kilohana Plantation**, cheer sugar cultivation's past in a rum and cocktail tasting at Kōloa Rum Co, then dine at The Plantation House by Gaylords on the lānai of the restored manor nearby.

05 Sleep in a rustic bungalow on the beachside grounds of **Waimea Plantation Cottages** (pictured left) – restored sugar-workers homes from three Kaua'i plantations, dating from the 1880s.

01 Strap on a headlamp, plop in a tube and float through **Hanamā'ulu Ditch** – irrigation flumes dug in the 1870s – on scenic Līhu'e Plantation while learning about Kaua'i's sugar past.

04 Only rubble and a sturdy brick chimney remain of Ladd & Company's 1835 **Old Sugar Mill of Kōloa**, the location of Hawai'i's first commercial sugar enterprize.

02 An 1850s sugar plantation is now the site of **Grove Farm Museum**, dedicated to showcasing sugar-era Hawaiiana.

FROM TOP: MICHAEL BARAJAS/SHUTTERSTOCK, CHASE CLAUSEN/SHUTTERSTOCK

21 West Side WANDER

SCENERY | CANYONS | BEACHES

Wander along Kaua'i's west and north sides and be wowed by natural wonders: striated, red-hued Waimea Canyon; mysterious Ni'ihau Island; the 12-mile-long stretch of sugary sand at Polihale Beach; and the misty end-of-the-road Kalalau Lookout, offering sweeping Nāpali views from above.

MARJOLAINE TREMBLAY/GETTY IMAGES

How to

Getting around You'll want a rental car and a full day to explore.

When to go Nāpali Coast views are more likely to be mist-free in early morning.

Good to know On Hwy 550 between Waimea and road's end there are no gas stations and only one eatery.

Barking Sands This nickname for a section of Polihale Beach describes sounds emitted by its textured grains in the wind or when walked upon.

BRESTER IRINA/SHUTTERSTOCK

Because of the island's rugged and swampy topography in the northwest, the road that rings Kaua'i has a gap of almost 20 miles. This has insulated most of the island's west side from merely curious travelers: to access its remote attractions, a little extra effort is required – routing along the South Shore and taking one of two out-and-back roads.

MARISA ESTIVILL/SHUTTERSTOCK

End of the Road First

Since most visitors sightsee up Hwy 550, you can beat crowds and get coastal views that are more likely to be mist-free by going to the end of the road early and first, making all stops on your way back south. The last of the two end-of-the-road scenic overlooks, **Pu'uokila**, affords Nāpali's best views without a helicopter, boat tour or long hike. It overlooks the **Kalalau Valley** flanked by undulating

Russian Ruins

En route to Waimea are remnants of the 1817 Russian fort, **Pā'ula'ula State Historic Site**. Built as an outpost for Russian-American Company traders, the fort represented one man's failed attempt to secure a sandalwood monopoly and several Hawaiian islands for the Russian flag. Today it's little more than rubble.

Top left View from the Pu'uokila lookout
Bottom left Alaka'i Swamp trail (p126)
Above Pā'ula'ula State Historic Site

green sweeps of mountains and the ocean beyond; it's not uncommon for a rainbow to arc across this otherworldly scene. The dirt trail that extends beyond the lookout turns into a series of boardwalks that run through the mossy, high-elevation **Alaka'i Swamp**.

Kōke'e Forest & Waimea Canyon

Following Hwy 550 south, you'll hit **Kōke'e State Park** (kokee.org), home to an informative natural-history museum, cabins (former Civilian Conservation Corps barracks circa 1935–42) and **Kōke'e Lodge Café & Bar**, the road's only restaurant, around mile marker 17. The forested upland area is a great place for a hike or a picnic. Every autumn, the large grassy lawn fronting the museum hosts the Eo e Emalani Festival, a celebration of the life and times of Hawaiian Queen Emma and commemoration of her journey into the Alaka'i Swamp with traditional hula, *oli* (chants) and *pā'ū* (skirt-wearing women horseback) riders.

Happenin' Hanapēpē

Another interesting stop on the island's west side – especially if you visit on a Friday afternoon – is the offbeat artists' town of Hanapēpē.

The former Chinese rice-farming community is a hodge-podge of aging galleries, antique stores and mom-and-pop shops. The town comes to life under arcs of twinkle lights from 5pm to 8pm each Friday for **Art Night** (hanapepe.org/art-night), when businesses stay open late, pop-up food vendors offer new dining options and musicians serenade passersby. Don't miss the **swinging bridge** spanning the Hanapēpē River behind town – a version of it has been here since the early 1900s.

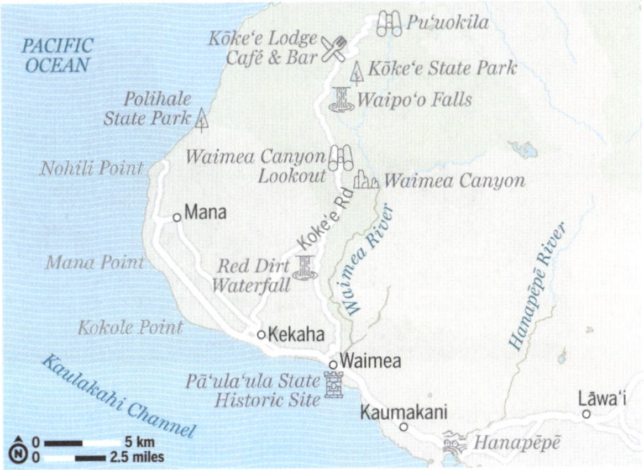

Left Hanapēpē swinging bridge
Below Red Dirt Waterfall

Further south, numerous pullouts overlook the stunning red-and-green **Waimea Canyon**. At around 3000ft deep, it's about half the Grand Canyon's depth. The striated layers each represent past eruptions of the now-weathered volcano that formed Kaua'i some 5.6 million years ago. Stop at the pullout around mile marker 12 to see **Waipo'o Falls**, tucked into the corner of a canyon. And stop again at the **Waimea Canyon Lookout** around mile marker 10, for the best panoramic views. Continue to the roadside **Red Dirt Waterfall**, where a small cascade navigates rust-red hills in an oddly Martian display.

Ni'ihau Lookout & Polihale Beach

Backtrack to the fork, around mile marker 7, and take **Koke'e Road** toward the coast. Along the way, before leaving higher elevation, pull over for the best views of mysterious Ni'ihau (p128), 'The Forbidden Isle,' 17 miles offshore. Then take Hwy 50 west all the way to the dirt trails that back **Polihale State Park**. Find a spot to park and clamber over the dunes for a private slice of the beach's vast uninterrupted expanse.

Nearly to Ni'ihau

THE FORBIDDEN ISLE BECKONS

'The Forbidden Isle' is nothing if not alluring. The mysterious, privately owned eighth Hawaiian island is visible from Kaua'i, yet remains off-limits to outsiders. Its isolated culture hints at pre-colonial Hawai'i and, offshore, the wildlife and topography are unparalleled.

Left Ni'ihau coastline **Middle** Ni'ihau shell lei **Right** Hawaiian monk seal

Preserving the Past

The hulking mass of 1280ft Pānī'au, the highest point on the arid 72-sq-mile island of Ni'ihau, looms large off Kaua'i's west coast. This distant view is the closest most people will ever get to the island.

Ni'ihau remains little changed by outside influence since it was purchased by a Scottish ranching family from King Kamehameha V in 1864 for $10,000 in gold and a promise to protect its residents and their traditional way of life. Today, some 70 Niihauans reside in Pu'uwai Village on the island's western side. There are no cars, paved roads, law enforcement, doctors or indoor plumbing. Traditional knowledge and pastimes continue – fish are caught with spears and nets, and meat is procured with knives and ropes. And while the Hawaiian language was almost entirely extinguished elsewhere, Niihauans continued speaking it, forming their own dialect, and remaining the last connection to Hawaiian linguistic antiquity.

Christianity is widespread and some modern concessions have been made – there's a small solar-operated school with computers, food is cooked on kerosene stoves, and water and groceries come from Kaua'i weekly. Islanders have always been allowed freedom of movement, but since a polio epidemic in 1952, Ni'ihau has remained insulated from outsiders. The only way onto the island itself is with an invitation from a resident. As economic enterprises dried up – including a ranch that once employed most residents – many islanders have left for greener pastures. Only around 10% of the island's population at the time of purchase remains.

ALVIS UPITIS/ALAMY

SHELBY DANIELLE/SHUTTERSTOCK

Landing on Ni'ihau

The Robinson family began offering controlled and limited glimpses of the island in the late 1980s; both options visit remote parts of the island and don't interact with locals. Half-day beach excursions offer the chance to beachcomb and enjoy the mystique of a Ni'ihau beach. Longer 'safari' excursions allow hunting access to help control populations of imported African ungulates, feral sheep and Polynesian boar, which remain unchecked by islanders' subsistence hunting. See **Niihau Helicopters** (niihau.us) for info.

> There are no cars, paved roads, law enforcement, doctors or indoor plumbing. Traditional knowledge and pastimes continue.

Take-Home Treasures

Another way islanders sustain themselves is by selling *lei pūpū* (shell garlands) made from rare, minuscule shells woven together into layered strands of pink, red, black, off-white and gold. It can take master craftspeople up to six months to make a necklace. These are displayed in Hawai'i homes, to be worn on special occasions – the cheapest cost several hundred dollars, while some fetch upwards of $10,000, depending on shell quality and type.

Much of the oral history surrounding shell lei has been lost, but the tradition of crafting *lei pūpū* pre-dates Western contact, and they have long served as traditional adornments for *ali'i* (chiefs) and hula dancers. Ni'ihau is the primary source of this painstaking ancient craft as this is where the shells are most abundant. Find Ni'ihau shell lei in shops across Kaua'i.

Offshore

Though they don't contribute to Ni'ihau's economy, day-long snorkel and dive charters from Kaua'i visit Ni'ihau and Lehua, a small island nearby, without landing. Most depart Port Allen and Po'ipū and some cruise past the Nāpali Coast before making the rough Kaulakahi Channel crossing. A highlight is the almost-guaranteed close-up sightings of *'īlioholoikauaua* – 'dog that runs in rough water' – rare and endangered Hawaiian monk seals. Fewer than 1400 remain in the wild. Underwater, submerged lava tubes with cave openings 100ft wide, striated boulders recalling sunken cities, coral encrusted arches and seemingly endless vertical walls are backdrops to schools of large *ulua* (giant trevally), reef fish, rare-in-Hawai'i species like the knifejaw, and abundant sharks.

22 JURASSIC Jaunts

MOVIE SETS | JUNGLE | HELICOPTER TOURS

The rolling green ridge-line of Kaua'i's northern coast sets the scene for the opening credits of the original *Jurassic Park* movie released in 1993. Though blessedly devoid of dinos, the island's remote interior is infrequently visited and still feels wild. Visit the film's park entrance and soar above ancient volcano tops and waterfalls for timeless jungle views.

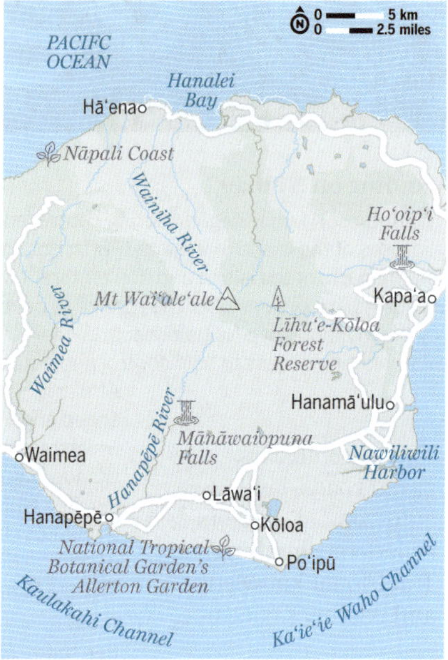

How to

Driving tours For *Jurassic* landscapes, skip movie tours (which lump in easy-to-reach sites with locations from other films) and book a 4WD tour to the harder-to-reach interior around Mt Wai'ale'ale.

Rain gear required Annual rainfall of 450in makes Kaua'i's interior one of Earth's rainiest locales.

Jurassic-less Park Kaua'i formed five million years ago, 60 million years after dinosaurs went extinct.

By Air

The *Jurassic Park* theme will play in your head as you approach the **Nāpali Coast** sea cliffs – the same aerial view featured in the film's arrival scene. Inland, you'll reach the 400ft **Mānāwaiopuna Falls**, where scientists and park owner John Hammond touched down; select tours give the full effect by landing at its base, allowing you to emerge into its mist. Then hover alongside the vast, green-walled expanse of **Mt Wai'ale'ale**, typically shielded from sight on land by a perpetual cloudy haze. Also called the 'Wall of Tears' for its many crevasses streaming with slender, sorrowful cascades, it played the iconic backdrop to the official park entrance.

Top left Allerton Garden, National Tropical Botanical Garden **Bottom left** View of Mānāwaiopuna Falls from helicopter cockpit

RITU MANOJ JETHANI/SHUTTERSTOCK

BENNY MARTY/SHUTTERSTOCK

High in the Sky

Most of Kaua'i is inaccessible and wild, making a helicopter tour the only way to glimpse remote valleys and timeless waterfalls, and appreciate the island's time-eroded shield-volcano form. For the best photos on helicopters, avoid light-colored clothing, which can reflect off the windows.

Over Land

Imagine being stalked by dinosaurs in the fern-carpeted forest around **Waikoko Stream**. You'll need a 4WD to travel the bumpy unpaved road into the **Līhu'e-Kōloa Forest Reserve**. Close by, twin towering wooden posts signal the sides of the once torch-bedecked Jurassic Park gate. North of Kapa'a, take the short **Ho'oip'i Falls** hike; the waterfall served as the mine where an amber-sheathed mosquito was unearthed, starting it all. On the South Shore, the **National Tropical Botanical Garden's Allerton Garden** houses the imposing Moreton Bay fig trees whose buttress roots shielded a nest of hatched eggs in the original film.

23 BIRD'S the Word

SEABIRDS | CLIFFS | WETLANDS

Due to the dearth of native land-based predators, Kaua'i is home to an astounding mix of wetland, sea and forest birds. Bring binoculars to spot spiraling shearwaters and Laysan albatross nesting along Kīlauea's lighthouse-capped cliff. Or follow trails through forest and shrubland for the best chance of spotting rare Hawaiian honeycreepers, six of which are only found here.

ROSANNE TACKABERRY/ALAMY

How to

Finding birds Private guides can assist in detecting forest birds' subtle cues, but sea and wetland birds are easily spotted road- and cliff-side, in the air and via boat charters.

When to go Forest and wetland birds are year-round residents. Winter months bring migratory shorebirds from colder climes. At Kīlauea Point, huge Laysan albatross soar in the sky November through July, and March through November brings wedge-tailed shearwater nests along the lighthouse walkway.

PHOTO RESOURCE HAWAII/ALAMY

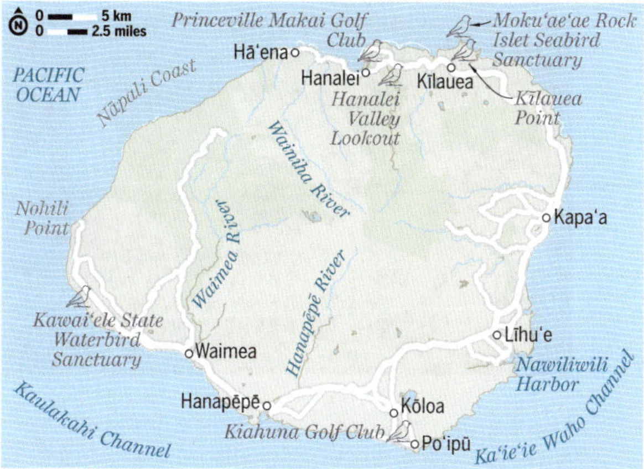

Top left *Aeʻo* (Hawaiian black-necked stilt) **Bottom left** *ʻAmakihi* (yellow-green honeycreeper)

Wetland birds Since settlement, Hawaiʻi has lost about 15% of its wetlands statewide, but native wetland birds – most of which look similar to genetically distant mainland cousins and whose populations dipped with habitat loss – are rebounding on Kauaʻi. North Shore taro *loʻi* (fields) and wildlife refuges have helped bolster populations of endangered *aeʻo* (Hawaiian stilt), moorhen, coot and the mallard-looking native duck – it's the only place on Earth where these birds have overlapping breeding populations. Look for them from the **Hanalei Valley Lookout** inland from Hanalei town, or in the **Kawaiʻele State Waterbird Sanctuary** on the west side near mile marker 30 on Hwy 50.

The state bird, nēnē (Hawaiian goose), is a true success story on Kauaʻi: nearly extinct when 50 individuals were introduced in the 1990s, the island now sports more than 2400, the state's largest population. Golf course greens are a surprising place to encounter them: try **Kiahuna Golf Club** outside Poʻipū or the **Princeville Makai Golf Club**.

Seabirds In the air around the sea cliffs of **Kīlauea Point** and the just-offshore **Mokuʻaeʻae Rock Islet Seabird Sanctuary**, find rambling seabirds, including red and brown footed boobies, great frigatebirds, shearwaters and tropicbirds. It's also the best place to spot Laysan albatross when around 150 lifelong mated pairs come to breed a single egg each winter.

Common birds In addition to ubiquitous chickens (p134), many colorful global transplants mingle throughout Kauaʻi: house sparrows from North America, the warbling white-eye from Japan, rose-ringed parakeets from Southeast Asia, the common myna from Africa (introduced via India), red-crested cardinals from South America and doves from Asia.

Forest Birds

Kauaʻi's native forest birds are high on every serious birder's list. Numbers have declined drastically, but if you're lucky and head *mauka* (up the mountain), you might glimpse them. Both Kalalau Valley viewpoints are good lookouts for red *ʻapapane* (honeycreeper) – find them feeding on the scarlet *lehua* blossoms of *ʻōhiʻa* trees. A walk down the Pihea Trail at the end of the paved highway may produce other honeycreepers – the small, yellow *ʻanianiau* or the green *ʻamakihi* – and the curious Kauaʻi *ʻelepaio* (monarch flycatcher) occasionally perches within reach. For the best chance of spotting the beautiful but elusive curved-bill *ʻiʻiwi* (scarlet honeycreeper), hike down to around the 1.5-mile marker.

Recommended by Jim Denny, *birding guide and author of* The Birds of Kauaʻi

Wild Chickens

LOVED AND HATED, FERAL FLOCKS ROAM KAUA'I

Proudly emblazoned on T-shirts, tea-towels and stickers, commemorated as bobbleheads and in island confections, spotted roaming the McDonald's drive-through and the reason many hotels offer earplugs – Kaua'i's chickens are enmeshed with the island's image and part of its tropical, rural charm.

FELIX NENDZIG/SHUTTERSTOCK

Left Wild chicks **Middle** Mother hen and chicks **Right** Cockerel

Find them in parking lots, neighborhoods, resort grounds, at tourist stops and prowling the interior jungle like their wild ancestors – Kaua'i's chickens are truly everywhere. They've become island icons, almost as emblematic of the Garden Isle as the Nāpali Coast.

So, How Did This Happen?

Many allege the ancestral chickens were flushed free from coops in backyards and on small farms during the island-ravaging hurricanes of Iwa and Iniki in '82 and '92. Left to fend for themselves, they faced few wild predators as adults. Even mongoose – a widespread sugarcane-era import to control rats – who are known to delight in a dinner of chicken eggs, were never unleashed here. The birds found much to eat in the way of wild fruit, seeds, human castoffs and insects. With clutches averaging a full-carton dozen, and birds reaching sexual maturity in four months, 40 years on...*voilà!*

Deeper Origins

Hui O Laka, the nonprofit that runs the Kōke'e Museum and associated facilities inside western Kaua'i's Kōke'e State Park, noted that chickens flocked there as early as the 1950s when a few that congregated around the visitor center were 'promoted as a wildlife visitor attraction.' Fattened with cracked corn by workers and visitors, a small and tame flock blossomed for decades; populations exploded following the hurricanes.

In 2015, when curious genetic scientists showed up to test those post-hurricane flocks, they found those early flocks may not have been chickens after all. Or, at least,

FELIX NENDZIG/SHUTTERSTOCK

BACKYARDPRODUCTION/GETTY IMAGES

not chickens as we think of them: a suite of recognizable breeds domesticated in Europe and the Americas. Instead, Kaua'i's chickens carried clear genetic markers that indicated these were the not-too-distant Hawaiian ancestors of red jungle fowl – a pheasant-like chicken domesticated 7000 years ago then carted along in voyaging canoes by Polynesians along their Pacific-spanning diaspora. Allowed to flourish unchecked upon arrival (archeological evidence shows them on Kaua'i as early as 1200), these birds were cut off from outside genetic influence – possibly for centuries – by the islands' far-flung location. In short, though now diluted by hurricane-spread farm birds, Kaua'i's feathered treasures retain links to a uniquely Kauaian chicken lineage – undisturbed for maybe 1000 years.

Kaua'i's chickens carried clear genetic markers that indicated these were the not-too-distant Hawaiian ancestors of red jungle fowl.

Squawking Menace

Kaua'i's chickens have a few fatal flaws. They don't only crow at dawn, causing some accommodations to have earplugs on hand for disgruntled guests. Chickens also cause other more serious problems, including carrying avian diseases that may be transmissible to rare, endemic forest birds, digging up native plants, and acting as road hazards. A law passed in 2024 now requires county departments to collabroate with state agencies to manage local chicken populations. Some approaches include trapping birds, using contraceptives to limit egg clutches, and increasing public outreach to limit feeding.

Answering the Obvious

With an abundance of creatures that typically feature as tasty menu items roaming free – why aren't Kaua'i's chickens rounded up for an epic feast? The answer is, well, complicated. Most islanders view the birds as part of the landscape, even endearing – they also feed on cockroaches and venomous centipedes, reducing numbers of things of which humans are even less fond. Their diet and roving lifestyle make for tougher, gamier and stringier meat than the plump, grain-fed broilers to which many palates are accustomed. And, with so many places to hide, it would be near impossible to round up enough to stem the island-wide 'problem.'

24 TARO Trail

ISLAND EATS | CULTURE | COMMUNITY

Taro was one of the few subsistence plants brought across the Pacific by Polynesians and was so critical to early Hawaiians' survival that it features prominently in the *kumulipo* creation chant. Kaua'i's North Shore is home to two-thirds of Hawai'i's total taro acreage, making it the best place to learn about this culturally significant, life-giving plant.

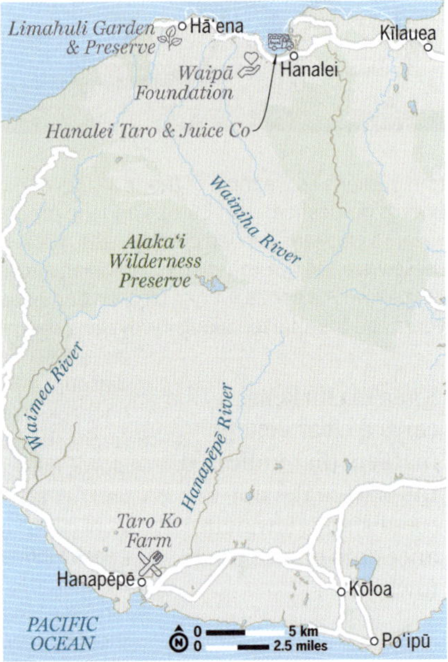

How to

When to go Though *kalo* grows year-round, larger harvests often take place in August and September.

Farm support Please don't trespass in taro patches; support farms by purchasing products in Hanalei.

South Shore taro Get crunchy taro chips fresh from **Taro Ko Farm** in Hanapēpē.

What is Taro?

One of around 24 Polynesian 'canoe plants' brought on Pacific settlement voyages, taro – *kalo* in Hawaiian – is a resilient root vegetable with a long and significant history. All parts of the hardy plant – tear-shaped leaves, shoots and corm (starchy root) – found a place in the Hawaiian diet and medical arsenal. Grown in both wet and dry *lo'i* (patches) some 300 varieties were developed to suit the islands' varied growing conditions. Cultivating and consuming taro fell out of favor after Western contact (less than 1% of cultivated taro acreage remains from its heyday), but it's slowly rebounding in popularity, marking an important connection to the past.

Top right Taro fields, Hanalei
Bottom right Limahuli Garden & Preserve

PHOTO IMAGE/SHUTTERSTOCK

STEVENGAERTNER/GETTY IMAGES

Ways to Try Taro

Laulau plate lunch Leaves wrapped around salty meat.

Poi A pounded cultural staple.

Taro mochi cake Cake made with soft layers of taro sponge.

Kūlolo Taro/coconut dessert with the consistency of fudge.

Recommended by Lyndsey Haraguchi-Nakayama, *fifth-generation taro farmer @HanaleiTaro*

Taro on Kaua'i

Several North Shore organizations help bolster appreciation for this sacred crop. **Limahuli Garden & Preserve** has beautifully restored, 700-year-old terraced rock walls once used in farming upland taro.

The state's largest family-owned taro farm, **Hanalei Taro** operates the **Hanalei Taro & Juice Co** food truck selling its taro-centric products in Hanalei. Nearby, the **Waipā Foundation** (waipafoundation.org) offers tours of its agriculturally rich property – including of its wetland taro fields, allowing visitors to get an up-close look at the plants unique growing conditions.

Common Reef **FISH**

03

02

01

06

05

04

07

01 Threadfin butterflyfish
Chevron-patterned body; long filament and black spot on dorsal fin.

02 Raccoon butterflyfish
These yellow fish sport a black eye band that resembles raccoons.

03 Arc-Eye hawkfish
Can be reddish or greenish. Has a red, yellow and blue circle around and behind the eye.

04 Longnose butterflyfish
Boasts the longest Hawaiian fish name: *lauwiliwili nukunuku 'oi'oi,* meaning 'the leaf of the *wiliwili* tree, sharp (or best) beak.'

05 White mouth moray
The most-sighted moray species – it's the only one that hunts in daytime. Recognized by bright white spots and inner mouth.

06 Yellow tang
Their bright yellow bodies form large schools visible from the surface.

07 Indo-Pacific sergeant
Curious blue-striped fish; occasionally greets snorkelers.

08

09

11

10

12

13

08 Moorish idol
Elegant black-, yellow- and white-striped fish with long dorsal filament. Think Gill in *Finding Nemo*.

09 Palenose parrotfish
All start as gray females; only some morph into recognizable colorful males (green, blue and lavender). Chomps coral, expels sand.

10 Achilles tang
Pretty, blue and black fish with white outlines and orange on its tail. Common in the surge zone and close to shore.

11 Reef/Wedgetail triggerfish
The state fish – *humuhumunuku-nukuāpua'a* – part of which means 'nose like a pig.' Grunts like a pig when threatened. Look for the telltale 'v.'

12 Hawaiian cleaner wrasse
Slender purple-and-yellow fish seen wiggling to attract clients or actively cleaning fish.

13 Saddle wrasse
Tri-colored, vertical-banded dark-blue, orange and green fish.

01 ERIC ISSELEE/SHUTTERSTOCK, **02** PETER DOUGLAS CLARK/SHUTTERSTOCK, **03** THOMAS KLINE/DESIGN PICS/GETTY IMAGES, **04** ERIC ISSELEE/SHUTTERSTOCK, **05** JENNA SZERLAG/DESIGN PICS/GETTY IMAGES, **06** FIVESPOTS/SHUTTERSTOCK, **07** DMITRY RUKHLENKO/SHUTTERSTOCK, **08** RICH CAREY/SHUTTERSTOCK, **09** DAVID FLEETHAM/ALAMY, **10** VOJCE/SHUTTERSTOCK, **11** RICKARD ZERPE/WIKIMEDIA/CC BY 2.0, **12** MAQUILADORA/SHUTTERSTOCK, **13** VLADIMIR WRANGEL/SHUTTERSTOCK

Listings

BEST OF THE REST

Additional Adventures

Wailua Kayak Adventures

Follow veteran guides down 4.4 miles of the Wailua River to a rainforest path and a 120ft hidden waterfall with swimmable pools (adult/under 12 $100/50).

Makai Princeville Course

All the views without the hefty greens fees. The informative Sunset Golf Cart Tour at this golf course (two-person cart $120) offers up its usually private stunning vista.

Da Life Outdoors Kauai

Strap in and rappel down a series of remote waterfalls, the largest 60ft high, inside the otherwise off-limits Hulēʻia National Wildlife Refuge (per person $224).

Lydgate Farms

Tour this award-winning chocolate farm, learning about the cacao-growing process and munching on delicious chocolate samples (adult/child $145/115).

Fun Freebies

Tunnels (Makua) Beach

The wide arc of this beach, 6 miles west of Hanalei, cups a shallow reef with excellent snorkeling in the calmer summer months.

Salt Pond Beach

Outside Hanapēpē, this beach fronts Kauaʻi's last red-clay flats. They're still in use by traditional Hawaiian practitioners, who distill the ocean's essence for cooking and healing.

Spouting Horn Blowhole

Adjacent to the Kukuiʻula Small Boat Harbor, the blowhole – featured in Hawaiian lore – hisses then rockets sea spray up to 50ft when surf surges through the lava tube beneath.

Kīkīaola (Menehune Ditch)

Kīkīaola, outside Waimea, features mysterious stonework attributed to some of the earliest island arrivals.

Glass Beach

At industrial ʻEleʻele beach, waves have tumbled debris from a decades-old seaside dump into a quirky stretch of shoreline where sand and smooth, colorful sea glass mingle.

Eats That Represent Kauaʻi

Kauaʻi Juice Co $

Earth-savvy Kauaʻi Juice Co (kauaijuiceco.com) cold presses nourishing fruit and nut juices from island-grown ingredients. Return your glass bottle for cheaper seconds.

Koloa Fish Market $$

This market in downtown Kōloa is a must-stop for take-out *poke* and rice bowls with ocean salad. Selection changes daily, but avocado ʻahi and Korean *poke* are highlights.

JUERGEN_WALLSTABE/SHUTTERSTOCK

Sand from Glass Beach

Eating House 1849 $$$

Sample upscale 'plantation cuisine' from one of Kaua'i's legendary chefs, Roy Yamaguchi, at this South Shore restaurant.

Decent Diners & Dives

AMA Restaurant $$

The views star at this outdoor ramen and Japanese fine-dining outlet, especially when sunset illuminates Hanalei Wildlife Refuge, the clouds and the looming peaks beyond.

Pink's Creamery $

Dairy-based comfort foods unite with Hawai'i flair here in Hanalei. Choose from sweet island-inspired ice creams such as banana mac-nut brittle or savory Hawaiian grilled cheese (muenster and pineapple).

Tahiti Nui $$

Get your kitsch fix at the rattan-soaked Tahiti Nui, an authentic tiki bar with excellent umbrella-topped mai tais in downtown Hanalei.

Japanese Grandma's $$

A tiny cafe that serves homestyle, small-plate Japanese cuisine from its location abutting the clothing racks of trendy Blü Umi lifestyle boutique in Hanapēpē.

Kalaheo Café & Coffee Co $$

A worthwhile stop on the way to west-side attractions, this cafe does breakfast best (from 7am) and serves its own brand of coffee.

Livin' the Lifestyle

EHA Culture

Blends designs reminiscent of old Hawaiian quilting patterns with cozy cotton Turkish towels in vibrant colors.

Havaiki Oceanic and Tribal Arts

The owners of this gallery in Hanalei spent 18 years sailing the Pacific collecting one-of-a-

CHASE CLAUSEN/SHUTTERSTOCK

Waimea Canyon lookout

kind folk art from far-flung island locales; over 400 artisans' works are for sale.

Hanalei Surf Co

Shop popular surf brands or rent boards and beach chairs from this longtime local business.

Sway Hanalei

Modern aloha and beach wear, home goods and local artists' originals mingle at this charming boutique.

Half-Day (or Less) Hikes

Okolehau Trail

Ascend 1250ft to take in views of Hanalei Bay via this 5-mile round trip. Look for endemic wetland birds in the abutting Hanalei Wildlife Refuge near the trailhead.

Ho'opi'i Falls

Near Kapa'a, seek out these two cascades. The 2.4-mile rock and mud trail through vine-covered forest is easy but begins in a neighborhood – please park with aloha.

Waimea Canyon & Cliff Trails

Off Hwy 550 mile marker 14, head through forest to several spectacular canyon overlooks then partially into the canyon for views of 800ft Waipo'o Falls.

MAUI

ADVENTURE | OUTDOORS | NATURE

RESEARCHED BY SARAH SEKULA; UPDATED BY AMY BALFOUR

- **Trip Builder** (p144)
- **Practicalities** (p146)
- **Upcountry Magic** (p148)
- **Made on Maui** (p150)
- **Peaks & Panoramas** (p152)
- **Farm Fresh** (p154)
- **Paddle Out** (p156)
- **Whale Central** (p158)
- **Maui Gone Wild** (p160)
- **Stellar Sights** (p162)
- **Heavenly Hāna** (p164)
- **Small Town, Big Art** (p166)
- **Monster Waves** (p168)
- **Listings** (p170)

ANDREW BERTINO/SHUTTERSTOCK

MAUI
Trip Builder

Maui is home to a handful of microclimates, including rainforests, alpine deserts and lava fields. There are lush bamboo forests to explore and even a national park with a 10,023ft volcanic summit. If you're ambitious, experience them all in one vacation.

CLOCKWISE FROM BOTTOM LEFT: SCOTT MEAD/DESIGN PICS/GETTY IMAGES, HIROAMANO/SHUTTERSTOCK, EPICSTOCKMEDIA/SHUTTERSTOCK

Practicalities

EQROY/SHUTTERSTOCK

ARRIVING

Kahului Airport (OGG) Maui's primary gateway; lots of airlines offer nonstop flights.

Kapalua Airport (JHM) Commuter airport in West Maui near Kā'anapali and Lahaina.

Hāna Airport (HNM) Commuter airport in East Maui. Fly on Mokulele Airlines, or if you're staying at **Hāna-Maui Resort**, book a flight on its nine-seat Cessna; the hotel provides airport shuttles. No car-rental or rideshare services in Hāna.

HOW MUCH FOR A

Loco moco $20

Packaged Maui Gold $49

Large shave ice $8

WHEN TO GO

JAN–DEC
Warm days, mild nights all year.

DEC–MAR
Accommodations pricier during peak season.

NOV–APR
A chance to see humpback whales.

NOV–MAR
Best time to see surfers catch big waves rolling through. Rainy season.

GETTING AROUND

Car A rental car is the easiest way to explore Maui. There are lots of major car-rental companies at the Kahului Airport. Uber and Lyft are available on Maui, except for remote areas like Hāna.

Bus & shuttle You won't be able to explore all of Maui by bus, but if you have time and patience, it's an option for some sightseeing. Roberts Hawaii Express Shuttle and SpeediShuttle can be booked online.

Ferry Expeditions Ferry runs between Maui and Lāna'i, departing from Mānele Harbor.

TOP: SERGI REBOREDO/ALAMY
BOTTOM: JAREKG/GETTY IMAGES

EATING & DRINKING

The American-owned pineapple and sugar industries imported laborers from around the world. As a result, Maui has a Trans-Pacific palate. This means it's easy to find *poke* prepared many different ways, fresh *malasadas* (a Portuguese recipe) and other examples of eclectically influenced cuisine, such as crab mac salad and Spam *musubi* (fried Spam on rice, wrapped in dried seaweed).

Maui Brewing Co's Pineapple Mana Wheat is a local beer worth sampling, and the Hawai'i Food & Wine Festival is held annually.

Best fresh seafood
Mama's Fish House (p171)

Must-try
Ululani's Hawaiian Shave Ice (p156)

CONNECT & FIND YOUR WAY

Wi-fi Widely available except in remote areas such as Haleakalā National Park and much of the road to Hāna. Major retail stores and some restaurants offer free wi-fi. To find free wi-fi hotspots, go to cca.hawaii.gov and search 'DCCA designated hotspots.'

Navigation For the most part, GPS will get you where you need to go.

WHERE TO STAY

Maui has everything from super high-end resorts to unique Airbnbs (one, in fact, has alpacas grazing in the backyard).

Location	Pros/Cons
Kā'anapali	Lots of upscale resort options; sunny and dry. Pricey; limited parking.
Kīhei	Seaside condos; nightlife and shops. Touristy and crowded; some condos may close per new housing law.
Nāpili	Bayside condos; great restaurants and pretty beach. Limited nightlife.
Hāna	Hāna-Maui Resort is the only hotel on the east side. Go for peace and quiet. No nightlife; poor cell service.
Wailea	High-end hotels. Beautiful, paved 1.5-mile coastal beach walk. Pricey; beaches are crowded during high season.
Makawao	Boutique hotel and historic section with walkable shopping and dining. Often rainy.

DINING OUT

For Maui's best restaurants, make a reservation as far ahead as possible. For Mama's Fish House (p171), sometimes reservations are needed months in advance.

MONEY

Most places accept credit cards, but keep cash handy for farmers markets and such. Exchange currency at Kahului Airport, ATMs are common.

25 UPCOUNTRY Magic

DAY TRIP | ADVENTURE | LANDSCAPES

The bucolic Upcountry area, which includes Kula, Ha'ikū, Pukalani and Makawao, is known for its inland expanse of rolling hills, a colorful 10,023ft volcano and even a misty redwood forest. In other words, it's the unexpected side of Maui. Stop to breathe in the scent of eucalyptus trees, nibble on gourmet goat cheese and paraglide among the clouds.

SARAH SEKULA

How to

Getting around Some tours shuttle guests to the Upcountry areas, but a rental car is what most people opt for.

When to go All year. Come springtime look for purple-flowering jacaranda trees.

Top tips Bring a light jacket or sweatshirt for roaming around. Bring heavier layers if you visit Haleakalā's summit, where it's important to prep for anything from fierce winds to sunshine; it even snows occasionally in winter.

JESSIE BANG/SHUTTERSTOCK

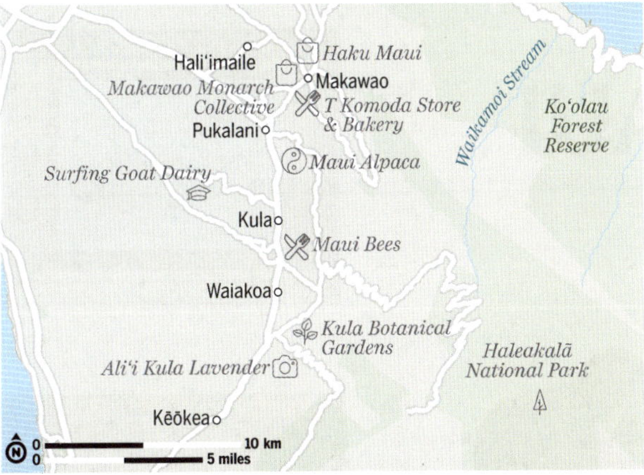

Rise early for stick donuts at **T Komoda Store & Bakery** in historic Makawao, full of boutiques, food trucks and *paniolo* (Hawaiian cowboy) charm. Make your own flower crown at **Haku Maui**, an adorable boutique on Baldwin Ave. Spend one-on-one time with angora rabbits, do a yoga session with alpacas or find your zen in a sound-healing session at **Maui Alpaca**.

In Kula, **Ali'i Kula Lavender** farm has 55,000 lavender plants and 20 varieties of lavender. The garden – packed with wisteria, Italian cypress and grapevines – is photo-worthy, indeed. Learn the art of cheese making and goat milking at **Surfing Goat Dairy**. Stroll through **Kula Botanical Gardens** to hug the brilliant rainbow eucalyptus trees.

Upcountry's showstopper is, hands down, the national park: **Haleakalā**. If you're not up for driving the winding roads, go with an outfitter like **Hike Maui**, which leads groups on fun jaunts through the park in the summit area and also in the Kīpahulu District.

Named for its now-dormant volcano, Haleakalā National Park is thought to be one of the quietest places on Earth. This otherworldly place is considered sacred and is the only place on Earth you will see the Haleakalā *'āhinahina* (silversword plant).

Mark Twain once said Haleakalā's summit sunrise was the 'sublimest spectacle' he'd ever witnessed. However, the sunset is equally mind-blowing, and the park much less crowded at that time.

Top left Haleakalā summit trail
Bottom left Goat at Surfing Goat Dairy

Shells & Swimsuits

In Makawao visit **Makawao Monarch Collective** for puka-shell necklaces, prints by local artisans, silk dresses and fine art; and **Makai Glass Maui** for sea-inspired blown-glass sculptures.

Don't miss **Kūlua**, a sustainable, Native Hawaiian–owned clothing brand, for shirts, dresses and jewelry.

Forget your swimsuit? **Dos Gardenias** in Pā'ia is a small boutique with lots of options – bikinis, rash guards, one-pieces and more.

Head to Kula to pop into **Maui Bees** for homemade granola, artisanal honey and food to go; while **Haleakalā Creamery** offers fresh chèvre, jarred caramel and 'goatlatos' (ice cream), all made from fresh goat's milk.

Made

ON MAUI

01

02

03

04

05

06

01 Extra pluck
For the musically inclined, ukuleles made of koa or mango wood are a must-have.

02 Maui masterpieces
A watercolor painting or block print from a local artist are easy to transport back home.

03 Sweet treat
Bringing Maui Gold pineapples home as gifts is a no-brainer (check your country's biosecurity restrictions)

04 Comfy and cozy
Hawaiians have been making quilts sporting bold tropical prints for more than 200 years.

05 Lovely lavender
Bring lavender soap home to your *'ohana* (family) to keep them smelling lovely.

06 Tangy taste
Liliko'i (passion fruit) jam tastes delicious on just about anything. Toast, scones, shave ice, pie, cocktails. The list goes on and on.

07

08

09

10

11

12

07 Kick back
Alcoholic drinks come in many varieties here, from POG (passion fruit, orange and guava) IPAs to Maui Blanc pineapple wine and Maui Brewing Co coconut porters.

08 The bee's knees
Prep those taste buds for honey flavors like macadamia blossom, lavender and wildflower. The good news: you can't go wrong.

09 Spill the beans
Coffee fan? Yellow *caturra*, red *catuai*, *typica* and *mokka* beans are grown here.

10 Flowers galore
From intricate flower crowns to lovely lei, this traditional greeting or ceremonial statement is a fragrant gesture, indeed.

11 Aloha spirit
First appearing in the 1920s, the aloha shirt is a classic way to make a totally tropical fashion statement.

12 Shell yeah!
Gold-filled puka hoops. Cowrie necklaces. Pearl bracelets. Shell jewelry is not hard to find!

01 BOBKOV EVGENIY/SHUTTERSTOCK, **02** TOMEKBUDUJEDOMEK/GETTY IMAGES, ANDREA_HILL/GETTY IMAGES, **03** DAVYDENKO YULIIA/SHUTTERSTOCK, **04** TED STRESHINSKY PHOTOGRAPHIC ARCHIVE/GETTY IMAGES, **05** PANNONIA/GETTY IMAGES, **06** NIKCOA/SHUTTERSTOCK, **07** BIG BLINK CREATIVE/SHUTTERSTOCK, **08** DIONISVERA/SHUTTERSTOCK, **09** ACHANFOTO/SHUTTERSTOCK, **10** MR DOOMITS/SHUTTERSTOCK, **11** INCHIC/SHUTTERSTOCK, **12** ZIEDONIS/SHUTTERSTOCK

26 PEAKS & Panoramas

HIKES | LANDSCAPE | COASTAL VIEWS

Add a little extra oomph to your vacation with some trail time. With many accessible trails to choose from, you can expect everything from waterfalls to dreamy ocean views to bamboo forests – all well worth the trek. Just don't forget to pack your hiking shoes.

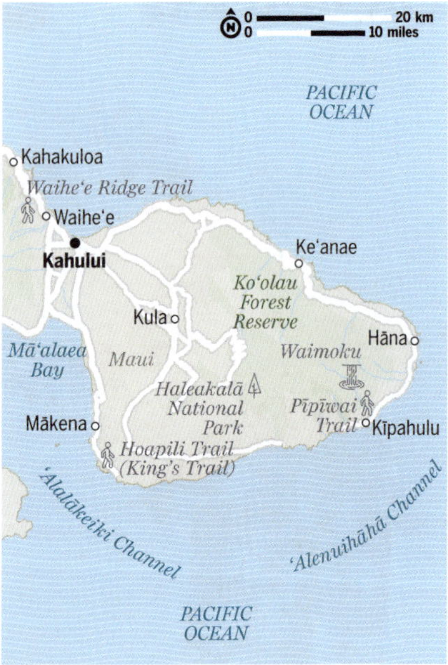

How to

Are we there yet? Some trails (Waihe'e, we're talking about you) are tougher than others. Plan extra time if you are not in tip-top shape and so you can leisurely snap photos.

When to go Consistent temps make hiking enjoyable all year. Early birds score uncrowded trails and parking. Avoid holidays when trails can be packed.

Top tip At higher elevations drink extra water to ward off altitude sickness.

The **Waihe'e Ridge Trail** (5 miles round trip) starts out very steep. Don't worry, it does level out, though it gets steep again at the top (1563ft). Your reward: views of Moloka'i, O'ahu, *Jurassic Park*–like jagged cliffs and waterfall squiggles in the distance.

Inside the Upcountry section of **Haleakalā National Park**, try Keonehe'ehe'e (Sliding Sands) Trail for a spectacular look inside a volcano crater the size of Manhattan. Plan for twice as long for the uphill hike out. Beginners: go to the first lookout. Experts: do the 11-mile trek to Halemau'u. In summer, look for endemic silverswords, a rare shimmering spiky plant that blooms only once in its lifetime.

Top right Hikers, Haleakalā National Park **Bottom right** Banyan tree, Pīpīwai Trail

MARIDAV/SHUTTERSTOCK

MNSTUDIO/SHUTTERSTOCK

Trail Mix

With 30 miles of trails, it's impossible to be bored at **Haleakalā National Park**. The topography is diverse: some trails are green and junglelike, and others are a desolate alpine desert.

Have a few days on your hands? Consider trekking to a wilderness cabin in Haleakalā's crater. Go to recreation.gov and search Haleakalā.

In the Kīpahulu District of Haleakalā National Park (4 miles round trip), traipse through rainforest, bamboo forests and banyan trees on the **Pīpīwai Trail**. The finale: the 400ft **Waimoku** falls. Don't forget bug spray!

Join resident goats on the **Hoapili Trail** (5 miles round trip), which is a section of the King's Trail, for views of the jagged coastline. Wear your sturdiest shoes (you will be trekking on uneven lava rocks) and slather on sunscreen (most of the trail is exposed). Once a crucial road reserved for Hawaiian royalty, the pathway looped around Maui, unifying the island's 12 districts in the 16th century. Besides some reconstruction done in 1824, this section of the path, near Keone'ō'io Bay in South Maui, looks much like it did in antiquity.

27 Farm FRESH

FARMS | FOOD | FUN

Many of Maui's farms are in the Upcountry area, which is known for its consistent rainfall, cooler temps (typically 10 degrees cooler than the coast) and rich volcanic soil. But no matter where you park your beach umbrella, on Maui there will be a farmers market close by. Banana bread with *liliko'i* jam, anyone?

SARAH SEKULA

How to

When to go Farmers markets are open year-round. As with most things in Hawai'i, get there early before popular items sell out.

Farm meals Have a lavender-scones-and-tea-picnic at **Ali'i Kula Lavender** farm or pop over to **O'o Farm** where the meals are to die for. Pro tip: look around for Jackson's chameleons scaling the coffee plants. It's common to see the slow-moving lizards on trees and plants anywhere in the Upcountry.

THELITTLECACTUS/SHUTTERSTOCK

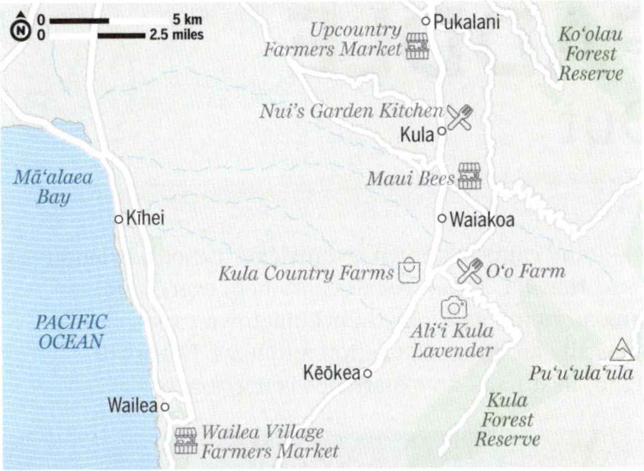

On Tuesday mornings **Wailea Village Farmers Market** is *the* place for fresh fish, local flowers, produce of all sorts and locally sourced fresh juices and elixirs.

The **Upcountry Farmers Market** in Pukalani is a must. It's the largest market on Maui. You'll find everything from just-picked coconuts to live music, crafts, produce and good eats.

In Kula, big appetites will appreciate **Nui's Garden Kitchen** food truck for pad thai and smoothies.

Pick strawberries (in spring) at **Kula Country Farms**, and score *liliko'i* jam, blueberries and beautiful protea flowers. Views of **Mā'alaea Bay** and **Kahului Bay** do not disappoint.

Maui Bees is a farm and market in Kula that offers tours and beekeeping workshops and sells house-made focaccia, farm-fresh produce and, of course, seasonal honeys.

Short on time? Shop for local produce online at **Maui Hub** (mauihub.org). It's got everything from Okinawan sweet potatoes to kabocha squash to blueberry lemonade kombucha. Order during the week for pickup in Ha'ikū, Lahaina, Central Maui, Kīhei, Hāna and Upcountry at weekly designated pickup times. You can also buy produce grown at **Kumu Farms** at the wonderful **Country Market at Maui Tropical Plantation** in Wailuku. Maui-grown coffee and Moloka'i venison are also for sale here.

Left Freshly made rolls at O'o Farm **Below** Country Market at Maui Tropical Plantation

Fun Fruits

Maui is home to more than 800 farms.

Apple bananas, about half the size of traditional bananas and a bit sweeter, can be found at farmers markets and grocery stores year-round. So can breadfruit, coconuts, papaya and pineapples.

Dragon fruit is about 90% water, is packed with antioxidants and tastes like a mix between a kiwi and a pear.

Since the 19th century, *liliko'i* (passion fruit) has been growing in Hawai'i. It's tangy and sweet and you will find it in salad dressings, jams, tropical drinks, pies – you name it. Grab it at a farmers market and scoop the seeds out for a fun snack.

28 PADDLE Out

OCEAN | WORKOUT | WILDLIFE

Double-hulled, ocean-going canoes, known as outrigger canoes, brought the first Polynesian settlers to Hawai'i. Today, regattas are held every summer and children start competing as young as 10 for their hometown canoe clubs. As an island visitor you can easily get in on the action and learn the art of Polynesian canoeing firsthand. Best part: no experience is necessary.

SARAH SEKULA

How to

Getting here The **Kihei Canoe Club** is in North Kīhei across from **Ululani's Hawaiian Shave Ice** (ululanishawaiianshaveice.com). You know you're in the right place when you spot bright red and gold *wa'a* (canoes).

When to go All year long. Canoes go out in the mornings before it gets too windy.

The views Turquoise-blue water, green sea turtles, and humpback whales (from December to May).

GREG ELMS

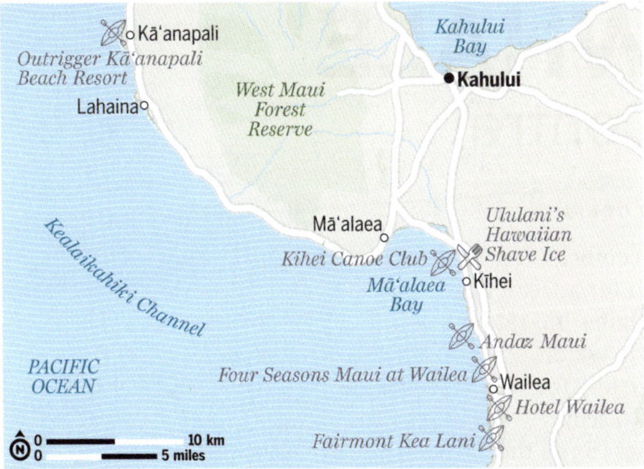

Top and bottom left Kihei Canoe Club

Canoeing with the club The Kihei Canoe Club offers visitor paddle sessions every Tuesday and Thursday morning, weather permitting. Paddlers begin by greeting the morning with a traditional chant. Afterward, a *mahalo* (thank you) chant expresses gratitude to the ocean, the land and *kūpuna* (ancestors, elders).

Depending on conditions, paddlers head out onto Mā'alaea Bay to a large reef (where green sea turtles love to hang out) or north toward **Keālia Pond** and **Sugar Beach**. The good news: regardless of the route, it's gorgeous in all directions. During February and March you are nearly guaranteed a whale sighting.

Through the sun-dappled, turquoise waters, it's possible to also spot red pencil sea urchins, butterflyfish and dolphins. Keep those peepers peeled for mantas and loads of tropical fish, too.

Local hotel tours Sign up for canoe experiences if you are a guest at one of the following Wailea spots: **Fairmont Kea Lani**, **Four Seasons Maui at Wailea**, **Andaz Maui** and **Hotel Wailea**. Several commercial outfitters also offer outrigger canoe trips, mostly along the South Maui coast.

Nautical know-how Before fiberglass and carbon fiber, canoes were made of indigenous woods. The hull was dug out of a single acacia koa log.

Wind & Waves

Hawai'i's official team sport is outrigger canoeing. Preteens and adults well into their 60s compete for their hometown canoe club during the summer regatta season.

Outrigger canoes can travel across channels from island to island, oftentimes attracting dolphins and whales.

Outrigger paddling is a low-impact activity engaging the shoulders, arms, latissimus dorsi and trapezius muscles.

The first Polynesian settlers to Hawai'i arrived in large double-hulled, oceangoing canoes.

I've had a newborn whale swim up to me as its mother kept a wary eye.

Told by Iokepa Nae'ole, *Outrigger Kā'anapali Beach Resort's Beach Activities Manager, who has been paddling competitively since age 12*

29 WHALE Central

WHALES | PHOTOGRAPHY | OCEAN

Visit Maui from December through May, and you're in for a treat. This is when humpback whales migrate from Alaska to Maui's warm waters to breed and give birth. Luckily for you, there are many ways to score some serious cetacean time. Here's the lowdown to help you maximize your whale watching.

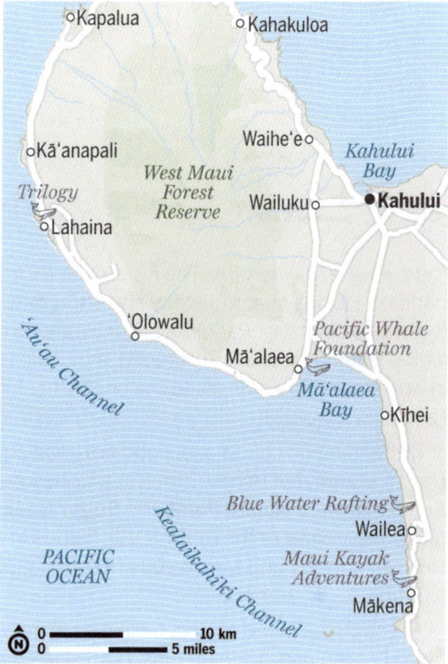

How to

Getting here Zodiac, catamaran, stand-up paddle-board (SUP) or kayak.

When to go December to May. January to March is peak season.

How much Tour prices range from an $85 commercial trip to a $1500 private charter. Or rent a kayak (around $125 per day) or SUP ($30 to $35 per day). Budget concerns? Bring your own snorkel gear and listen to whales sing underwater for free.

Need to know All oceangoers must stay at least 100yd from humpback whales.

Lounge on a luxury catamaran with **Trilogy** (sailtrilogy.com). It has a two-hour tour from Mā'alaea and Kā'anapali with snacks, fun facts from a whale naturalist and hydrophones so you can hear the whales.

From Kīhei, on Maui's southwest side, **Blue Water Rafting** (bluewaterrafting.com) launches its Express Whale Watch. Not only do you look for the giants, but you will also get to snorkel Molokini Crater, where visibility sometimes exceeds 150ft. It's home to loads of marine life and more than 30 coral species. Bring your GoPro along: dunk it in the water for the chance to capture a whale on camera.

Top right Whale watching with Pacific Whale Foundation
Bottom right Humpback whale

DAVID FLEETHAM/ALAMY

MANUEL BALESTERI/SHUTTERSTOCK

Whale Talk

Breaching Propelling all (or most of) the body above water.

Spy hopping Taking a look around by popping the head above the surface.

Bubble-net feeding When a group of whales circle up and blow bubbles as a way to feed on fish.

Peduncle throw Whale swings tail and the rear part of its torso above water, often for mating purposes.

Fluking Lifting tail above water before taking a dive.

Be a marine biologist for the day with **Pacific Whale Foundation** (pacificwhale.org) tours out of Mā'alaea Harbor. Spend two hours asking naturalists all the questions you want and learn about the data they're collecting. All while enjoying breakfast, lunch or dinner and cocktails.

Burn calories while whale watching with **Maui Kayak Adventures** (mauikayakadventures.com) from Mākena Landing. Not only do you paddle among the massive mammals but you also snorkel. Look for angelfish, octopus, butterflyfish and moray eels. Gorgeous red pencil sea urchins make for great photos, too.

Maui

GONE WILD

02

01

04

03

06

05

01 Water ballet
Prepare to be wowed by Hawaiian spinner dolphins. They love to put on a show with jumps, spins and flips.

02 Serious cephalopods
If you've seen *My Octopus Teacher* on Netflix, you know how incredible these creatures are. They have beaks and a toothed tongue!

03 Invasive species
Did you know the plural of mongoose is mongeese? They are often spotted scurrying across the road.

04 Shark watch
Many sharks can be found in Hawai'i. Do not swim in murky water. This is often when sharks mistake humans for prey.

05 Whaley cool
Plan your trip during whale season (December to May) when thousands of whales show up and serenade each other (and you).

06 Spiky critters
Red pencil sea urchins are plentiful in shallow waters.

07 Graceful giants
Manta rays have wing-

07

08

09

10

11

12

13

spans up to 20ft across and can breach nearly 10ft in the air.

08 Rise and shine!
From parking lots to forests to beaches, you will spot wild chickens everywhere in Maui.

09 Watch out
Centipedes are venomous and can sting. Steer clear and watch those multiple legs from a distance.

10 Rare goose
Hawai'i's state bird, the nēnē (nay-nay), is one of the rarest birds in the world. Found at Haleakalā's summit.

11 Tongue twister
Humuhumunuku-nukuāpua'a (triggerfish) is not only fun to say, it's fun to see. Part of the name means snout like a pig.

12 What a hoot
The yellow-eyed *pueo* (short-eared Hawaiian owl) are endemic to the Hawaiian Islands.

13 Beach blobs
One of the most endangered marine mammals in the world, Hawaiian monk seals can be found lounging seaside.

01 LANCE SAGAR/SHUTTERSTOCK, **02** TABOOMA/SHUTTERSTOCK, **03** DWI PUTRA STOCK/SHUTTERSTOCK, **04** CHARLES O'REAR/GETTY IMAGES, **05** IDREAMPHOTO/SHUTTERSTOCK, **06** MADELEINE PLATT/SHUTTERSTOCK, **07** RICH CAREY/SHUTTERSTOCK, **08** MODERN META PHOTOGRAPHY/SHUTTERSTOCK, **09** MR. SUTTIPON YAKHAM/SHUTTERSTOCK, **10** JANE MCILROY/SHUTTERSTOCK, **11** MELISSA BRANDES/SHUTTERSTOCK, **12** FRANK FICHTMUELLER/SHUTTERSTOCK, **13** BENNY MARTY/SHUTTERSTOCK

30 STELLAR Sights

STARS | LEARNING | CULTURE

Maui has everything one could ask for when it comes to experiencing a memorable cosmic display: little light pollution, epic star visibility and pretty rad weather all year long. So go ahead, shoot for the stars. It's your chance to gain celestial navigation and wayfinding know-how, wind down and maybe see a meteor shower.

How to

When to go Winter: see the brightest stars thanks to clearer skies and longer nights; look for Orion, Taurus, and the Pleiades. Spring: Southern Cross and Alpha Centauri. Summer: gaze directly into the heart of the galaxy. Fall: nebulae and star clusters.

Star power *Hōkū* means star. *Le'a* means gladness. *Hōkūle'a* is the name of Hawai'i's zenith star and means star of gladness. Visit Honolulu's Bishop Museum (p51) to learn about the voyaging canoe of the same name.

Twinkle Twinkle

There are 88 constellations in the sky. With Maui's latitude of 20 degrees north, you can view 80 of the 88 constellations throughout the year.

When the sun sets, **Haleakalā's** summit gets even more dramatic. **Maui Stargazing** (mauistargazing.com) helps astronomy enthusiasts spot nebulae, star clusters and galaxies through a massive Dobsonian telescope.

The Tour of the Stars program at the **Hyatt Regency Maui Resort and Spa** has been running for two decades. Bring your camera to photograph the night sky.

The **Ritz-Carlton, Maui Kapalua** offers a Stars and

Top right Stargazing, Haleakalā summit **Bottom right** Dusk, Haleakalā summit

SHAYKATH/SHUTTERSTOCK

JONATHAN LINGEL/SHUTTERSTOCK

Seeing Stars

Different stars pass over different places on Earth. The Polynesian navigators knew that Arcturus and the Pleiades passed over Hawai'i.

Eddie Mahoney *is NASA ambassador and director of astronomy at Hyatt Regency Maui Resort & Spa*

S'mores activity where guests learn how Hawaiian navigators used the stars, waves, currents, fish, ocean temperatures and wind to sail the high seas. Afterward, dine on the catch of the day, sushi and specialty cocktails at **Alaloa Lounge** in the lobby and sway to live tunes each night.

Top of the World

For more info on stargazing at Haleakalā's summit, visit nps.gov/hale and search for stargazing.

There's an App for That

Check spaceweather.com and heavens-above.com every night to see what's in view.

31 Heavenly HĀNA

RAINFOREST | NATURE | WATERFALLS

There is certainly something special about Maui's remote east side. Its curvy roads pave the path to bamboo forests, black-sand beaches, caves and waterfalls galore. These swoon-worthy sights, however, have led to overtourism. Because the highway sees thousands of rental cars a day, we encourage visitors to skip the drive and go with a tour company.

ROSANNA U/GETTY IMAGES

Good to Know

- Traffic is a problem, especially for locals. Pull over to let faster drivers pass.
- Avoid private property and areas without visitor signage.
- **Hike Maui**, **Get Your Guide** and **Valley Isle Excursions** offer Hāna tours. Or skip the drive with **Maverick Helicopters**.
- If you 'make your own' parking spot, your vehicle could be towed.

Trip Notes

Getting here Hāna is about 50 miles from Kahului Airport. Tours to Hāna are an all-day affair.

When to go Dry season (April to October) is best. Avoid rainy season (November to March).

Pro tip If you suffer from motion sickness, this may not be the adventure for you. The road has more than 600 hairpin turns and 59 narrow bridges.

Fuel up Hāna Town is the only place to get gas.

01 In Pā'ia watch world-famous windsurfers carve up waves at **Ho'okipa Beach Park** and snap photos of turtles snoozing beachside (keep a distance of at least 10ft).

03 **Wai'ānapanapa State Park** (pictured left and far left) is famous for its black-sand beach and trails that were once a pathway for Hawaiian royalty. Permit needed.

02 The 20-minute walk to **Twin Falls** is popular, so parking is a problem. Going with a tour company is best.

04 Hike to **Fagan's Cross** and rest at **Hāna-Maui Resort**, a boutique hotel where waves lull you to sleep. The lava-rock cross was built in the early 1960s as a monument to Paul Irving Fagan Sr.

05 While most Hāna beaches are not ideal for swimming or snorkeling, on a calm day, **Hamoa Beach** makes for a good snorkel stop.

FROM TOP: VICTORIA LIPOV/SHUTTERSTOCK, GREG ELMS, DEJETLEY/SHUTTERSTOCK

32 Small Town, BIG ART

DAY TRIP | ART | CULTURE

Strolling through downtown Wailuku is like going on an Easter-egg hunt: there are treasures around every corner. With the West Maui Mountains as your backdrop, search for murals representing *mauka* to *makai* (from the mountains to the ocean) themes. There are more than 25 oversized works of art in all.

PHOTO RESOURCE HAWAII/ALAMY

Arts Alive

Maui Historical Society Hō'ike'ike at the Bailey House Showcases cultural artifacts (pictured) and contemporary work.

Native Intelligence Hawaiian artwork from woodworkers, fashion designers and more.

Friends & Faire For jewelry workshops.

Recommended by Matthew Agcolicol, *Pangeaseed Seawalls mural project @matchyou*

Trip Notes

Getting here Wailuku is 10 minutes west of Kahului Airport.

When to go For the best mural views, go early when cars are not parked in front of the walls. Keep in mind: most vendors close by 5pm.

Beyond the art Snack on pudding-filled *malasadas* (Portuguese-style donuts) at **Four Sisters Bakery** (1968 E Vineyard St).

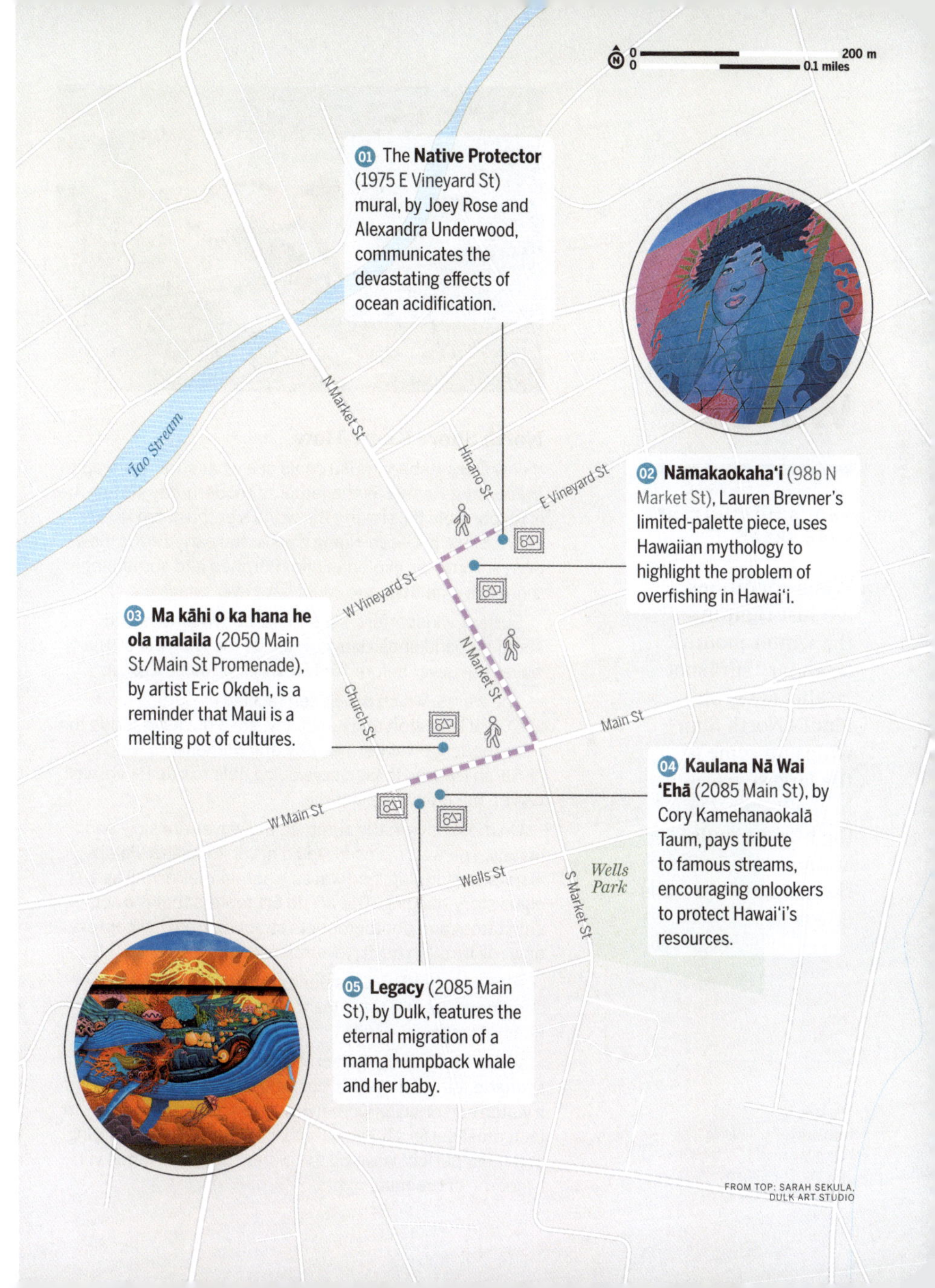

01 The **Native Protector** (1975 E Vineyard St) mural, by Joey Rose and Alexandra Underwood, communicates the devastating effects of ocean acidification.

02 **Nāmakaokahaʻi** (98b N Market St), Lauren Brevner's limited-palette piece, uses Hawaiian mythology to highlight the problem of overfishing in Hawaiʻi.

03 **Ma kāhi o ka hana he ola malaila** (2050 Main St/Main St Promenade), by artist Eric Okdeh, is a reminder that Maui is a melting pot of cultures.

04 **Kaulana Nā Wai ʻEhā** (2085 Main St), by Cory Kamehanaokalā Taum, pays tribute to famous streams, encouraging onlookers to protect Hawaiʻi's resources.

05 **Legacy** (2085 Main St), by Dulk, features the eternal migration of a mama humpback whale and her baby.

FROM TOP: SARAH SEKULA, DULK ART STUDIO

Monster Waves

MAUI'S MOST INTENSE SURF BREAK

When conditions are just right in the winter months, legendary surf spot Pe'ahi (Jaws) on Maui's North Shore whips up some of the largest waves in the Pacific. Only the bravest souls attempt to ride the skyscraper-sized walls of water.

Left Surfer, Pe'ahi **Middle** Tyler Larronde competing in the 2016 Jaws Big Wave Championships **Right** Surfer, Pe'ahi

CURIOSO.PHOTOGRAPHY/SHUTTERSTOCK

North Shore Know-How

If only Duke Kahanamoku could see what surfers are up to these days. Known as the father of modern-day surfing, he is responsible for stoking the world's enthusiasm for the sport. Since his wave-riding days in the early 1900s, however, surfing has exploded and morphed into something more extreme than one could have ever imagined.

Surfers, windsurfers, kitesurfers, bodyboarders and stand-up paddleboarders now tackle the gnarliest of gnarly waves like never before. And Pe'ahi is *the* place to do it.

The waves, which have been tackled by surfing icons like Laird Hamilton and Kai Lenny, are a bucket-list ride for the experienced watermen or waterwomen. Pro windsurfer Sarah Hauser, in fact, says being able to ride Pe'ahi well can be the quest of a lifetime.

On most days in the summer, the waves are slow and steady. The water is calm. You'd never know that Pe'ahi is notorious for big, bad waves – sometimes as tall as an eight-story building. The 40- to 60-footers that attract spectators and photographers shooting from helicopters only roll through from November to March.

About four or five days during that timeframe, when conditions are just right, giant waves break in front of Pe'ahi's jagged sea cliffs.

When Pe'ahi is firing, it creates a worst-nightmare scenario for most people, but a thrilling challenge if you're a waterman or waterwoman up for a colossal challenge. In fact, most surfers think of it as both the most intimidating and most perfect wave on the planet. Surfing it lands you a lifetime of bragging rights.

EPICSTOCKMEDIA/SHUTTERSTOCK

JARVIS GRAY/SHUTTERSTOCK

Force of Nature

The nickname Jaws comes from the early days when big-wave surfers first started frequenting this spot. When the surf really kicks up, it feels as unpredictable and vicious as a shark attack.

If you want to see the waves yourself, it's a matter of luck – being on Maui on the right day at the right time when the swell rolls through can be tricky. Keeping a constant eye on the **Jaws Big Wave Championships**, which take place between mid-November and the end of March most years, is one way to plan. Event organizers constantly monitor the waves during that time. When it's go-time, competitors have 72 hours' notice.

In fact, most surfers think of Pe'ahi as both the most intimidating and most perfect wave on the planet. Surfing it lands you a lifetime of bragging rights.

Of course, watching people race down the waves is best done by boat or Jet Ski. But that's not something readily available to most visitors. Instead, bring binoculars or a telephoto lens and watch from the cliffside perch. From here, you'll hear the roar of the waves below pounding the deep-water reef.

Swell Seeker

A lot of people get seriously injured. I took several survival courses designed for big-wave surfers. It doesn't make the situation totally safe but reduces risks.

When conditions are right, Jaws is a perfect giant wave. Its shape, its A-frame, its closeness to the cliffs make it very special. In order to access it somewhat safely, we launch on a Jet Ski. Once we get to the wave I rig my sail on the Jet Ski, attach it to my board and I'm off. If I fall in the impact zone, the Jet Ski picks me up. During a wipeout you get tossed violently and try your best to find the balance between being tight and loose.

As told by Sarah Hauser, *Guinness World Record holder for the largest Pe'ahi wave windsurfed by a woman @hauserlifestyle*

Listings

BEST OF THE REST

Adventurers Only

Swell Maui Surf Lessons

Private and semiprivate lessons for everyone, from newbies to more advanced surfers looking to add tricks to their repertoire. Learn the art of surfing from the pros on Maui's west-side breaks.

Blue Hawaiian Helicopters

Get a bird's-eye view of Maui on a helicopter tour that takes you over West Maui, Hāna and Haleakalā. Some tours land at ʻUlupalakua Ranch, on the slopes of Haleakalā.

Paraglide Maui

Take a tandem or solo flight that you'll be talking about for years. Thanks to the Upcountry location, the launch site is protected from the tradewinds and allows paragliding sessions seven days a week.

Blue Water Rafting

Bounce over the waves in a motorized raft to see remote sea caves and arches along the Kanaio Coast. Trips start at the Kīhei boat ramp and stop for snorkeling on the return.

Maui Roadsters

Explore the island in a vintage ride. It's a surefire way to meet new friends and to have a great post-vacation story. Choose from four 1957 Porsche 356 Speedsters.

Rest & Recovery

Spa at the Resort at Kapalua Bay

Splurge on a session that embraces the spirit and bounty of the islands, from a *lomilomi* massage inspired by the flow of the ocean to a soothing body polish enhanced by the scents of tropical plants.

Kilolani Spa at Grand Wailea

Treatments change with the Hawaiian lunar calendar at this new spa at the Grand Wailea. You can also decompress in the sauna or saltwater pool, both in the Hydrotherapy Gardens.

Flower Power

Haku Maui

String your own beautiful lei while learning Hawaiian history and traditions during a workshop at this lei shop in downtown Makawao.

Aliʻi Kula Lavender

Breathe in the sweet botanical smells. Take a tour and collect a bouquet (this spot is home to about 55,000 lavender plants).

Snap Happy

Mermaid Memories Maui

Bring out your inner Ariel with a mermaid photo shoot. Tails, tops, fins, crowns and ocean-themed jewelry provided. Choose from underwater photos or sunset beach portraits.

Blue Hawaiian Helicopters

Foodie Fare

Humble Market Kitchin $$$

From the brussels sprouts and cauliflower appetizer to the herb-seared fresh catch, you'll get your fill at this upscale eatery serving seasonal faves with Asian flair. Added bonus: ocean views.

Nuka Maui $$

An *izakaya* restaurant and sushi bar serving up delightful sushi, seafood and salads. Think: miso eggplant starters, tempura shrimp udon and black sesame ice cream.

Café des Amis $

Have a culinary feast of French, Mediterranean and Indian cuisine. In other words, nosh on crepes, curry wraps and Greek salads in one fell swoop.

A'A Roots $

Creative plant-based crowd-pleasers at this stylish Nāpili cafe include chilled noodle bowls, avocado toast and acai bowls loaded with fresh tropical fruit. Salads, juices and smoothies too.

Mama's Fish House $$$

Stuffed *kanpachi,* Antarctic toothfish and *liliko'i* (passion fruit) crème brûlée. The menu changes daily, but you can expect to be wowed regardless of when you go. Book three to six months ahead.

Ku'ia Estate Chocolate Factory $$$

Tour the largest chocolate factory in Hawai'i, get schooled on the cacao-growing process and take in rooftop views. Did we mention? You get to nibble on nine different chocolates.

Wooden Crate at Lumeria Maui $$$

Garden views. Check. Mountain views. Check. This farm-to-table eatery offers a three-

Café des Amis

course prix fixe menu. Enjoy fresh eats while learning about sustainability.

Baya Bowls $

Settle in at a picnic table beside wild DT Fleming Beach for acai bowls loaded with fresh local fruit, organic granola and swirls of Maui honey. Simply delicious...and totally photogenic.

Cocktails & Corks

Three's Bar & Grill $$

With an extensive wine list, you'll surely find the perfect match for your meal. Coconut-crusted fish tacos and fries tossed in *furikake,* sriracha aioli and mochi crunch are hard to beat.

Pint & Cork $$

For memorable house-crafted cocktails, this high-energy gastropub is a no-brainer. Toughest part is choosing which whiskey to down – there are more than 100.

Monkeypod Kitchen $$

The consistent crowds outside this island favorite say a lot. Settle in for tasty drinks like the No Ka Oi (ocean vodka, Thai basil and lime topped with honey *liliko'i* puree).

33 A Weekend on LĀNAʻI

SOLITUDE | ADVENTURE | WILDS

Home to about 3000 residents, Lānaʻi (lah-nuh-ee) has no stoplights, no chain restaurants and about 30 miles of paved roads. Travelers come to recharge and explore wild landscapes. You'll get the same gorgeous views as on the other islands without the crowds.

CULTURA EXCLUSIVE/STUART WESTMORLAND/GETTY IMAGES

How to

Getting here Fly into the small one-runway airport. A cab is $15 per person to Lāna'i City and should be arranged ahead of time. Resorts will send a shuttle. Or if you're on Maui, take the 1¼-hour ferry between Mānele Harbor and Mā'alaea Harbor for $66. As you travel through the 'Au'au Channel, keep your eyes peeled for sea turtles, dolphins and whales.

When to go Year-round.

Did you know? White-spotted axis deer outnumber residents on the island. You may also see sheep and turkeys.

TOM SIMAK/GETTY IMAGES

Pet project Consistent snuggles. Endless naps. A catfurteria. Life is good if you're a feline at the **Lāna'i Cat Sanctuary**, a 4-acre cat shelter in the center of the island. Altogether there are about 600 adoptable cats. Dozens will greet you with meows. Others will continue to nap in baskets perched in trees.

LIBRARY LADY AMY/FLICKR/CC BY 2.0

Below the surface Divers visit specifically to check out **Cathedrals**, a series of undersea caverns along Lāna'i's southern coast. Snorkelers appreciate **Hulopo'e Beach**, where meeting resident parrotfish, pencil urchins and *honu* (green sea turtles) is easy to do. Dolphins sometimes take a breather here, too. On a good day, 100-plus feet of visibility is common. Because it is a protected area, remember to leave shells and stones where they are. Make a day of it – there are barbecue grills, restrooms, showers and picnic tables.

Get Fancy

Many visit Lāna'i simply to lounge at the **Four Seasons Resort Lāna'i**. Relax by the lagoon-shaped pool overlooking **Hulopo'e Beach**, practice downward dogs in a yoga class and dine on Japanese cuisine at cliffside Nobu Lanai. Board the hotel's luxe boat to get waterlogged with a snorkel or dive.

Top left Hulopo'e Beach
Bottom left Cathedrals dive site
Above Lāna'i Cat Sanctuary

Talk story Chat with historians about Lāna'i's ranching and pineapple-plantation roots at the **Lāna'i Culture & Heritage Center**. The small museum offers a glimpse into the past with Hawaiian artifacts.

Take a trek Hike to **Pu'u Pehe** (Sweetheart Rock), located off the island's southern Mānele Bay, for sunrise. Start at Hulopo'e Beach where there's public parking and take the short hike uphill. You can't miss the giant rock protruding from the ocean floor. Drive through desert-like terrain for the quick walk to **Kaiolohia** (Shipwreck Beach) where, thanks to strong tradewinds and large swells, many ships have grounded.

Four-wheel it Before embarking on a 4WD journey, note that the sites listed below are sacred, and should be respected as such.

Take in views of Moloka'i and O'ahu from a 1600ft rock garden known as **Keahiakawelo** (Garden of the Gods). The haphazard boulders dotting the lunar-like landscape might

Schooners to Steamships

Thanks to Lāna'i's fierce tradewinds and strong swells, the island's north shore is home to at least a dozen shipwrecks. From Kaiolohia, an 8-mile stretch of sand also known as Shipwreck Beach, you can photograph a rusting oil tanker from the 1940s resting on the shallow reef. Stick around to hike along the shoreline where it's common to find leopard cones and sea slug shells. Note: you need a 4WD to get to this beach. Wear sturdy shoes since it requires some rock scrambling. Get directions ahead of time as the roads are unmarked.

Left Shipwreck off the coast of Kaiolohia **Below** Keahiakawelo

remind you of the Colorado spot bearing the same name. Note: you will need a 4WD to get there. Taking rocks or stacking them here is prohibited.

The 4WD will also come in handy for the unpaved roads leading to **Kaunolū** – a historic fishing village that once welcomed King Kamehameha and his warriors. Hike across the stream to find **ancient petroglyphs** etched in the rocks. Wander past sacred rock walls at **Halulu Heiau** (a sacrificial temple) across the gulch until you reach the cliff's edge. Once there, take in views of Shark Island. This spot is known as **Kahekili's Leap**. Warriors used to dive off the edge here to gain respect.

You only live once Choose your own adventure at **Lāna'i Adventure Park**. If heights are your thing, try ziplining with dreamy views of the Kaiholena Valley. Score more thrills at the aerial tower, an elevated obstacle course with two tiers. It's a 90-minute mental and physical challenge. Prefer to stay grounded? The electric mountain-bike tours take you to photogenic spots like Keahiakawelo and Pālāwai Basin.

Did you know? There are petroglyphs scattered across the island. The **Luahiwa Petroglyphs**, about 10 minutes outside of Lāna'i City, are the easiest ones to find.

MOLOKA'I

ADVENTURE | OUTDOORS | CULTURE

RESEARCHED BY SARAH SEKULA; UPDATED BY AMY BALFOUR

- **Trip Builder** (p178)
- **Practicalities** (p180)
- **Hike in Hālawa** (p182)
- **Farm Frolics** (p184)
- **Fringe Benefits** (p186)
- **No Coastal Crowds** (p188)
- **Pedal Power** (p190)
- **Shell Yeah!** (p194)
- **Catch of the Day** (p196)
- **Listings** (p198)

BENJAMIN S FISCHINGER/SHUTTERSTOCK

Seek out locally grown papaya, dragon fruit, *liliko'i* (passion fruit) and lychee at **Kumu Farms** (p185)
12min from Moloka'i Airport

Smash open a macadamia nut shell – they're tough! – for a fresh sample at **Purdy's Macadamia Nut Farm** (p185)
14min from Kaunakakai

Gather fragrant flowers at **Molokai Plumerias** to construct your own lei (p185)
8min from Moloka'i Airport

Chow down on loaves of fresh, hot bread in **Kaunakakai** (p199)
12min from Moloka'i Airport

MOLOKA'I
Trip Builder

Moloka'i is drastically different from the other islands. It's the least developed, the least touristy and home to the least amount of people. That's exactly its appeal. Step back in time and experience a place where people still practice the ancient art of throw-net fishing and hold a strong desire to keep Hawaiian traditions alive.

CLOCKWISE FROM TOP LEFT: ASHOK SAXENA/ALAMY, ZUMA PRESS, INC/ALAMY, DAVID FLEETHAM/ALAMY

Practicalities

DOUG HOLLAND/SHUTTERSTOCK

ARRIVING

Ho'olehua Airport (MKK) Moloka'i is small – about 38 miles long and 10 miles across – and so is its airport. That said, getting to Alamo Rent a Car (the only major car-rental company on the island) is easy. It's a short walk across the street from baggage claim. From Alamo you are about 15 minutes from the main town, Kaunakakai. Pro tip: many refer to it simply as Moloka'i Airport.

HOW MUCH FOR A

Large pizza from $16

Gallon of milk $8–10

Gallon of gas $5.30

GETTING AROUND

Car There's no public transportation, so a rental is the best way to explore Moloka'i. Rideshare services aren't available. Rental-car numbers are small, so book early.

Taxi Fares start at $15 to get from the airport to Kaunakakai. Credit cards and cash accepted. Note: there are only a few taxis on the island, so book ahead.

Bicycle If you're in good shape, cycling is an option. Molokai Bicycle rents bicycles and bike racks. Having a rental car in addition to a bike would be a smart idea.

WHEN TO GO

JAN–DEC
Warm days, mild nights and uncrowded year-round.

JAN
The Ka Molokai Makahiki Festival showcases hula, arts, crafts and games.

MAY
The birth of hula is celebrated at the Molokai Ka Hula Piko Festival.

MAR–OCT
See plumeria in bloom.

EATING & DRINKING

Burgers come in many forms at **Moloka'i Burger**, which also sells sandwiches, fried chicken and island-style plates. Try the **Fish N' Shrimp** food truck for delicious seafood platters – the fish is uber-fresh. A semifinalist for a James Beard Award, the beloved **Kanemitsu Bakery & Coffee Shop** (pictured top) has been around for more than 90 years and sells pastries galore. Come evening, use the alley window to order Moloka'i sweet bread topped with cinnamon, cream cheese or jelly. **Moloka'i Pizza Cafe** (pictured bottom) is exactly what you'd expect from a pizza joint: fresh pizzas, milkshakes, soft-serve ice cream and salads.

Best pastries
Kanemitsu Bakery & Coffee Shop (p199)

Must-try seafood
Fish N' Shrimp

CONNECT & FIND YOUR WAY

Connectivity Wi-fi is available at **Kamoi Snack-n-Go** and **Moloka'i Public Library**. Cell-phone reception islandwide is spotty and in many areas impossible to get. Make any important calls on a landline before you head out to explore.

Navigation The island isn't too difficult to navigate; there is only one two-lane highway that stretches from one end to the other.

WHERE TO STAY

Hotel Moloka'i is the island's only hotel. Not to worry, though, there are condos and cottages available. You can even stay on a working ranch.

Location	Pros/Cons
Kaunakakai	Widest range of options at all price points; main shopping and supply hub. Noisier and busier than elsewhere. Hotels, ranch and cottages available.
Hālawa Valley	Close to nature and the island's only accessible waterfalls; quiet and uncrowded. Few amenities. Accommodations at Pu'u O Hoku Ranch are a solid option.
Maunaloa	If you are staying on the west end, this small village is the only place to grab groceries. Condos available for rent.

FILLING UP

Kaunakakai has the island's only two gas stations.

MONEY

ATMs can only be found at Bank of Hawaii, American Savings Bank and Molokai Community Federal Credit Union in Kaunakakai. Carry cash.

34 Hike in HĀLAWA

CULTURE I WATERFALLS I HIKE

Since Moloka'i is a jumble of privately owned land, there are not many opportunities for travelers to trek solo. Hiking, for the most part, requires a guide or a permit. The good news is that having a guide means, in addition to getting exercise and seeing beautiful sights, you will experience Moloka'i through the eyes of a local.

PHOTO RESOURCE HAWAII/ALAMY

How to

Getting here & around About 1½ hours from the airport and an hour from Kaunakakai. The scenic drive has you passing ancient fishponds, Kalua'aha Church (the first Christian church on the island, built 1833) and Kūmimi Beach.

When to go Year-round.

Booking Book online at halawavalleymolokai.com or leave a message at 808-542-1855.

NORINORI303/SHUTTERSTOCK

The hike and spectacle of the 250ft **Moa'ula Falls** and **Hipuapua Falls**, which cascade down the back of the lush Hālawa Valley, are a highlight of a visit to Moloka'i. The twin falls are reached via a straightforward 2-mile trail lined with historical sites. To protect these sites, and because the trail crosses private property, you are required to visit the falls with a local guide.

There are numerous cultural sites along the path, and you'll pass through lush tropical foliage during the walk: look out for the bright orange blossoms of African tulip trees and the brilliant green of beach heliotrope trees.

The crescendo of the hike is the dreamy falls. Most people thrill at the bracing plunge into the pools at the bottom. Walks can easily take three to five hours, depending on the abilities of those in your group – expect muddy conditions and the occasional need to clamber over river boulders.

Reputable guides include **Greg Kawaimaka Solatorio** (halawavalleymolokai.com), who represents a family that has lived in the valley for generations. His tours include extensive cultural demonstrations. **Kalani Pruet** (molokaiflowers.com), who runs a flower farm, also offers hikes and makes a mean smoothie from the fruit he gathers at his lush spread of land. **Eddie Tanaka, Jr** (facebook.com/mysticalmolokai), whose house you pass between mile posts 20 and 21, is also an option.

Top left Hālawa Valley Falls trail
Bottom left Hipuapua Falls

Top Tips

In Hālawa Valley, your shoes will get wet while crossing streams. Bring a rain jacket. Wear your swimsuit if you'd like to take a dip at the waterfall. The hike is suitable for most skill levels, though you should be nimble enough to traipse across slippery rocks, duck beneath tree limbs and navigate through dense brush.

Hike the nearby moss-enshrouded rainforest of **Kamakou Preserve** (nature.org). Permits from the Department of Health are required for visits to **Kalaupapa National Historical Park** (nps.gov/kala).

35 FARM Frolics

OUTDOORS I NATURE I FARMS

Living off the land is a huge part of the culture on Moloka'i. An ideal way to learn about it is to talk story with islanders who are doing just that. From a family-run tea farm to a plumeria paradise to a working ranch that includes 14,000 acres of protected lands – take your pick.

STEVEN GREAVES/GETTY IMAGES

How to

When to go All year long.

Give the gift of fruit Kumu Farms ships boxes of strawberry papayas and Maui Gold pineapples to mainland US.

Mobile market Sust'āinable Moloka'i offers an online farmers market. Order at sustainablemolokai.org and pick up your Moloka'i-grown produce at various locations on the island.

REGULA HEEB-ZWEIFEL/ALAMY

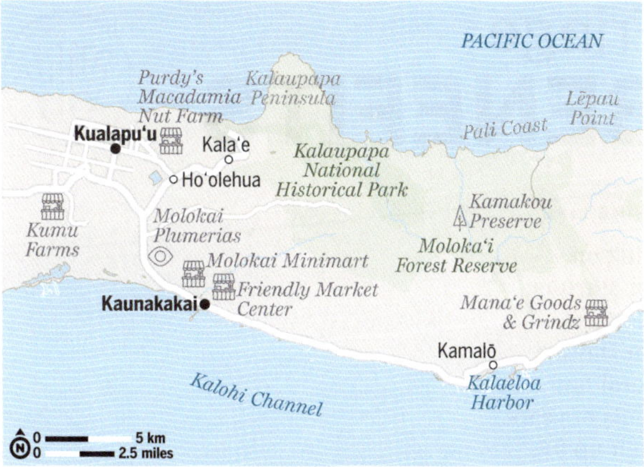

Go nuts Look for Central Moloka'i bounty at **Purdy's Macadamia Nut Farm**, where enthusiastic nut farmer Tuddie Purdy leads tours of his 90-year-old orchard. Crack open macadamia nuts on a stone with a hammer, then try the incredible macadamia-blossom honey, scooped up with slices of fresh coconut.

Flower power Pick flowers at **Molokai Plumerias** in Kaunakakai, an orchard packed with thousands of plumeria trees. Then talk story while sewing the flowers into a lei under the shade of a tree. For maximum blooms, visit March through October. Call for an appointment.

Farm goodness When hunger strikes, stop by **Kumu Farms** (mile marker 8) for Moloka'i-grown produce. You'll find papaya, apple bananas, fresh macadamia nuts, kale, Swiss chard, jam, *liliko'i* (passion fruit) butter and hot sauce. Pick up local **Molokai Meli** *kiawe* honey, made by a family of beekeepers, at **Friendly Market Center**, **Mana'e Goods & Grindz**, **Molokai Minimart** and more.

Local knowledge The best way to find out about things on Moloka'i is to scour the bulletin boards, check the local paper, *Moloka'i Dispatch,* and to ask questions. Quite often you'll find a home-based business that sells vegan food or a farmer who sells raw honey on the side of the road. Many of the best things are not advertised online.

Top left Molokai Plumerias
Bottom left Mana'e Goods & Grindz

#Ranchlife Rocks

At family-owned **Pu'u O Hoku Ranch** (the name means 'Hill of Stars') guests can choose from three remote cottages, including an awesome one on the beach, and even an entire lodge. There is an organic farm here, too. The setting is truly magical, as the ranch is surrounded by 14,000 acres of protected land. There are good views over the open, green lands out to sea. A roadside shop sells refreshments, ice, organic honey and locally made gift items.

36 Fringe BENEFITS

OCEAN | ADVENTURE | MARINE LIFE

Snorkeling and diving on Moloka'i is a real treat. For starters, the island is home to the longest continuous fringing reef in Hawai'i – 28 miles long – where coral has steadily grown for thousands of years. Plus, water visibility is often up to 140ft. Here's where to have a flipper-kicking good time underwater.

How to

Getting here Based at Kaunakakai Harbor, **Molokai Fish & Dive** has three boats for diving and whale watching. It's Moloka'i's only PADI-certified dive and snorkel outfitter.

When to go All year. Diving with hammerheads on the agenda? May to November is your best bet.

Need to know There are more than 40 dive sites, ranging from newbie-level to advanced. If you aren't a certified diver, Molokai Fish & Dive offers discover scuba dives.

Below the Surface

On a calm day, **Mokuho'oniki** (Elephant Rock) makes for an ideal snorkel session. This small island at Moloka'i's eastern tip is home to large schools of fish and lots of healthy coral in lovely shades of yellow, pink and purple. Note: this one is for experienced snorkelers only.

Snorkel at the fringing reef (Hawai'i's largest) in search of finger coral, triggerfish, *kala* (unicorn fish), *manini* (convict tang), trumpetfish and green sea turtles. During whale season, you may either hear or see whales, too. Due to the lack of visitors, the reef remains in very good condition. Request a visit to

Top right Mokuho'oniki
Bottom right Scalloped hammerhead shark

DAVID FLEETHAM/ALAMY

DAVID FLEETHAM/ALAMY

Wind & Waves

With sometimes harsh winds and swirling currents, it's no surprise that the translation of **Pailolo Channel** loosely means 'crazy fisherman.' Separating Maui and Moloka'i, the channel is about 1 mile from Moloka'i's east end.

one of the seven blue holes to the east of Kamalō. Here the reef is bisected by impressive underwater canyons.

Shark Nerds

For an adventurous dive, sign up to explore the **Pailolo Channel**, where you'll be in search of scalloped hammerhead sharks. If you're lucky, you'll witness them swimming in large groups (sometimes more than 100) during this blue-water drift dive. If you're really, really lucky, a Hawaiian monk seal will show up, too. As if that wasn't enough, it's not uncommon to see blue dragon nudibranchs, moray eels, barracuda, spinner dolphins, eagle rays, manta rays and other pelagic sharks.

This is considered an advanced dive, so you must have 25 dives under your belt to sign up.

37 No Coastal CROWDS

WAVES I WILDLIFE I NATURE

Beach bars, surf schools and loud music are all things you won't find on Moloka'i's beaches. What you will find is peace and quiet and no crowds. In fact, it's possible to have an entire stretch of sand all to yourself.

BILLY MCDONALD/SHUTTERSTOCK

Trip Notes

Getting here & around Exploring by rental car is best. Since cell service is spotty it could be tough getting a taxi back.

When to go Year-round.

Hawaiian saying *Mālama i ke kai, a mālama ke kai iā 'oe* means 'care for the ocean, and the ocean will care for you.'

Water Safety

There are no lifeguards watching the beaches on Moloka'i. That said, it's crucial that no matter what water activity you choose, you go with someone. Conditions can change quickly.

Visit hioceansafety.com to learn about dangerous shore breaks, currents and wind.

02 **Pāpōhaku Beach** is one of Hawai'i's largest and longest white-sand beaches. Three miles by 100yd, to be exact. With the rough shore break, it's not a swimming beach.

03 **Kepuhi Beach** (pictured left) is a Hawaiian monk seal hangout. You might spot Kepuhinui, a monk seal born on the island named by local second-graders. The name means 'the great one of Kepuhi Beach'.

05 On the east side at **Hālawa Beach Park**, take your pick between Kawili and Kama'alaea beaches. If it's calm, grab the snorkel gear. If there are waves, surfers will entertain.

01 Families love **Kapukahehu Beach** (Dixie Maru Cove). Its crescent-shaped sandy cove is sheltered from windswept waves, meaning it's safe for swimming.

04 Centrally located, **One Ali'i Beach Park** was a favorite of Hawaiian royalty. Today, you'll appreciate the picnic facilities, restrooms and parking.

FROM TOP: BILLY MCDONALD/SHUTTERSTOCK, DAVID FLEETHAM/ALAMY

0 — 20 km
0 — 10 miles

38 PEDAL Power

OUTDOORS I ADVENTURE I VIEWS

There's not much traffic to speak of on Moloka'i, no stoplights and most roads are well paved. That makes it ideal for roaming around on two wheels. You'll pass by ancient fishponds, traverse over red-dirt roads and maybe even spot turkeys.

JOHN DE MELLO/ALAMY

How to

Getting here & around Molokai Bicycle provides a bike rack to attach to your vehicle.

When to go Year-round.

Solo journey Believe it or not, there's a very good chance you will not encounter other cyclists during your journeys.

Need to know Molokai Bicycle is the only traditional bicycle-rental shop on the island. It can drop bicycles off at your accommodations depending on where you are staying.

BILLY MCDONALD/SHUTTERSTOCK

Cycling Routes

Mountain biking If you rent a mountain bike and want a challenge, try the forest reserve road from Homelani Cemetery to Waikolu Lookout. After a hard 10-mile climb, you'll be rewarded with a dramatic view of the valley and the shoreline. The first 5 miles of the route are hot and dry. When you enter the forest, it's a whole different story. Ten miles up and you're smack-dab where scenes from *The Lost World: Jurassic Park* were filmed. The 2774-acre preserve is packed with 250 rare Hawaiian plants, many of which cannot be seen anywhere else on the planet.

Road cycling From Kaunakakai, ride to Hālawa Valley (27 miles) on the northeast tip of the island. The 900ft climb at Pu'u O Hoku Ranch (25-mile mark) will have your calves burning. Once you see the valley, take a dip.

BRIAN CAISSIE/GETTY IMAGES

Cycling Tips

- Start rides as early as possible to beat the sun and tradewinds.
- Either hug the white line or stay to the right of the line.
- Watch out for *kukus* (thorns) everywhere.

Tips from Phillip Kikukawa, *owner of Molokai Bicycle*

Top left Mountain bikers, Kalaupapa Overlook (p192) **Below left** Road cycling, Moloka'i **Above** Pāpōhaku Beach (p192)

While you're here, check out the two good swimming beaches.

From Kaunakakai, take Kala'e Hwy 470 for 4.2 miles to where you'll see 1000 palm trees planted in the 1800s by King Kamehameha V. Pick up snacks at **Kualapu'u Market**. Head 4 miles to the **Kalaupapa Overlook** and **Pālā'au State Park**. Breathe in pine and eucalyptus aromas along the way (10 miles, elevation gain about 1700ft).

The ride to Maunaloa town from Kaunakakai is about 16.5 miles with a total of 1360ft of climbing. On the way, the tradewinds are typically in your favor. Coming back, not so much. At the 15.5-mile marker, opt for the 1000ft drop down Kalua Koi Rd to Kepuhi Beach. Dig your toes in the sand at Hawai'i's largest beach, **Pāpōhaku Beach**. Pay Kapukahehu (aka Dixie Maru Cove) a visit while you're at it. Even though it's paved, the road is still super bumpy.

Kamakou Preserve

The island's highest mountain, Kamakou, is home to Kamakou Preserve. This fragile rainforest is packed with endangered native plants, trees, birds and insects not found anywhere else on the planet. It's important to protect this environment and to go with a guide. Molokai Outdoors will take you to the **Waikolu Lookout**, navigating the steep descents, rises and turns in a 4WD. To protect the forest from diseases, visitors should wear brand-new gear or fully decontaminate existing gear. Wash gear in warm soapy water, remove debris and soil, and spray soles with 70% rubbing alcohol.

Left Kamakou Preserve
Below St Joseph Catholic Church

Perfect Pitstops

East from Kaunakakai

- 2 miles: Hotel Molokaʻi
- 10 miles: Kamalō Wharf
- 10.5 miles: St Joseph Catholic Church
- 14.5 miles: Our Lady of Seven Sorrows Catholic Church, built by Father Damien
- 16 miles: Manaʻe Goods & Grindz, Pūkoʻo Harbor
- 20 miles: Good swimming beach
- 21 miles: Climb to Puʻu O Hoku Ranch begins
- 25 miles: Puʻu O Hoku Ranch Store, descent to Hālawa begins
- 26 miles: Hālawa Overlook

West from Kaunakakai

- 8.7 miles: Kumu Farms

North on 470 from the Maunaloa Hwy (460)

- 2 miles up 470: Kualapuʻu town
- 3.9 miles up 470: Ironwoods Golf Course and Country Club
- 4 miles up 470: RW Meyer Sugar Mill Museum
- 6 miles up 470: Pālāʻau State Park/Kalaupapa Overlook

Shell **YEAH!**

01

02

03

04

05

06

01 Stuck on you
'Opihi (limpet snail) can be found clinging to rocks. The conical shells of this gastropod resemble a mini mountain.

02 Beautiful but beware
Marble cones, textile cones, striated cones. All beauties. Beware, though, many cone shells in Hawai'i are venomous.

03 Holey grail
Puka shells have a naturally formed *puka* (hole) in the middle. You'll find them used in shell jewelry.

04 Drupe, drupe, hooray
Found dotting shallow reefs and rocky shores, drupes are fairly easy to find.

05 Sea snail
Triton's trumpet shells are the largest sea snail in Hawai'i and can grow up to 20in long.Covered in algae on the ocean floor, they are often overlooked.

06 Sea donuts
Wana (sea urchin) shells are sometimes a lovely shade of lavender and resemble a pincushion. Often seen at 30ft or more.

07

08

09

10

11

07 Hello sunshine
A beautiful rarity, sunrise shells have hints of red, orange, yellow, pink and purple.

08 Wave worn
The assortment of sea glass in Hawai'i is quite impressive. Lavender, turquoise, chartreuse. Even the occasional yellow or red.

09 Gorgeous glossies
Shaped like half an egg, *leho* (tiger cowrie) shells were used by ancient Hawaiians as fishing lures to catch octopus.

10 Salty marvels
Why do so many marbles wash up on shore? No one can say for sure. Find them in rocky areas below the tide line.

11 Nighttime critters
Pu'oni'oni'o (Hawaiian partridge tun shells) have a beautiful spiral pattern. The snail's body can grow to be a foot wide.

Note: take care of beaches, and the critters who rely on them, by leaving shells where you find them.

01 MARC BRATLAND/GETTY IMAGES. **02** MAYINA/GETTY IMAGES. **03** AKAISER/SHUTTERSTOCK. **04** PJRSTUDIO/ALAMY. **05** FOTANA/SHUTTERSTOCK. **06** JENNY DETTRICK/GETTY IMAGES. **07** DANITA DELIMONT/SHUTTERSTOCK. **08** DENNIS FRATES/ALAMY. **09** ROBYBRET/SHUTTERSTOCK. **10** ELENA MOISEEVA/SHUTTERSTOCK. **11** JON G. FULLER/VWPICS/ALAMY

Catch of the Day

THE ANCIENT ART OF THROW-NET FISHING

Hawaiians have been feeding themselves from the ocean for centuries. This is especially true on Moloka'i, where much of the diet comes from fishing, hunting and farming. While the grocery store may be more convenient, many choose to be self-sufficient to stay connected with their surroundings and to offset the soaring cost of living.

Left Throw-net fishing **Middle** Diver spearfishing **Right** *Uhu* (parrotfish) for sale

BLASIUS ERLINGER/GETTY IMAGES

Fishing Lore

Traditional fishing beliefs in Hawai'i include never talking about it in advance – the fish might hear you! – and not eating pineapple beforehand or bringing bananas with you. Although most fishers don't credit these beliefs, many still follow them as a nod to age-old practices.

Throwing the Net

How exactly do you go throw-net fishing? Simply put, it's complicated. For starters, the conditions should be just so. Water clarity needs to be good enough to spot the fish. Waves should not be too big because you don't want to damage the net or get injured trying to retrieve it. The sun should be in front of you so you aren't casting shadows.

If you've got all that going for you when you reach your fishing spot, study the reef. See the way the water rushes over the rocks. Throw-net fishing is a lesson in patience. Just like the *'a'ama* (crab), you must move stealthily.

Next requirement: good balance. You must tiptoe surreptitiously over craggy lava rocks. You don't want the *kala, uhu* and *awa* to know you are stalking them. With the balance of a gymnast, you crouch down while continuing to hop from one uneven rock to the next. After careful consideration you finally cast the net, much like you would toss a Frisbee.

Even gathering the net is complicated. Made from monofilament with little weights around the edges, the *upena* (net) can weigh up to 10lb. First, hold it up in a loop, and measure it to about hip height. Part of it goes under the elbow then swings over your shoulder. The other part of the net goes over your knee like a hula skirt. And so on.

DANIEL JAMES FUENTES/SHUTTERSTOCK

WIRESTOCK CREATORS/SHUTTERSTOCK

If you have the patience and skill, an extraordinary catch could yield up to 100 fish or so from a single throw. However, traditionally Hawaiian culture says only take what you need to feed your family.

Favorite catches include *kala* (unicorn surgeonfish), *palani* (surgeonfish), *uhu* (parrotfish), *ama* (mullet), *manini* (convict tang) and *awa* (milkfish). *Moi* (Pacific threadfin) is the cream of the crop because it's tricky to catch. It's culturally significant because in ancient times the flaky white meat was reserved for chiefs.

> Throw-net fishing is a lesson in patience. Just like the *'a'ama* (crab), you must move stealthily.

Catch yourself one of those, steam it with some ginger, green onions, peanut oil and soy sauce, and you've got yourself a flavorful dinner.

Spearfishing for Dinner

Hawaiians eat two to three times as much fish as the rest of the United States. So it comes as no surprise that there are many different methods of catching it. Spearfishing, for example. Donning full-body, hooded wetsuits and weight belts, spearfishers train themselves to hold their breath up to six minutes at a time. With aluminum spear in hand, they then dive down 100ft and hover just above the ocean floor. The most important thing is to relax. Even though your brain is sending a signal after 30 seconds that you should breathe, you actually have much longer.

Dive Deep

A traditional cultural practice, spearfishing has been passed down from generation to generation and is often described as a meditative and therapeutic process. After all, you are immersed in a surreal landscape of spherical coral and forced to be 100% focused and in the moment. If you are a good spearfisher, you are completely relaxed. While it can be calming, it has its dangers. Shallow-water blackouts (aka fainting underwater) can occur when divers hyperventilate underwater, run out of oxygen and drown; not to mention sharks are attracted to caught and speared fish.

Listings

BEST OF THE REST

Nature's Calling

One Ali'i Beach Park and Pāpōhaku Beach

Bring a tent and snooze beachside (permit required). Come nighttime, look for shooting stars. During the day, stick to lounging on the white sand. The water is too shallow for swimming.

Kapuaiwa Coconut Grove

King Kamehameha V had a slew of palm trees planted in this spot across from Church Row in the central part of the island. While you are snapping photos, beware of falling coconuts.

Molokai Bicycle

Best way to get to know the island is on two wheels. Molokai Bicycle will set you up with a car rack and arm you with all the info you need to explore.

Pālā'au State Park

At the top of Kala'e Hwy, take the short trail to a sweeping view of historic Kalaupapa. A phallic-shaped stone along the trail is said to enhance fertility.

Kapukahehu Bay

This stretch of sand is ideal for snorkeling, swimming and bodyboarding on a calm day. If the surf's not up, this cove is typically empty.

Molokai Outdoors

Private island tours. Downwind kayaking tours launching from Hotel Molokai (call the front desk to book). Moped rentals (book online at molokaioutdoors.com). This outfitter has a bit of everything, including knowledgeable, local guides.

Kaloko'eli Fishpond

Moloka'i's shores are dotted with fishponds constructed out of lava rock and coral. Some date to the 13th century. Two ponds at this site have been restored and are maintained by community members.

Music with a Meal

Hotel Moloka'i

The yet-to-be-named restaurant at the retro Hotel Moloka'i will host live music after it opens in 2026. We feel certain *'ukulele* strumming will pair perfectly with dinner and a tropical drink at this oceanfront spot. Views of Lāna'i and Maui don't hurt either.

Paddlers Restaurant and Bar

From karaoke to disco night to jazz jam sessions, this eatery will have your toes tapping. Get yourself a Kona Big Wave Golden Ale (most nights have a full bar), nosh on *pūpū* (appetizers) and hit the dance floor.

RALF BROSKVAR/SHUTTERSTOCK

Phallic-shaped stone, Pālā'au State Park

Reel 'Em In

Alyce C Sportfishing

If catching a 1000lb marlin tops your list, book a deep-sea fishing charter. Guests may keep fish if they've got a place to grill it.

Hallelujah Hou Fishing

Hop aboard an 18ft tunnel-hull boat for a catch-and-release fly-fishing trip on the expansive sea flats.

Kaunakakai Harbor and Pier

Makes for a great photo during golden hour. On a clear day, you can see the south coast and Lāna'i. You will no doubt see locals fishing here.

Gifts Galore

Big Wind Kite Factory

Need a gift to bring home? This shop in Maunaloa is a surefire way to find one. Handmade kites, funny postcards, antiques, puzzles, snorkel gear, books and *'ukulele*.

Kupu a'e

Find wearable art in the form of batik silk scarves, wraps and wall hangings from this family-owned business off Maunaloa Hwy.

Molokai Art from the Heart

Shell jewelry and paintings of all sorts.

Burgers, Coffee & Sweet Bread

Hula Bean Cafe $

Popular menu items include bacon breakfast paninis, kale smoothies, milkshakes and caramel mocha frappuccinos.

Kanemitsu Bakery & Coffee Shop $

Nominated for a James Beard Award, this wildly popular shop in Kaunakakai sells pastries galore. Come evening, ask for Molokai sweet bread topped with cinnamon, cream cheese, butter or jelly.

BILLY MCDONALD/SHUTTERSTOCK

Kaunakakai Harbor

Mana'e Goods & Grindz $

On the drive out to Hālawa Valley, this is a good pitstop for drool-worthy banana pancakes, chicken tenders, funnel cakes and barbecue pork sandwiches.

Moloka'i Burger $

Serves burgers, fried chicken, shrimp baskets and tater tots in a casual setting at mile marker zero in Kaunakakai. Breakfast available too.

Friendly Market Center $

This popular family-owned, small-scale grocery store opened in 1953. Stop here for fresh produce, snacks and cold drinks.

Culture & History

Molokai Museum & Cultural Center

Beginning in 1866, Hansen's disease patients were banished to the remote Kalaupapa Peninsula. At this modest museum, learn about their stories. The gift shop has island maps and local crafts.

Church Row

Seven churches, each of a different denomination. Some date back to the 19th century. Across from the Kapuaiwa Coconut Grove on the *mauka* (mountain) side of Hwy 460.

HAWAI'I ISLAND (THE BIG ISLAND)

VOLCANOES | ROAD TRIPS | LOCAL VIBE

RESEARCHED AND UPDATED BY MEGHAN MINER MURRAY

- **Trip Builder** (p202)
- **Practicalities** (p204)
- **Lava Lands** (p206)
- **Hawai'i Island's Varied Terrain** (p210)
- **Brew Thru** (p212)
- **Kona's Dark Sea** (p214)
- **Hawaiian Heritage** (p216)
- **Surf's Turf** (p218)
- **Hāmākua Coasting** (p220)
- **Mālama Hawai'i** (p222)
- **Local Treats** (p224)
- **Inland Ocean Tastes & Tours** (p228)
- **(Some) Features of a Hawaiian Landscape** (p230)
- **Conflict on the Mauna** (p232)
- **Listings** (p234)

J NEL/SHUTTERSTOCK

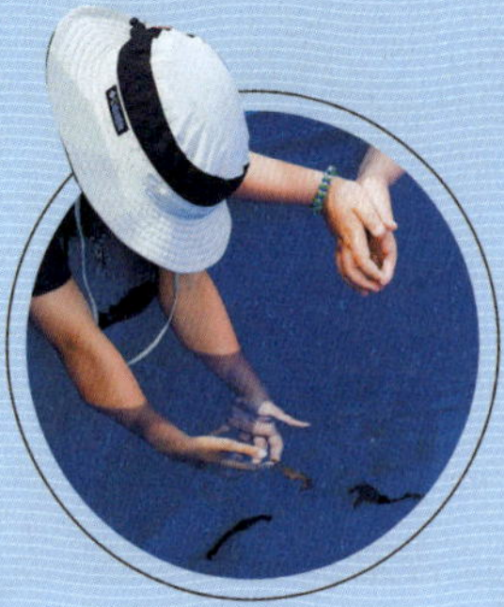

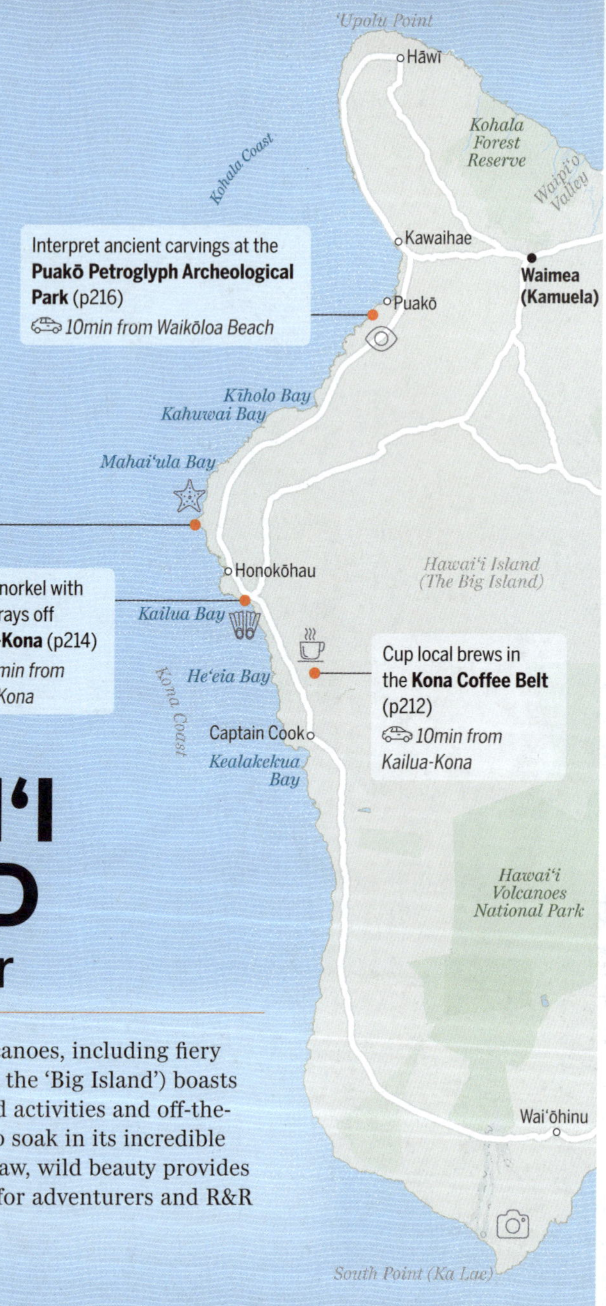

Interpret ancient carvings at the **Puakō Petroglyph Archeological Park** (p216)
10min from Waikōloa Beach

Commune with a seahorse in **HOST Park** (p228)
15min from Kailua-Kona

Night snorkel with manta rays off **Kailua-Kona** (p214)
10min from Kailua-Kona

Cup local brews in the **Kona Coffee Belt** (p212)
10min from Kailua-Kona

HAWAI'I ISLAND
Trip Builder

With five distinct volcanoes, including fiery Kīlauea, Hawai'i Island (aka the 'Big Island') boasts the perfect mix of structured activities and off-the-beaten path opportunities to soak in its incredible diversity of landscapes. Its raw, wild beauty provides an ever-changing backdrop for adventurers and R&R seekers alike.

CLOCKWISE FROM TOP LEFT: WENDY WHITE/ALAMY, FAINA GUREVICH/SHUTTERSTOCK, ITSMELAVICTOIRE/SHUTTERSTOCK, SHAUN BUSUTTIL

Practicalities

ADRIANOK/SHUTTERSTOCK

ARRIVING

Ellison Onizuka Kona International Airport (KOA) The larger hub, 7 miles north of Kailua town and 19 miles south of the Waikōloa Beach area. Taxis, rideshares and shuttles are sparse – book in advance. Rental cars available.

Hilo International Airport (ITO) The closest airport to Hawai'i Volcanoes National Park, a 30-mile drive. It's 4 miles from Hilo, and mostly receives interisland travelers. Rental cars available.

HOW MUCH FOR A

Loaded acai bowl $15

Rental car per day $35–150+

Guided manta snorkel $150

WHEN TO GO

DEC–FEB
Peak tourist and whale season. Rainier on windward side.

MAR–MAY
Shoulder season. Warm weather. Merrie Monarch hula festival in Hilo in April.

JUN–AUG
Second peak season. Warmest weather and calmest waters.

SEP–NOV
Slowest season. Ironman triathlon in October. Kona coffee harvest starts in August.

GETTING AROUND

Rental cars Offer the most flexibility to explore spread-out highlights. Most rental companies prohibit off-roading, even if you opt for a 4WD, so a standard vehicle will usually be best.

Roads Māmalahoa Hwy rings the coast with the exception of the northern valleys, across which there is no access. The high-elevation Saddle Rd cuts through the island's center connecting Hilo and Kailua-Kona.

Savings Prices can vary wildly depending on seasonal demand – check online (discounthawaiicarrental.com) for no-commitment deals that can be altered up to a day in advance.

TOP: MARIDAV/SHUTTERSTOCK
BOTTOM: SCEDIT/SHUTTERSTOCK

EATING & DRINKING

Many high-end restaurants are in resorts where prices can sour the experience. Fortunately, casual, decent options abound, and gems do exist. Some of the best *grinds* (local food) come from pop-up vendors and roadside shacks. Don't discount farmers markets for fresh produce.

Hawai'i Island is a great place to try *poke* (pictured top) and other fresh fish – the waters off Kona are among the best for pelagics like mahimahi and marlin. Visit Ola and Kona breweries in Kailua-Kona for flights of island-brewed beer (pictured bottom), tropical seltzers and more.

Best Hawaiian food
Kaaloa Super J's (p235)

Must-try beach bar
Lava Lava Beach Club (p235)

CONNECT & FIND YOUR WAY

Connectivity Most towns and resorts offer wi-fi access. But plenty of places still have little or no connectivity, allowing you to go 'off-the-grid.' Most major US cell carriers offer widespread coverage; Verizon seems to have the fewest dead zones.

Navigation Hotel concierges, word-of-mouth and a few brochure stands touting tours are the extent of traveler services.

WHERE TO STAY

The bulk of accommodations – and the highest prices – are in the sunny, beachy Waikōloa area. However, it's possible to find sleeping options across a wide geographical and budgetary range.

Location	Pros/Cons
Kailua-Kona Town	Walking distance to shopping, dining, beach and historical sites; some nightlife.
Waikōloa Resort area	High-end, self-contained resort-style accommodations; beaches. Crowds and distance from most island highlights.
Kohala	Luxurious seclusion. Far from most island highlights.
Hilo	Closer to waterfalls and Volcanoes NP. Rainier weather.
Volcano	Best for visits to Volcanoes NP. Far from amenities and other island highlights.
Puna	Off-the-grid jungle lodging. BYO everything.

TRI-PARK PASS

If you're spending multiple days in Hawai'i Volcanoes and Pu'uhonua o Hōnaunau, or also visiting Maui's Haleakalā, this year-long pass offers big savings.

MONEY

Expect to pay more than in most continental US locales. Credit cards are widely accepted, but carry smaller bills for roadside stands and small shops.

39 LAVA Lands

VOLCANOES | GEOLOGY | PELE

Hawai'i Volcanoes NP has an often-glowing lava lake and geothermal activity, but evidence of the island's volcanic might is not constrained within park boundaries. Visit neighborhoods besieged by lava, explore a cave-like lava tube, and bask on one of the world's newest black-sand beaches to appreciate Pele's creative forces.

MNSTUDIO/SHUTTERSTOCK

How to

Getting around You'll want a car and two days to explore lava lands both in and outside the park; no package tours take in both.

When to go Red lava views are never guaranteed, but after-dark visits during active periods afford the moodiest views of fountaining lava or the pooling orange glow standing out from the landscape. The largest crowds congregate around dusk and dawn.

Eruption updates Kīlauea's dynamic environment means plans to experience it should be flexible and based on current activity. Check updates online (nps.gov/havo/planyourvisit/conditions.htm).

KNELSON20/SHUTTERSTOCK

Park Highlights

A good first orientation to the park is the **Welcome Center**, where you'll find park rangers, up-to-date information on eruptive activity, road and trail closures, bathrooms and gift shops. At the time of publication, the primary Kīlauea Visitor Center – which also houses natural history displays and historical exhibits – was closed for renovations. Instead, visitors are directed to the Koa Room at the Kīlauea Military Camp (KMC) just a little over a mile inside the park.

From the center, follow the **Sulfur Banks Trail** over boardwalks through a steamy lunar landscape and native rainforest pocked by geothermal activity. The path connects to **Crater Rim Trail**, which skirts the northern edge of **Halema'uma'u Crater's** spectacular maw. Drive or walk the 2 miles to **Kīlauea Iki Crater** (little Kīlauea), a 1959 eruption site that formed

'Ōhi'a Trees

Iconic *'ōhi'a lehua* trees populate Kīlauea's slopes. With its firework flowers that feed native birds, *'ōhi'a* are often lava's first colonizers helping to transform rock into soil. A fungal disease called Rapid 'Ōhi'a Death (ROD), which has decimated these sacred trees, can be transferred via soiled shoes, so use boot-wash areas.

ES3N/GETTY IMAGES

Top left Kīlauea Iki Crater
Bottom left Nāhuku (p208)
Above *'Ōhi'a lehua* tree

a lava lake. Take the loop hike into the crater and across the dried lava lakebed (3.3 miles). Head next into the damp recesses of the well-lit **Nāhuku** (Thurston Lava Tube), formed by a stream of lava 500 years ago. Pack a picnic for your drive down the park's steep, 19-mile **Chain of Craters Road**. Take in historic craters, pits, fissures and expansive ocean views en route to the wild coast.

Pāhoa's Newest Landscapes

Outside the park, in the Puna District, recent eruptions have impacted the town of **Pāhoa**. Look for the **mural of Pele**: the revered and feared Hawaiian goddess is said to live in Kīlauea and have sway over eruptions. Orient yourself at the community-run **Pāhoa Lava Zone Museum** before heading to the **Pāhoa Transfer Station**. Not your typical tourist site, the dump was besieged by lava in 2014; molten rock oozed through a chain-link fence, putting the town on high alert for months. Continue south on Cemetery Rd to where the 2014 flow crossed the road on your way to **Leilani Estates**. The still-occupied neighborhood was shocked when fissures opened and started spewing lava into the streets in 2018. **Ahu'ailā'au** – the mound that formed atop

Other Park Lands

An hour's drive from Hawai'i Volcanoes' main attractions is the **Kahuku Unit** (nps.gov/places/kahuku.htm), a rarely visited 116,000-acre parcel of former ranch and Hawaiian crop lands on Maunaloa volcano. It's been a bit longer since lava visited here – the mid-19th and early 20th centuries – but its remnants are equally interesting. A highlight requires a full-day's hiking into a forested pit crater. When a parcel of land sunk 230ft below the rest of the surrounding landscape hundreds of years ago, it took a parcel of native forest with it. Its steep-walled confines now protect a haven of endangered native plants and forest birds, and offer a rare glimpse into an ancient Hawaiian landscape.

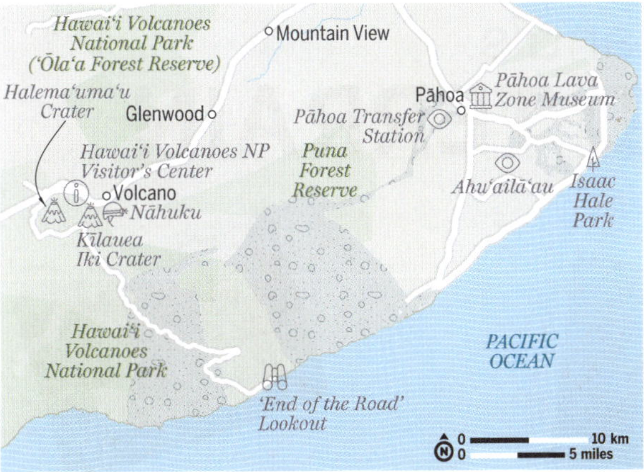

the largest fissure as it spewed lava up to 200ft into the air – was ground zero for that eruption, the most destructive in 200 years. From the **Fissure 8 Viewing Area** you can see the rocky expanse that consumed hundreds of homes as lava flowed to the sea. From the incredible **'End of the Road' Lookout** just beyond Lava Tree State Monument, take in the blanketed landscape.

A Region Transformed

To explore the black lavascape left by the 2018 flow, you'll have to backtrack into town to follow a series of roads south of the lava flow to the coast. A new coastal road crosses over a dried black lava river; surreally, you encounter patches of spared green trees in its midst. This route brings you to **Isaac Hale Park**, a former small boat harbor and site of **Pohoiki Black Sand Beach** on your right. This strip of black sand was created when the 2018 flow hit the sea – hot lava shattered into tiny and remarkably smooth particles that blanketed the coast. It's also close to where the other side of the same lava flow took out Pahoa-Pohoiki Rd at the 'End of the Road' Lookout. As that flow branched and continued toward the coast, it blanketed seaside communities, rare aquatic ecosystems and filled in an entire bay, creating 845 acres of the island's newest land.

Left Hiker, Kahuku Unit, Hawai'i Volcanoes National Park **Below** Pohoiki Black Sand Beach

Hawai‘i Island’s

VARIED TERRAIN

01

02

03

04

05

01 Tropical Rainforest & Waterfalls
Large swaths of Hawai‘i’s low-elevation windward coasts – from Waipi‘o Valley (pictured) to Puna – and mid-elevation leeward coasts are flush with verdant, wet jungle.

02 Tropical Farmlands
Areas with a summer dry or, unusually, a winter dry season exist; such as, the semi-forested Kona/Ka‘ū Coffee Belt.

03 Savanna-esque
Look *mauka* (inland) when driving through the Ka‘ū District for acacia-dotted grasslands reminiscent of African savanna.

04 Temperate Rainforest
Lush ferns, olive-green mosses and gnarly *‘ōhi‘a lehua* look positively primordial in the cooler rainforest areas around Volcano town.

05 Old(er) Growth & Native Forest
On some volcano slopes and in Kahuku Unit pit craters live scattered stands of towering koa – traditionally used for canoes and surfboards.

06

07

08

09

10

11

06 Polar Tundra
Don your parkas! Maunaloa and Maunakea's high-elevation summits with low rainfall and cold temperatures qualify as polar tundra terrain.

07 Desert Grasslands
Find huge swaths of brown, dry grasses north of Kailua-Kona by following Hwy 190 toward Pu'uwa'awa'a Forest Reserve.

08 Lush Grassland
Head to Waimea and the Scenic Kohala Mountain Rd for Norfolk pine and green rolling pastures.

09 Cloud Forest
Head up Hualālai volcano's high-elevation slopes for a magical misty walk through a cooler rainforest perpetually in the clouds.

10 Wind-Whipped Coast
The island's northern and southern tips get regular gusts. Great for panoramic white-capped sea views.

11 Tropical Beaches
Find palm-backed warm sands and clear waters along the coast north of Kailua-Kona and fringing Puna.

01 WESTEND61/GETTY IMAGES, **02** BILLY MCDONALD/ALAMY, **03** DORK MADDER/SHUTTERSTOCK, **04** JIM WEST/ALAMY, **05** BILLY MCDONALD/ALAMY, **06** MIKEUK/GETTY IMAGES, **07** C. BLICKWINKEL2511/SHUTTERSTOCK, **08** DESIGN PICS INC/ALAMY, **09** RS SMITH PHOTOGRAPHY/SHUTTERSTOCK, **10** GEORGE BURBA/SHUTTERSTOCK, **11** ATOMMY/SHUTTERSTOCK

40 BREW Thru

COFFEE | SCENERY | FESTIVAL

Maunaloa's tropical leeward slopes provide the perfect climate to cultivate world-renowned Kona coffee. Road trip through the Kona Coffee Belt's farms and rural hamlets, stopping to tour some of the different estates and learn about how they grow and roast their signature coffee beans. For total immersion, overnight in a guesthouse amid the coffee rows.

DANITA DELIMONT/ALAMY

Coffee Fest

November's week-long **Kona Coffee Cultural Festival** (konacoffeefest.com) awards the region's outstanding brews and brings coffee-themed events and activities to locations throughout Kona. Don't miss its **Hōlualoa Village Coffee & Art Stroll**, when the art town offers your best chance to cup dozens of smaller farms' offerings for side-by-side comparison.

Trip Notes

Getting around You'll need your own transportation. Kona's coffee region sits between 700ft to 2500ft of elevation following Māmalahoa Hwy south from Kailua-Kona for roughly 40 miles.

When to go Flowering: February to May. Harvest: August to December.

'Ono Kona Kona Coffee Council describes the region's brews as: 'rich, medium-bodied and slight acidic...a heady aroma and complex, winey, spicy taste.'

Authentic Only beans grown within a 30-mile-long strip are allowed to be called Kona coffee; Kona blends must have at least 10% Kona coffee.

01 Tucked toward the end of coffee country, the **Coffee Shack** welcomes breakfasters from 7am for a hot cuppa cliffside with panoramic coastal views spanning 20 miles.

02 Venerable **Greenwell Farms** (pictured left and far left), grower and brewer of Kona coffee since 1850, offers 45-minute, seed-to-cup tours of its well-oiled Kealakekua operations.

03 At **Buddha's Cup** some coffee grows with the aid of crystals, pyramidal symbolism and blu-light therapy. Tour croplands by UTV and taste unconventional award-winners.

04 Tours of the well-manicured garden grounds of **Mauka Meadows** are decidedly high-end and culminate at a tasting overlooking an infinity pool and the ocean.

05 **Kona Coffee & Tea's** massive upland farm is just the start of its operations – it mills and roasts then serves its coffee via its popular Kailua-Kona cafe on Palani Rd.

FROM TOP: DMITRI KOTCHETOV/ SHUTTERSTOCK, JIM WEST/ALAMY

41 Kona's DARK SEA

ADVENTURE | DIVING | WILDLIFE

Dip into the ocean at night and get up close and personal with some of the island's most enigmatic residents. Join an inshore snorkel or diving tour to glimpse massive mantas during their acrobatic nightly feast through an underwater light show, or scuba in the inky black deep, hundreds of fathoms above the seafloor and amid a micro-menagerie of glittering plankton.

ONTHERUNPHOTO/GETTY IMAGES

How to

When to go Nightlife occurs year-round; warmer water and fewer trip-canceling storms occur in late summer.

Manta sites There are two: Keauhou (south) or Makako Bay (north). Makako's topography better suits divers; Keauhou has its own harbor and is popular for short snorkel trips.

Options Choose from three night ocean experiences: manta dive, manta snorkel and blackwater dive. Scuba certification required for all dives. Any confident swimmer can manta snorkel.

SEAN STEININGER/SHUTTERSTOCK

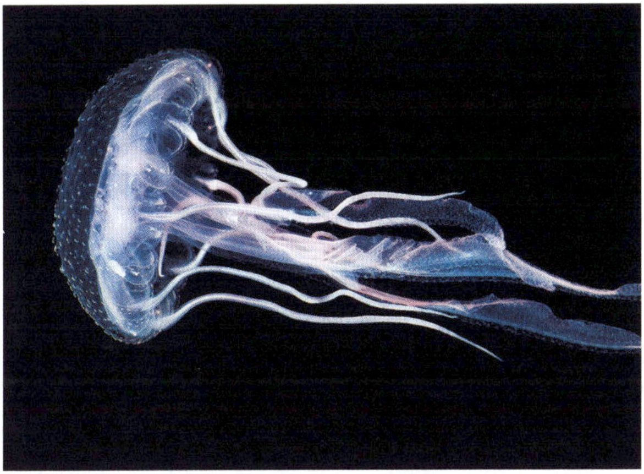

JEFF MILISEN/ALAMY

Left Mauve stinger jellyfish
Far left top Manta ray viewing
Far left bottom Manta ray glides over divers

Most visitors expect to enter the ocean on a Hawai'i trip, but in Kona you should consider it at night. Sunset awakens a new cast of characters. Inshore, majestic manta rays more than 12ft across filter feed in backflipping loops on clouds of zooplankton attracted by bright waterproof lights. The lights create a football stadium–like effect and you'll have a front-row seat. When mantas turn their black-spotted white bellies toward the surface – each as unique as human fingerprints – guides can identify regulars like 'Darth Raydar,' 'Big Bertha' and 'Sugar Ray.' **Manta Pacific Research Foundation** (mantapacific.org), a nonprofit advocate, maintains a database of Kona's 350+ named mantas and recent sightings.

Kona's steep drop-offs close to shore mean it's a short boat ride to open-ocean conditions...and creatures. Five miles out – well beyond manta tours – divers hover, tethered to the boat, above water 5000ft deep. During the day, weird and wonderful creatures navigate a dark world, but when low-light conditions are mimicked at the surface, a profusion of tiny life – gelatinous jellies, translucent octopus and bioluminescent blobs – dance upward. This migration happens worldwide, but Kona is among the few places offering tours to drift in its midst. Like floating through a galaxy of living stars, scuba divers become cosmonauts exploring the last frontier and encountering alien life – new species are discovered all the time.

Offshore Wonders

Critters spotted on Kona's blackwater dives:

Larval lobster A tiny, spider-looking creature, thinner than paper, will grow into something delicious dipped in butter... lobster!

Miniature kraken We see lots of squid on blackwater dives, but the miniature kraken, or enope squid, is probably the most iconic.

Dolphins I love seeing animals interact, and perhaps the most impressive are dolphins hunting squid. It is easy to forget that they are, in fact, apex predators.

Net-casters We're sometimes rewarded with an awe-inspiring sight: Earth's longest animal, a type of siphonophore or net-caster, that can reach 150ft long!

Jeff Milisen, *author of A Field Guide to Blackwater Diving in Hawai'i*
@jeffmilisen

42 Hawaiian HERITAGE

HISTORIC SITES | HAWAIIAN CULTURE | HEIAU (TEMPLES)

Wander among the low rock walls of fishing village ruins to conjure up images of pre-colonial life. Discover a boulder field of chiseled petroglyphs or the impressive rock pedestal of an ancient heiau (temple). From fishponds to a summer palace and a statue dredged up from the sea, reminders of traditional Hawai'i hide in plain sight.

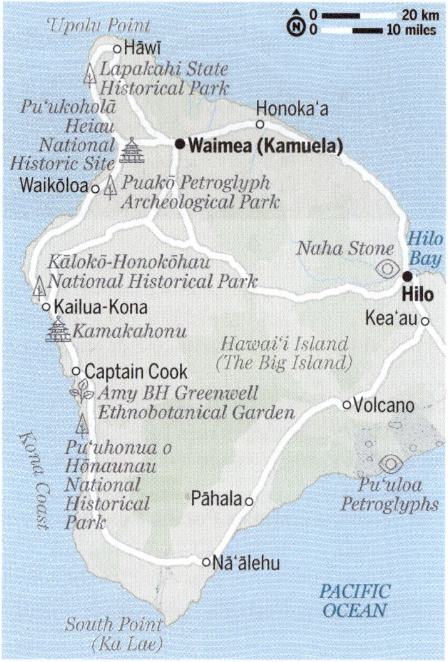

How to

Getting here Significant historic sites can be found islandwide.

When to go Petroglyph viewing is best early or late when shadows accentuate and illuminate details.

Remember While these sites are historically important, many continue to be culturally and spiritually significant. Please respect *kapu* (forbidden) signs by not entering restricted areas.

Chiseled into rocks are human figures, dot matrixes, even Latin letters and guns. Likely crafted from the 13th to 19th centuries, the specific meanings of these *ki'i pōhaku* (petroglyphs) are unknown. See them at the **Puakō Petroglyph Archeological Park**, the **Pu'uloa Petroglyphs** in Hawai'i Volcanoes NP, and inland from the traditional fishponds of **Kālokō Honokōhau National Historical Park**.

At **Lapakahi State Historical Park**, a partially restored traditional fishing village includes a canoe house, reconstructed thatched home, burial mound, fishing shrine and several heiau. Further from the sea within present-day **Amy BH Greenwell**

Top right Petroglyph, Puakō Petroglyph Archeological Park
Bottom right Pu'uhonua o Hōnaunau National Historical Park

ANDYSARTWORKS/SHUTTERSTOCK

ART BOARDMAN/SHUTTERSTOCK

Authentic Hula

April brings **Merrie Monarch** to Hilo. An illustrious showcase of the traditional art of hula, the festival features *hālau* (hula troupes) from across the state competing in both *kahiko* (ancient) and *'auana* (modern) dance, as well as a huge artisan fair.

Ethnobotanical Garden are rocky ruins of the Kona Field System, a network of agricultural terraces. **Pu'uhonua o Hōnaunau National Historical Park** contains sacred grounds villagers would seek out after breaking laws under the ancient *kapu* system of governance; a place of refuge.

Just before Hawai'i Island-born and -raised Kamehameha united the islands in 1810, he had the massive **Pu'ukohola Heiau** constructed to the war god Kū. Among the many sites that commemorate Kamehameha are Hilo's **Naha Stone**, a boulder he overturned in a show of might, and **Kamakahonu** at the Kona Pier, site of his last residence and personal heiau (access is *kapu*). A statue of him sits near his birthplace in **Kapa'au**.

43 Surf's TURF

BEACHES | SWIMMING | SURFING

It's not all white sandy beaches – as with its inland topography, the variety in Hawai'i's shoreline astounds. From colorful sands to scenic backdrops and sport-centric haunts, match your MO with its best beach. Whether your priority is lounging, swimming, snorkeling, sightseeing or surfing, Hawai'i has a beach for that.

How to

Getting around Beyond state and county beach parks, much of the coast can be challenging to get to, requiring a hike or 4WD.

When to go Inshore waters are warmer from June to September. Winter brings the highest surf.

Good to know Most of the popular beaches are on the island's western side.

Rental equipment Unless a beach fronts a hotel, nearby equipment rentals may be scarce. Rent in town.

Unusual sands **Punalu'u** is the most easily accessible of Hawai'i's black-sand beaches and a great place to spot sea turtles. Native Hawaiian community-managed **Ho'okena Beach Park** sports a surprising salt-and-pepper combo of lava and coraline sands.

Water sports Surfed for centuries, **Kahalu'u Bay** has a regular reef break on its north end; it's great for beginners, with lessons and rentals available. More advanced surfers opt for the tucked-away **Kohanaiki Beach Park (Pine Trees)**. Offshore winds at **'Anaeho'omalu (A-Bay)** on the South Kohala Coast are popular with windsurfers, while paddleboarders frequent inshore waters.

Top right Hāpuna Beach
Bottom right Punalu'u beach

KRIS S/GETTY IMAGES

ROBERT HARDING VIDEO/SHUTTERSTOCK

Beach Access

All shoreline is public, and private properties must provide beach access. Resorts have designated parking for this purpose, though it can be limited. Arriving before 9am or after 2pm affords your best chances of scoring a spot.

Lounging and swimming The Kohala Coast's long stretch of white-sand **Hāpuna Beach** is popular for a reason. Scenic but small **Manini'ōwali Beach (Kua Bay)** has calm, clear waters great for a dip.

Snorkeling There's no beach to speak of at **Two Step** on Hōnaunau Bay, but this beloved snorkeling spot – named for its natural lava rock entry steps – has dense reef and an abundance of colorful fish. The water fronting the **Captain Cook Monument** on Kealakekua Bay is another top-notch reef, but you'll have to take a boat or hike in; kayaks require permits to land.

44 Hāmākua COASTING

WATERFALLS | JUNGLE | WILD HORSES

The 45 miles of coast north of Hilo boast some of the state's most scenic vistas. Deep jungle ravines punctuated by sinuous waterfalls compete with blue ocean views. Admire gorgeous 'Akaka Falls, meander down vine-enshrouded Old Māmalahoa Hwy and find tropical blooms in a botanical garden en route to windswept Waipi'o Valley, home to a remote community and taro farms.

MRKOO83/IMAZINS/GETTY IMAGES

Into Waipi'o

Waipi'o Valley has been an important Hawaiian settlement for centuries. Today fewer than 100 residents call it home. They're fiercely private and wary of outsiders, so don't wander uninvited. The road down is so steep most rental companies prohibit the drive. For local insight and access, try **Waipio Valley Shuttle** (waipio valleyshuttle.com).

Trip Notes

Getting around Start from Hilo to maximize time along the route.

When to go Drive between November and March to spot whale spouts; abundant rains also make waterfalls larger.

Stay awhile Rentals and homestays allow you to remain in this sleepy region for days; most have ocean views and some sport private waterfalls.

Early bird To avoid large tour groups at popular 'Akaka Falls, aim to arrive before 11am.

01 Two waterfalls tumble into jungle streams at **'Akaka Falls State Park** (pictured left); the namesake cascade plummets 442ft. Don't miss a stop at **Honomu Goat Dairy** on the way (weekends only); it offers free 'goat therapy.'

02 Step into the carefully curated jungle at **Hawai'i Tropical Botanical Garden**, where over 2000 species of palms, orchids, gingers and more line streamside nature trails and boardwalks.

03 Hāmākua has excellent conditions for growing finicky vanilla orchids. Visit **Hawaiian Vanilla Co**, the US's first commercial vanillery, for dreamy milkshakes and take-home treats.

04 Mom-and-pop shops operate out of late-19th- and early-20th-century buildings, holdovers from the sugar-plantation era. Pop into **Andrade's Honakaa Café** for Portuguese-meets-Hawai'i home cooking; the family has been a mainstay in town for five generations.

05 In magical **Waipi'o Valley** 2000ft sea cliffs protect a fertile valley and windswept beach. Waterfalls play backdrop to a remote community and herds of wild horses.

FROM TOP: JOSHUA WHITCOMB/SHUTTERSTOCK, FAINA GUREVICH/SHUTTERSTOCK

45 Mālama HAWAI'I

CULTURE | VOLUNTEERING | ENVIRONMENT

Mālama means to care for or to nurture, and giving back to the land is part of the Hawaiian way. Enrich your sense of place and meet dedicated locals by combing the shorelines for plastic debris in an organized beach cleanup, or pulling invasive weeds and planting saplings as part of a native forest restoration project.

ABBY DARRAH/WIKIMEDIA/CC BY 4.0

How to

Where to look Carefully vet volunteer organizations before registering. Then consider activities you may have done anyway. Planning to whale watch? The Hawaiian Islands Humpback Whale National Marine Sanctuary has citizen science shoreline whale counts (oceancount.org). Hiking fan? Friends of Hawai'i Volcanoes National Park (fhvnp.org) organizes monthly restoration of native forest trails.

Added benefits Some hotels offer freebies for volunteers of affiliated programs (gohawaii.com/malama).

CAMPPHOTO/GETTY IMAGES

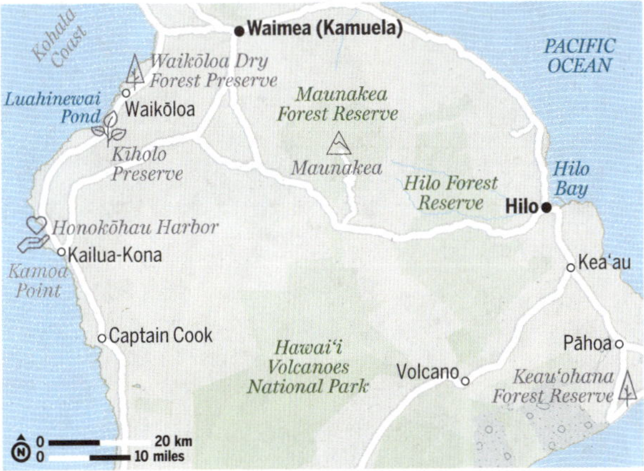

To *mālama* can take many forms: active engagement, passive support and even awareness to minimize harm.

See new places Some volunteer opportunities will take you to parts of Hawai'i most residents never see. Monthly opportunities to clean, pull invasive plants or plant native vegetation around a traditional *loko i'a* (fishpond), in the otherwise off-limits **Kīholo Preserve**, are offered via the Nature Conservancy and Hui Aloha Kīholo. The Mauna Kea Forest Restoration Project has sapling-planting days of native trees like koa and *māmane* in high-elevation plots (5000ft to 11,000ft), providing habitat for the critically endangered *palila* honeycreeper bird only found on **Maunakea's** slopes. Ocean Defenders' Alliance partners with dive shops to keep underwater areas debris-free – like highly trafficked **Honokōhau Harbor**. Just inland from Kona's popular resort area, the **Waikōloa Dry Forest Preserve**, home to the beautiful native *wiliwili* tree, hosts twice-monthly days to restore native drought-resistant vegetation to this unique area. And Hawai'i Environmental Restoration hosts regular volunteer days in the **Keau'ohana Forest Reserve**, promising a learning opportunity while revitalizing the biggest native lowland forest system in the state.

Money talk If tours are involved or you take something home, fees may be associated, but typically you do not pay to *mālama*. That said, volunteer organizations usually welcome donations.

Top left Endangered *palila* (honeycreeper) **Bottom left** Kīholo Preserve

Time Limited

So, you don't have days or hours to give – that's OK! *Kōkua* (give back) by making mindful decisions and minimizing your impact on the environment:

- Wear reef-safe sunscreen and avoid touching coral.
- Respect *kapu* signs.
- Pick up three pieces of beach trash.
- Report monk seal sightings to the NOAA Marine Wildlife Hotline: (888) 256-9840.
- Listen to regional *mo'olelo* (stories) to perpetuate history and place significance.
- Purchase products, activities or tours that support *mālama* initiatives. Examples: the **Four Seasons Hualālai** (fourseasons.com/hualalai/spa) *'iliahi* (sandalwood) spa treatment experience, or **Hawaii Forest and Trail** (hawaii-forest.com) 'Giveback' tours to the Maunakea summit.

46 Local TREATS

MARKETS | FARMS | ROAD TRIP

The state's largest island, Hawai'i, boasts at least four times the agricultural acreage of its neighbors and an abundance of products to match. Taste the tropical bounty and meet growers at one of the nearly two dozen regular farmers markets, or head straight to the source for locavore eats.

TTD_ARK/ALAMY

How to

Getting around Note: farm tours require advance reservations.

When to go Great produce is grown year-round.

Stay awhile Overnight experiences range from quiet hands-off retreats to multi-month work-trade options; many shorter stay options list on vacation rental sites.

Definitely stop Roadside farm stands (some unattended with honesty boxes) are prevalent in rural areas. Bring cash and pull over for some of the freshest flavors around.

DANITA DELIMONT/ALAMY

Farm Tours

Growers small and large across the island open their doors for tours. The following is only a small selection.

Kona Historical Society's **Kona Coffee Living History Farm** in Kealakekua is a family-fun option that meshes working coffee-farm tours with an outdoor museum showcasing the coffee region's rich history. An affiliated 1870s general store and communal stone oven for baking Portuguese sweet bread are just up the road. **Big Island Bees**, a large organic honey producer, offers apiary tours and tastings of its popular macadamia and native *lehua* blossom honeys. One of the state's largest growers, **OK Farms**, provides tours of its fruit, spice, nut and chocolate orchards, and offers a unique vantage on Hilo's Rainbow Falls.

JIM WEST/ALAMY

Seasonal Produce

If you're a fan of something specific like mangoes, squash, finger limes, soybeans (edamame) or lychee, check with local food hubs – such as **Adaptations** (adaptationsaloha.com) in Kona or the **Locavore Store** (bigislandlocavorestore.com) in Hilo – to ascertain peak season.

Top left Big Island Bees
Bottom left *Hoshidana* (drying platform), Kona Coffee Living History Farm
Above Variegated lemons, OK Farms

Also check out **Hamakua Chocolate** for tours that help with cacao harvesting, sorting and processing for its chocolate bars.

Farm-to-Table Dining

It seems restaurants serving locally sourced ingredients are everywhere these days, but the following offer something extra – dining by starlight on a remote farm plot or creative feasts where nearly every ingredient is local.

On Kohala's slopes, working cattle property **Kahua Ranch** shares area history, gives roping demonstrations and serves its Big Island beef in an on-site sunset barbecue dinner. **Starseed Ranch**, an off-grid tropical permaculture food forest, offers several on-site dining options – come for a tour, farm-fresh *pūpū* (appetizers) and *'awa* (kava) ceremony, or stay for a three-course foraged feast. Multi-course private dinners by **Na'au** feature ingredients that have been personally

Find Local Grinds

Magic's Beach Grill (magicsbeachgrill.com) was our number one supporter throughout the pandemic buying local *'ulu* (breadfruit), *kalo* (taro) and purple sweet potatoes.

Right before Waipi'o, female owned-and-operated **Lilinoe Fruit Stand** (@lilinoefruitstand) sells cold cut coconuts and fresh fruit.

Hilo's **Kawamoto Store** (kawamotostore.com), an *okazuya* deli opened in 1947, sells the best local food.

Recommended by Holokai Brown, *operations manager at Hawai'i 'Ulu Co-op @hawaiiulucoop*

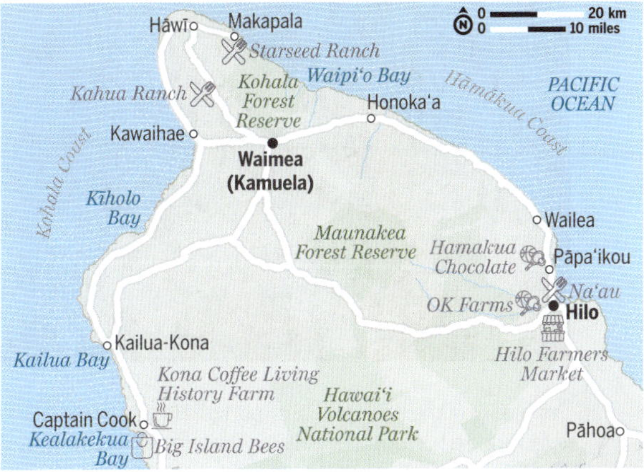

Left Magic's Beach Grill **Below** Fruit and vegetables for sale, Hilo Farmers Market

foraged, hunted and caught or locally procured by chef Brian Hirata – wild boar, *'ōhelo* berries, slipper lobster and *limu* (seaweed). They're worth the splurge; or look for Na'au's pop-up dinners held at Whitehaven Farm outside of Pepe'ekeo.

Farmers Markets

With nearly 20 formal farmers markets happening on different days islandwide, and numerous outlets selling locally grown offerings daily, you're sure to find fresh fruit and vegetable options nearby. See what's in season: try jams, kimchi, bread, smoked fish and more from value-add vendors; or grab a whole meal from on-site food trucks.

The **Hawaii Farmers Market Association** (hawaiifarmersmarkets.org) keeps a current list of where to go when, but for the largest regular offerings head to the upcountry *paniolo* (cowboy) town of Kamuela/Waimea on Saturdays, when three simultaneous markets in different corners of town offer all things locally grown and made. The **Hilo Farmers Market** happens most days of the week on the corner of Kamehameha Ave and Mamo St in downtown Hilo (the largest days are Wednesday and Saturday). A few blocks down, the **Locavore Store** functions like an indoor farmers market, offering everything from eggs, cheese and meat to produce, coffee and bath products.

FAR LEFT: MAGIC'S BEACH GRILL, LEFT: ALLISON H. SMITH/SHUTTERSTOCK

Inland Ocean Tastes & Tours

AQUACULTURE RESEARCH AND DEVELOPMENT MAKES FOR UNIQUE TOURS

Tours of one-of-a-kind biotechnology research and development ventures at Hawai'i Ocean Science & Technology Park (HOST Park) let you get up close with charismatic sea life or try aquacultured seafood while supporting new industries – some may help bolster Hawai'i's future food security.

Left Seahorse, Ocean Rider Seahorse Farm **Middle** Pan-seared abalones **Right** Lobster

AMAURY LAPORTE/FLICKR/CC BY 2.0

Just south of the Kailua-Kona airport on Hawai'i Island, scattered amid a barren desert of black lava rock, sits a hodgepodge of research facilities. Centered around a failed 1980s experiment to create energy from cold, deep seawater, dozens of new tarp- and tin-roofed buildings make use of old pump infrastructure. Appearances are deceptive – these are cutting-edge commercial aquaculture outfits, many of which offer unique experiences for the curious visitor.

Seahorse & Salt Farms

One building houses the only place in North America that you can reliably get a cuddly finger cling from a live seahorse's tail. The **Ocean Rider Seahorse Farm** is a start-up hoping to reduce pressure on wild-caught seahorses taken for the aquarium trade as well as bolster free-living populations. Tours include the opportunity to see several species, including the frilly Australian weedy sea dragon, as well as seahorses at various life stages.

Another enterprising local business evaporates water pulled up from the deep-sea pipes to create mineral-rich, flaky culinary salts and concentrated magnesium. **Kona Sea Salt** offers a sneak peek into its operations on tours of its seven-acre oceanfront property. Stay a little longer for a frigid foot soak in the old, cold and pure water or a sunset bonfire with cocktails/mocktails and small bites crafted with its salts.

Sustainably Sourced Seafood

Gaze offshore and you'll see large cages poking out of the sea. These pens are home to thousands of Kona kampa-

CHIARA SAKUWA/ALAMY

JOHN DE MELLO/ALAMY

chi, a type of amberjack, raised by HOST Park company **Blue Ocean Mariculture**. The company sells its harvest directly and to local restaurants. It also owns **Kona Cold Lobsters**, where Maine lobsters are imported as babies and raised to adult perfection in the arid lava fields.

A sister research and development company nearby created the world's first free-floating mariculture pen – an open ocean fish farm – with Lockheed Martin engineers. Its unique fish-raising format could help reduce pollution associated with traditional inshore farms worldwide. Algae and seaweed farms raise *limu* in large onshore vats; their harvest is used in human nutritional supplements and in research and development trails as lower-production energy feed for fish and livestock.

> These are cutting-edge commercial aquaculture outfits, many of which offer unique experiences for the curious visitor.

Still more companies grow cold-water creatures for Hawai'i's restaurant industry, using pumped-in deep seawater, which saves the heavy carbon cost of importing them. Visitors can pop into **Big Island Abalone** to tour facilities and taste Japanese abalone.

These decidedly non-traditional Hawai'i experiences offer a deeper dive into serious island issues like food security and sustainable seafood sourcing and ensure your tourist dollars support a greener Hawai'i.

Feeding the Aloha State

An estimated 85% to 90% of the state's food is shipped in by boat or flown on cargo planes. This contributes to a large carbon footprint, costs companies extra time and money to reach consumers, and ultimately leads to inflated food prices – part of the reason the Hawaii Foodbank estimated nearly one in three Hawai'i residents dealt with food insecurity in 2024–25. In addition to an increased reliance on local farms, research and development projects can help by growing new local food industries. Island-produced food is not only more affordable and easier on the environment but can also help Hawai'i weather literal storms and natural disasters, when it's vulnerable to shipping delays and food shortages.

(Some) Features of a
HAWAIIAN LANDSCAPE

02

01

05

03

04

01 Heiau
Often all that remains of these traditional temple sites are rock platforms or terraces. Sites were selected for their *mana* (spiritual essence).

02 Ahupua'a
Traditional wedge-shaped land division encompassing upland forests, terraced pastureland and shoreline. Some 1800 existed at the time of first European contact. For more information, see p100.

03 Ki'i pōhaku
Petroglyph rock carvings depicting people, canoes, turtles and more, adorning smooth, *pāhoehoe* lava rock. Their true meanings are unknown.

04 Hale
A building used as a house, lodge or hall. Traditional *hale* were often A-frame structures with thatched roofs.

05 Ala loa
Long trail or path connecting *ahupua'a* and significant sites across communities, following the most easily traversable points in the landscape, often along the coast.

01 NORINORI303/SHUTTERSTOCK, **02** JUAN WILSON/ISLANDBREATH.ORG2016, **03** ANDYSARTWORKS/SHUTTERSTOCK, **04** PETER FRENCH/DESIGN PICS/GETTY IMAGES, **05** YOU TOUCH PIX OF EUTOCH/SHUTTERSTOCK, **06** GARY GILARDI/SHUTTERSTOCK, **07** NORINORI303/SHUTTERSTOCK, **08** DOUG PERRINE/ALAMY, **09** STEVE ALLEN/SHUTTERSTOCK, **10** TMI/ALAMY, **11** LIBORK/SHUTTERSTOCK, **12** FUNBOXPHOTO/SHUTTERSTOCK, **13** KIERAN BURGESS/EYEEM/GETTY IMAGES, **CONTOURS** THEUS/SHUTTERSTOCK

06

07

08

09

10

11

12

13

06 Hālau
Used for canoe storage or hula instruction, these elongated huts are important meeting places.

07 Loko iʻa
An ingenious way to store or catch fish; a walled fishpond.

08 Loʻi
Terraced fields of food crops including *kalo* and, later, rice.

09 Puʻu
A hill or cinder cone.

10 Pā Pōhaku
Rock walls often built using the traditional *uhau humu pōhaku* (dry stacking technique), which requires a variety of stone sizes to hold the wall together without mortar.

11 Puka
Any hole or crevice including sea arches, caves and indentations in the landscape.

12 Mauka
Traditional directional term to indicate that something is inland or toward the mountain.

13 Makai
Traditional directional term still employed to indicate that something is toward the sea.

Conflict on the Mauna

A PLANNED TELESCOPE IS DIVIDING A COMMUNITY

Maunakea has long been hallowed ground for Native Hawaiians, who worship and revere the *mauna* (mountain) as central to the creation of humankind and as a physical home to the gods. Its summit is also the site of several world-class astronomical observatories.

CHRIS FINCH PHOTOGRAPHY/SHUTTERSTOCK

Far from the nearest major landfall, the remote Central Pacific enjoys incredible stargazing. Maunakea is the tallest point in the Pacific Basin and the tallest mountain on Earth when measured from its base at the seafloor (33,500ft compared to Everest's 29,035ft). The shield volcano's summit – with its dry atmosphere and wind shear allowing for an abundance of cloudless nights – is one of Earth's best spots for gazing deep into the universe. Since 1967 it has been the site of world-class telescopes. Today, there are 13, collectively the world's most scientifically productive astronomical site.

In 2009, organizers behind a powerful new telescope with a huge observation mirror 30m across — the Thirty Meter Telescope (TMT) — decided Maunakea was the best location to site their project. But not everyone agreed.

Long before the first telescope was erected here, Kānaka Maoli (Native Hawaiians) knew the mountain as Ka Mauna a Wākea, or 'the mountain of Wākea,' and revered it as the embodiment of the first-born son of Wākea, the Sky or Light Father, and Papahānaumoku, the Earth Mother, from which all human Hawaiians are descended. The entire mountain is regarded as a place of worship, the center of Hawai'i Island, and its connection to all things beyond. The problem with the new telescope for many Kānaka Maoli has less to do with the telescope itself – the sky and its stars play a significant role in their history, after all – and more to do with continued alteration and desecration of their sacred lands.

In 2014, following years of legal challenges and permitting issues, the $1.4 million TMT project held a groundbreaking ceremony at its proposed site. Groups of peaceful protesters waved signs, formed a blockade and lay on the

Left Maunakea summit **Middle** Demonstrators, Maunakea Access Rd **Right** Observatory, Mountain Ridge

ZUMA PRESS, INC./ALAMY

CHRISTOPHER CHAN/GETTY IMAGES

road thwarting access. After embittered court proceedings and community meetings, construction was green-lighted for July 2019. This time thousands of protestors amassed at the base of the only access road, creating a sophisticated sit-in camp that remained for nine months. At the height of tensions, the National Guard and police from three islands converged for crowd control of the peaceful protests.

Videos spread and galvanized support from Indigenous communities, Hollywood stars and allies worldwide. The camp community held strong – with many living on-site – until it was agreed construction would not proceed in December 2019. Additional construction delays were caused by the COVID-19 pandemic, and a few wind-torn tarped stalwart outposts persisted for years. To address claims of historical summit mismanagement by the University of Hawai'i at Hilo, in 2022 the state developed an oversight committee comprising astronomers, protest leaders and university representatives. The Mauna Kea Stewardship and Oversight Authority is expected to take full control of management of the summit from the university by July 2028 and will then control access to the summit, run the visitor center, oversee the telescopes' land leases (set to expire in 2033) and, crucially, hold the power to issue new permits. The TMT holds a sublease on one of the plots that expires in 2033.

Another setback for the TMT in 2025: facing severe funding cuts from the Trump administration, the National Science Foundation withdrew crucial budgetary support for the Thirty Meter Telescope Project in favor of the Giant Magellan Project in Chile. Still, unless the TMT project is officially called off, it's unlikely we've seen the end of the conflict on the *mauna*.

Respecting Maunakea

Maunakea stargazing is a trip highlight, and the visitor information station along the Access Rd at 9200ft is a great place to begin. Check for weather and other closures by calling (808) 935-6268 or checking online (hilo.hawaii.edu/maunakea). From there it's possible to learn about science conducted at the summit telescopes, see rare and Dr Seussian Hawaiian silverswords, hike up Pu'u Kalepeamoa for incredible sunset views and perhaps even observe the rings of Saturn or Jupiter's moons with the help of local enthusiasts. Hikers venturing into the Ice Age Natural Reserve trails must register here. As with all culturally significant places, it's important to be respectful. Do not move or remove anything and avoid exploring beyond marked roads and trails.

Listings

BEST OF THE REST

Hawai'i Lifestyle & Boutiques

Island Nation

A clothing, art and gift shop promoting all things Hawai'i and Native Hawaiian with a huge educational book selection. For the *keiki* (children): colorful toys, puzzles and games with a focus on 'Ōlelo Hawai'i. Everything is sourced in-state, much of it from Native Hawaiian makers. In downtown Hilo.

Pueo Boutique

Established clothing boutique with stylish island wear and accessories for women and *keiki*. Also, a great stop for locally made jewelry, bath products, bags and swimwear. In Kailua-Kona.

Firehouse Art Gallery

Fine art gallery run by the Waimea Arts Council (Kamuela) housed in the town's historic fire station and bunkhouse. Art sales run alongside regular and rotating exhibits and occasional classes.

Sig Zane

The chic Hilo storefront of authentic aloha-wear designer Sig Zane is worth a gander for its vibrant, symbol-laden offerings.

Adrenaline Activities

Kazumura Cave

Head underground and clamber through the gypsum chambers of Kazumura Cave, the world's longest lava tube created in a centuries-old eruption. Advanced tours up to six hours long take you into total darkness and require some rappelling; gear including climbing harness is BYO.

Ka Lae

The brave congregate at Ka Lae, or South Point, to leap off the US's southernmost landfall 40ft into the churning sea below. A rickety metal ladder aids the return trip.

Paradise Helicopters

Doors-off excursions by Paradise Helicopters couple heart-in-your-throat aerial views of otherwise inaccessible valleys, sea cliffs and, if you're lucky, steaming lava with a convertible-like sensory immersion. Departures from Kona airport.

Big Island Gravity (BIG)

Daily chances to strap yourself to an instructor and take in the rugged Kohala Coast from a 12,000ft, 45-second freefall skydive. Departs from the 'Upolu Airport outside Hāwī .

Wild Hawai'i Ocean Adventures (WHOA)

WHOA's zippy stand-up and hold-on vessel – the same kind Navy SEALs use – heads offshore so you can commune in-water with the likes of short-finned pilot whales, oceanic white-tip sharks, mahimahi and hammerheads. Departs Honokōhau Harbor.

DUDAREV MIKHAIL/SHUTTERSTOCK

Ka Lae

Sweet Treats

Two Ladies Kitchen $

The hole-in-the-wall Hilo location belies its popularity. The nearly three-decades-old Japanese confectionery is renowned throughout the islands; a floury workshop producing a colorful and flavorful assortment of mochi and *manjū*. Preordering is recommended.

Punaluʻu Bake Shop $

No journey through southerly Kaʻū is complete without a *malasada* (Portuguese-style donut) stop at Punaluʻu Bake Shop. It's the US's southernmost bakery and a hopping tourist stop. *Haupia* (coconut pudding), *lilikoʻi* (passion fruit) and chocolate glazed are highlights.

Dinner Delights

Lava Lava Beach Club $$

Fronting ʻAnaehoʻomalu Bay's turquoise waters, this is one of the few places on the island to dine toes in the sand. Come for the retro surf-shack vibe and (often) live music. Seating is first-come, first-served.

Kaaloa Super J's $

Tiny, family-run Kaaloa Super J's en route from Kailua-Kona to Puʻuhonua o Hōnaunau National Historical Park isn't much to look at but this local favorite has some of the most authentic Hawaiian food you'll find. Its specialty is *laulau* – salty chicken or fatty pork steamed in taro leaves.

Hilo Bay Café $$$

Housed in a stilted building overlooking the town and its namesake bay, this cafe has excellent sushi and some of the island's better high-end American/Hawaiʻi fusion fare – think Maui rum barbecue ribs and curried Hāmākua mushroom pot pie.

NIELSVK/ALAMY

Kona Boys

Merriman's $$$

The flagship location of a now islandwide farm-to-fork eatery, Merriman's fronts the rolling green pasturelands of chilly Kamuela (Waimea) and employs the friendliest staff in the industry. Sunday brunch is a highlight; reservations required for dinner.

Pineapples $$

Open-air Pineapples in downtown Hilo is as great for people-watching as it is for dinner; it has some of the tastiest seafood preparations around.

Water Toys

Kona Boys

A great place to rent surfboards, paddleboards and kayaks (two locations: Kona Pier and upland Kealakekua), Kona Boys also runs top-notch excursions. Knowledgeable guides impart local lore while riding in a *waʻa* (outrigger canoe) or on a guided kayak and snorkeling tour to the Captain Cook Monument.

Practicalities

ARRIVING 238

GETTING AROUND 240

SAFE TRAVEL 242

MONEY 243

RESPONSIBLE TRAVEL 244

ACCOMMODATIONS 246

ESSENTIALS 248

Right Nāpali Coast (p118)

EASY STEPS FROM THE AIRPORT TO WAIKĪKĪ

Most people will fly into Hawai'i via the Daniel K Inouye International Airport (HNL), formerly called Honolulu International Airport. Just 20 minutes from Waikīkī, the airport is largely open-air, and shuttles move between the concourses for easy transit. If you're skipping O'ahu, try to fly directly to the island you're visiting – it'll save you a couple of hours and reduce your carbon footprint.

AT THE AIRPORT

A.FLASSIG/SHUTTERSTOCK

SIM CARDS
There are multiple places to buy prepaid SIM cards at HNL, but you'll likely find better deals in Honolulu through stores like Walmart and Target. If you have a newer phone, check whether it's capable of loading an eSIM and look at the packages from airalo (airalo.com).

INTERNATIONAL CURRENCY EXCHANGE
You'll find the best exchange rates at banks such as Bank of Hawaii or First Hawaiian Bank. Feel free to exchange a little cash at the airport, but Hawai'i is very credit-card friendly, and you should be fine waiting to find a bank.

WI-FI HNL has free unlimited wi-fi supported by ads. Connect to 'HNL Free WiFi.' Coverage should reach the curbside pickup area.

ATMS ATMs are abundant in and out of the airport. Expect to see fees around $5 for out-of-network withdrawals.

CHARGING STATIONS There are several free charging stations throughout the airport that take two- or three-prong 120V plugs or USB-A, making it easy for you to keep your devices powered up.

TIPS FOR A SHORT TRIP

Take advantage of baggage storage services at the airport kiosk across from Baggage Claim 19. They also offer beach supply rentals (chairs, boogie boards, coolers etc) to make the most of a long layover.

GETTING TO WAIKĪKĪ

BUS Bus route 20 will take you into Waikīkī in central Honolulu. To catch the bus, go upstairs to the departures level and look for the bus shelter on the median. Adult fare is $3, and no change is given. There is no room for luggage and your bags should fit on your lap.

RENTAL CARS Rental-car services are located in the Consolidated Rent-A-Car (CONRAC) directly across from Terminal 2 outside Baggage Claims 26 and 31, with shuttles to bring you there from other terminals. There are 10 rental-car companies located in the CONRAC.

HOW MUCH FOR A...

Taxi
$35
20min

Shuttle
$25–27
20min

Bus
$3
1hr 10min

RIDESHARES
Pickups are located on Ground Level 1, in the median across from Baggage Claim 31, 19 and 20, and the outside end of Baggage Claim 6.

TAXIS
Located just outside the baggage claim areas. Look for taxi dispatchers in yellow shirts for service.

SHUTTLES These are probably the easiest way to get to your accommodations, especially if you aren't staying in Waikīkī. It's recommended that you book ahead of time (a must if you want a lei greeting), but there are airport kiosks as well. A private shuttle may be the best deal if you have a large group.

OTHER POINTS OF ENTRY

Other airports Aside from Honolulu's airport, many US and international airlines also fly into Kona (KOA) and Hilo (ITO) on Hawaiʻi Island, Kahului on Maui (OGG) and Līhuʻe on Kauaʻi (LIH). Each airport has rental car and shuttle services and is fairly close to its island's main hotel and resort areas (under an hour). Despite this proximity, give yourself ample time when traveling to and from the airport, as traffic can be pretty bad on all islands. Note that these airports are much smaller than Honolulu's and may not have as many services, so if you need to exchange money or buy a SIM card, be sure to check you'll be able to do so at your chosen airport, and consider if it would make more sense to enter via Honolulu. If you're heading to Molokaʻi or Lānaʻi, you'll have the most flight options if you go through Honolulu.

Cruise ship The only other way to enter Hawaiʻi is via cruise ship. Multiple cruise lines have one-way routes to the islands from various Pacific embarkation points.

TRANSPORTATION TIPS TO HELP YOU GET AROUND

Having a car is almost a necessity for most areas outside Honolulu, especially on the Neighbor Islands (islands other than O'ahu). Rental prices can be quite expensive during high season and Hawai'i's gas prices are generally higher than elsewhere in the US. If you're staying in Honolulu, consider taking the bus to lower costs and carbon emissions.

RENTAL CARS

Car rentals are pretty seamless across the islands, but try to book as early as possible, as they do sometimes run out. If you're looking for an alternative to rental-car companies, try browsing Turo (turo.com) to rent from a local.

RIDESHARES

These are abundant in Honolulu but less reliable on the Neighbor Islands. To support local, try downloading Hawai'i's homegrown rideshare app, holoholo (rideholoholo.com) – available on O'ahu, Maui, Kaua'i and Hawai'i Island with no surge pricing.

CAR RENTAL PER DAY

$40–100+

Gas approx $4.50/gallon

Overnight hotel parking $30–80

INSURANCE Hawai'i is a no-fault state, which means that if you get into an accident and don't have insurance, you'll be required to pay for any damage to your rental car – regardless of whether you caused the accident. Check whether your car insurance or credit card will cover collision damage during travel. Otherwise, consider opting for a collision damage waiver (CDW) when you rent.

BUS SERVICE O'ahu's bus system is extensive and will get you almost anywhere you want to go, particularly in Honolulu. For easy bus riding, pick up a HOLO card (holocard.net) at an ABC Store or Skyline Station.

BIKI BIKES Bike-share stations are scattered throughout urban Honolulu and offer a great way to see the city. Visit gobiki.org for more info. While some streets have dedicated bike lanes, many do not and bikers share the road with vehicles.

DRIVING ESSENTIALS

Drive on the right side of the road; steering wheel is on the left.

On a red light, you're expected to turn right from the far right lane.

Speed limits max out at 60mph. Residential areas are 25mph.

Blood alcohol limit 0.08% (0.02% for drivers under 21).

Try not to use your horn unless you're about to hit someone.

SKYLINE At the time of writing, O'ahu's Skyline system features 13 operating stops running from Kapolei to Kalihi, including one at the airport. You'll need a reloadable HOLO Card to ride, which you can purchase from automated machines at each station.

INTERISLAND FLIGHTS Hawaiian Airlines, Mokulele Airlines and Southwest Airlines run interisland flights. Several flights connect each island, including dozens from O'ahu, from before sunrise to nearly midnight.

FERRY SERVICE Hawai'i's only ferry service runs between Lahaina, on Maui and Lāna'i. It runs four times a day and takes about 45 minutes one way. For more information, visit go-lanai.com.

NO CAR? If you don't drive, all hope is not lost. So long as you're staying in a central tourism hub (think Waikīkī or the Kona Coast), it's possible to book guided tours to most attractions that will pick you up from your accommodations. You can also book private shuttles if you'd prefer not to have a guide. SpeediShuttle (speedishuttle.com) has services on all major islands.

NAOMI RAHIM/GETTY IMAGES

SAFE TRAVEL

Visitors to Hawai'i are most likely to run into safety concerns when at the beach or in the mountains. Tourist rescues are unfortunately common and strain local resources. Be prepared, heed signage and stay within your normal range of physical activity.

WAVES & CURRENTS Many Hawai'i beaches have dangerous currents and shorebreak at certain times of the year. Be aware of your own swimming capabilities, keep to beaches with lifeguards and heed posted signs. For more information on ocean safety, visit HIOceanSafety.com. To check real-time conditions, visit hawaiibeachsafety.com.

AQUATIC STINGS The most common stinging animals are Portuguese man o' wars, box jellyfish and sea urchins. A vinegar rinse or soak is the best quick treatment for all three. On windward beaches, check the sand for blue Portuguese man o' wars before you get in the water. Box jellyfish flood south-shore waters eight to 10 days after every full moon.

HIKING HAZARDS Rain, wind and erosion can make trails dangerous. Never hike alone, stay on marked trails and choose hikes on public land. Wear appropriate shoes and pack ample water and food. Don't hike if the weather report shows heavy rain approaching. If you're in a valley during a flash-flood warning, get to higher ground immediately.

VOLCANIC ACTIVITY This is limited to Hawai'i Island. While lava is very unlikely to be a threat, eruptions can cause irritating volcanic smog (vog). Earthquakes can also occur, though large ones are rare.

WILL FALCON/SHUTTERSTOCK

THEODORE TRIMMER/SHUTTERSTOCK

CAR BREAK-INS Theft from cars sometimes occurs across the islands. Ensure that your belongings are out of sight when you leave your car, especially if you notice broken glass in the parking area.

HURRICANES
Hurricane season is from July to November. Hurricanes rarely hit Hawai'i directly, but even a nearby storm can cause flash floods and hazardous winds as well as dangerously dirty nearshore waters in the following days.

TSUNAMIS
Warning sirens will sound in the event of an oncoming threat. If you're near the coast, head to higher ground immediately. Note that sirens are tested at 11:45am on the first workday of every month.

QUICK TIPS TO HELP YOU MANAGE YOUR MONEY

CREDIT CARDS Credit cards are widely accepted and are often a requirement for car rentals and hotel reservations. Visa and MasterCard are universally accepted, followed by American Express, Discover and JTB. Most stores and restaurants will also accept contactless payment via Apple Pay, Google Pay and Cash App.

CASH

It's good to have some cash on hand for tips as well as cash-only restaurants (which are uncommon, but not particularly rare).

SALES TAX

Hawai'i's general excise tax (GET) is 4%, but expect to see rates between 4.1% and 4.712% depending which island you're on.

CURRENCY

US dollar

HOW MUCH FOR A...

Dinner for two **$50**

Spam musubi **$2**

Reef-safe sunscreen **$10**

DUTY FREE There's duty-free shopping for foreigners in HNL airport as well as in Waikīkī. If you have a layover elsewhere in the US, you won't be eligible for duty free.

CURRENCY EXCHANGE

Find counters at the international airports or at major bank branches. Note that smaller Neighbor Island locations often do not offer currency-exchange services.

ATMS

These are widespread throughout the islands. Do note that on top of your own bank's fees, most ATMs will charge around $3 per withdrawal in transaction fees.

TIPPING This is not optional, and tips should never be withheld. Hawai'i's economy relies heavily on tourism and the service industry, and many people from all walks of life rely on tips to make a living. Plan to tip hotel porters, housekeeping and valets $2 to $5 every time you use their service. At restaurants, tips should be 18% to 20% unless gratuity is included in the bill. Tip bartenders at least $1 per drink. And taxi drivers should be tipped 10% to 15% of your fare.

GO OAHU CARD

If your itinerary is action-packed with sites and tours, consider a **Go City pass** (gocity.com/en/oahu), which offers bundled admission discounts. At the time of publication 40 different tours and activities were part of their packages, including Pearl Harbor memorial sites, *lū'au*, the Bishop Museum, 'Iolani Palace and the Polynesian Cultural Center on the North Shore.

POSITIVE-IMPACT TRAVEL

Tips to leave a lighter footprint, support local and have a positive impact on local communities.

ON THE ROAD

Public transportation Use public transit or visitor shuttles when possible to reduce impact on traffic, parking and emissions.

Heed signs Some areas are protected for cultural, ecological or safety reasons. Be respectful of posted signs, and don't cross private property. If you come across a sign that says *kapu* (taboo), that means keep out.

Take only photos, leave only footprints *Mālama* (take care of) Hawai'i's natural environment by leaving lava rocks, seashells and plants where they belong and properly disposing of all trash.

Rapid 'Ōhia Death (ROD) This quickly spreading fungal disease is killing Hawai'i's native keystone trees. To prevent spreading ROD – and to keep other invasive species out – be sure to clean your gear of seeds, soil or other organic matter before and after every hike as well as when you arrive and leave.

MICHAEL BARAJAS/SHUTTERSTOCK

GIVE BACK

Research a way to give back that best fits your schedule, your interests and your finances.

Connect with locals Do good through travel2change (travel2change.org), a nonprofit that gets visitors involved with local initiatives through free or discounted experiences.

Donate to help the homeless Organizations to check out include Project Vision Hawai'i (projectvisionhawaii.org), Project Hawai'i (helpthehomelesskeiki.org) and Pu'uhonua o Wai'anae (alohaliveshere.org).

Give back and earn discounts Participate in the Mālama Hawai'i Program (gohawaii.com/malama) and help to *mālama* the land, ocean or local community.

DOS & DON'TS

Do be mindful that Hawai'i is home for many people There's little separation between visitors and locals, and many activities are in residential neighborhoods.

Don't use location tags Post on social media without the tags.

Do be curious 'Talk story' with locals, learn about Hawai'i's complex history, step out of your comfort zone.

LEAVE A SMALL FOOTPRINT

Stay where you play To avoid driving all over the island, choose lodging close to the activities you want to do. To see the whole island, divide your trip into stays in different areas.

Fly directly to the island you're visiting Try to limit your trip to one island. Traveling between most islands requires plane travel, and unless you're staying long-term, it's worth it to focus on one island.

Protect the reef Use non-nano zinc sunscreen and don't step on coral.

RINGOSOUNDS/SHUTTERSTOCK

SUPPORT LOCAL

Do research ahead of time Many hotels and tour operators are run by companies from out of state. To ensure you're supporting local, check out their websites – most local businesses will proudly display that they're 'locally owned and operated.'

Shop at farmers markets These are great for locally grown produce and handmade goods.

Buy local House of Mana Up (houseofmanaup.com) in Honolulu only sells local makers.

CLIMATE CHANGE & TRAVEL

Lonely Planet urges all travelers to engage with their travel carbon footprint, which will mainly come from air travel. While there often isn't an alternative, travelers can look to minimize the number of flights they take, opt for newer aircrafts and use cleaner ground transport.

One proposed solution – purchasing carbon offsets – unfortunately does not cancel out the impact of individual flights. While most destinations will depend on air travel for the foreseeable future, for now, pursuing ground-based travel where possible is the best course of action.

The UN Carbon Offset Calculator shows how flying impacts a household's emissions:

The ICAO carbon emissions calculator allows visitors to analyze the CO2 generated by point-to-point journeys:

RESOURCES

sustainabletourismhawaii.org
travel2change.org
gohawaii.com/malama
ponopledge.com

UNIQUE AND LOCAL WAYS TO STAY

Accommodations in Hawai'i run from off-grid cabins to ultra-luxury estates, though even the more basic accommodations are pricier than elsewhere, especially during summer and winter. Year-round warm temperatures provide an excellent opportunity to pick a stay with easy access to nature.

HOW MUCH FOR A...

Resort condo
$250

Boutique hotel
$350

Off-grid cabin
$150

BILLY MCDONALD/SHUTTERSTOCK

BOUTIQUE HOTELS & B&BS
Among the many big-name hotel chains and resorts are a healthy handful of boutique hotels and B&Bs. Smaller and more intimate, these accommodations offer a more curated experience with decor, amenities and activities that cater to various narrow demographics. They're ideal for those who want the place in which they stay to be an important part of their visit. Like all accommodations types in Hawai'i, there's a huge range in prices – from about $150 per night to over $800.

LUXURY ESTATES
Located in some of the most stunning locations, luxury estates are multi-million-dollar properties that have been meticulously designed and decked out for comfort. Find high-end estates from $800 per night to upwards of $10,000. Most can accommodate six or more people, and renting an estate might be more affordable than you'd expect.

IMAGE SOURCE LIMITED/ALAMY

RESORT CONDOS Many owners of resort condos rent out their units while they're away. Staying in a condo offers more space and flexibility than a hotel room while also allowing access to many of the resort's facilities, making it great for families. Renting a condo can be cheaper than booking a room at the same resort.

R PENNA/SHUTTERSTOCK

OFF-GRID GLAMPING

More comfortable than a tent but closer to nature than your average hotel, glamping is a great choice for those looking for a multi-day stay surrounded by nature. Stay in a geodesic dome in a rainforest, an offgrid cabin in the middle of a lava field, or an A-frame on the beach. Though less common on O'ahu, glamping options abound on the Neighbor Islands – though do note that many are in more remote locations away from the conveniences of a town or city. There are glamping options for every comfort level and budget, ranging from a bare-bones wooden structure for $50 per night to a multi-room yurt for upwards of $300.

WHAT TO EXPECT

Most glamping accommodations will be at least partially off-grid, meaning they may rely on water catchment, solar panels, gray-water systems and composting toilets. You may not even notice the difference, but off-grid living does require a little more attention. Depending on location and usage, a solar-powered system may run out of power in the evening. Gray-water systems require eco-friendly soaps, so it may be best to use the soaps provided. If your accommodations have a composting toilet, be sure to carefully follow the directions provided.

BOOKING

It's best to book as early as possible, especially if you're traveling during the high season in the summer (June to August) and early winter (late-November through December).

O'ahu vacation rentals Be aware that most short-term vacation rentals outside resort areas are no longer allowed on O'ahu. If you book an Airbnb or VRBO for less than 30 days in a residential neighborhood, it may not be legal, so if you find one you like, be sure to confirm that it's permitted. Otherwise, you may not have accommodations if they're shut down before you arrive.

Hawaii Eco Living (hawaiiecoliving.com) Find eco resorts and ecotourism resources.

Aloha Condos (alohacondos.com) Condos for rent by owner.

GlampingHub (glampinghub.com) Unique close-to-nature accommodations.

Savvy (savvy.com) Large database of B&B stays.

Elite Pacific Vacations (evrhi.com) High-end vacation rentals.

Hawaii Hideaways (hawaiihideaways.com) Luxury booking concierge.

RAWPIXEL.COM/SHUTTERSTOCK

RESORT FEE

Hotels throughout Hawai'i often charge a 'resort fee' on top of your booked rate. Resort fees range from $25 to $60 per night. Check beforehand so you aren't surprised at checkout.

ESSENTIAL NUTS-AND-BOLTS

BUGS
Tropical weather means bugs are inevitable. Ants, cockroaches and geckoes in your accommodations don't necessarily indicate uncleanliness.

STREAMS & WATERFALLS
Don't enter waterfalls or streams with open cuts – leptospirosis, a bacteria present in Hawai'i's streams, can make you quite sick.

SUN INTENSITY
Hawai'i is in the tropics, and the sun can be more intense than elsewhere.

FAST FACTS

Time Zone
GMT-10

Country Code
+1

Electricity
120V/60Hz

GOOD TO KNOW

The US issues 90-day visas on arrival to citizens of 42 countries.

The legal drinking age is 21, and recreational cannabis is not legal in Hawai'i.

Wait for the crosswalk: drivers don't watch for jay-walkers.

Street parking may require a QR scan so don't forget your cellphone.

Don't put too much faith in your weather app – they don't usually tell the whole story.

ACCESSIBLE TRAVEL

Hotels Newer hotels have accessible rooms and facilities. Book well in advance.

O'ahu Offers the most activities with reliable wheelchair accessibility, including many of the top attractions.

O'ahu buses All are wheelchair accessible. O'ahu also has a paratransit service, TheHandi-Van (thehandivan.org), for those who are ADA Paratransit Eligible.

Trails Some are paved and suitable for wheelchairs and those with sight impairments.

O'ahu beaches Some offer all-terrain wheelchairs, particularly in Waikīkī.

Crosswalks Most do not have audible cross signals but do have curb cuts.

Accessibility resources Check out health.hawaii.gov/dcab/community-resources/travel-tips-for-people-in-hawaii

SHOES OFF
If you're invited into a local home, remove your footwear.

LOCAL BEER
Look for ridges at the top of aluminum cans signifying they were packaged locally.

MILD WILDLIFE
There are no bears, snakes, ticks, deadly spiders or rabies on Hawai'i's mountain trails.

BARGAIN SHOPPING
Though it's not exactly shopping local, families traveling together would be wise to do what many locals do to save money on meals, snacks and gas – visit Costco and buy in bulk (membership required). Honolulu's Costco is the world's busiest.

FAMILY TRAVEL
Rash guards Great for active kids who don't want to slow down to reapply sunscreen.

***Keiki* (child) discounts** Kids under 12, found at most attractions.

Check surf conditions Always check before heading to the beach. Don't expect to swim at any north-facing beaches during winter.

Local food Even for picky palates local food is easy. Try *mochiko* chicken, Spam *musubi*, shave ice and saimin.

Expect mud Make sure kids are dressed to get dirty on hikes.

HOMELESS
Hawai'i has a very visible homeless population. Many homeless people have jobs and families but simply can't afford Hawai'i's ever-increasing costs of living. Be mindful of your surroundings and be respectful to those you encounter. Use common sense when it comes to personal safety.

VIDAHAWAII/SHUTTERSTOCK

LGBTIQ+ TRAVELERS
Hawai'i has long been accepting of queer and nonbinary people. Look up the Hawaiian concept of *māhū* to learn how far back it goes.

Honolulu has the largest gay scene in the islands, but you'll likely find it lacking compared to other large cities.

Lei is an LGBTQ+ travel publication. Follow @leiculture on Instagram or visit its website (leiculture.com) for the latest in contemporary local queer culture.

Pride Guide Hawai'i (gogayhawaii.com) has island-specific info on all facets of gay-friendly travel.

Index

A

accessible travel 248
accommodations 246-7, *see also* camping, *individual locations*
activities 12, 19, 22-9, *see also* *individual activities*
ahupua'a 11, 33, 100-1, 230
air travel 238-9, 241
airports 238-9
'Akaka Falls State Park 221
Alaka'i Swamp 126
aloha 56-7
amusement parks 175
animals, *see also* wildlife, *individual animals*
  cat sanctuaries 173
  dogs shelter (hiking with) 120-1
aquaculture 228-9
architecture 76
art 18, 61, 74, 166
art galleries, *see* murals, museums & galleries
ATMs 243
ATV tours 19, 105

B

B&Bs 246
Banzai Pipeline 103
Barking Sands 125

000 Map pages

beach parks
  'Ehukai Beach Park 103
  Hālawa Beach Park 179, 189
  Ho'okena Beach Park 218
  Keawa'ula Beach Park 91
  Kohanaiki Beach Park (Pine Trees) 218
  One Ali'i Beach Park 189, 198
  Prince Kūhiō Beach Park 69
  Pūpūkea Beach Park 104-5
  Waimānalo Bay Beach Park 111
beaches
  accessibility 219, 248
  'Anaeho'omalu (A-Bay) 218
  Glass Beach 140
  Hāpuna Beach 219
  Hamoa Beach 165
  Hulopo'e Beach 173
  Kahuku 34
  Kaiolohia 174
  Kalalau Beach 118
  Kapukahehu Beach 189
  Kepuhi Beach 189
  Ko Olina Lagoons 111
  Laniākea Beach (Turtle Beach) 103
  Lanikai Beach 111
  Manini'ōwali Beach 219
  Pāpōhaku Beach 189, 192, 198
  Pohoiki Black Sand Beach 209
  Polihale Beach 127
  safety 242, 249
  Salt Pond Beach 140
  Sandy Beach 73, 92
  Shipwreck Beach 174
  Sugar Beach 157
  Tunnels (Makua) Beach 140
  Waikōloa 205
  Waimea Bay 111
  Wāwāmalu 73, 92
beer 249, *see also* breweries
bicycle travel, *see* cycling, mountain biking
bike-share stations 240
birds 14-15, 132, 134-5, 160-1, 223
bird-watching 31, 132-3, 223
black-sand beaches 218
blowholes 99, 140
boat travel 241
books 42
breweries 61, 121, 140, 147
bus travel 240
Byodo-In Temple 99

C

camping 86-7, 118, 247
canoeing 21, 24, 156-7, *see also* kayaking
car travel 40, 240, 248, *see also* scenic drives
carbon tax calculators 245

cat sanctuaries 173
chickens 134-5
children, travel with, *see* family travel
chocolate 16, 140, 226
climate 22-9, 41, 248
climate change 245
coffee
festivals 17, 24, 212
Hawai'i Island (The Big Island) 225, 226
Kona Coffee Belt 17, 212-13, **213**
Ko'olau 99
costs 239, 240, 243, 246
credit cards 243
cruise ships 239
culture & heritage 6-7, 10-11, 50-3, 196-7, 216-17, 222-3, *see also* food, history, language, lei
ahupua'a 11, 33, 100-1, 230
aloha 56-7
festivals 25, 28
hula 25, 28, 55, 126, 204, 217
landcare 10-11, 106-9, 222-3
lū'au 54-5
petroglyphs 175, 216, 230
currents 242
cycling 19, 48, 190-3, 198, 240

D

disabilities, travelers with 248
diving, *see also* snorkeling
Kona 214-15
Lāna'i 173
Moloka'i 186-7
North Shore, O'ahu 104-5
Pailolo Channel 21, 187
sharks, with 187
dogs, shelter (hiking with) 120-1
dolphins 160
Hulopo'e Beach 173
Kona 215
Mā'alaea Bay 157
Nāpali Coast 119
Pailolo Channel 187
Wai'anae Coast 91
driving, *see* car travel
duty-free shopping 243

E

ecosystems 210-11, 230-1
'Ehukai Beach Park 103
electricity 248
etiquette 249
events, *see* festivals & events

F

family travel 249
beaches 111
canoeing 156
hiking 79, 87
snorkeling 85
farm tours 16-17
Ali'i Kula Lavender 17, 170
Big Island Bees 225
Greenwell Farms 213
Gunstock Ranch 99
Hamakua Chocolate 226
Hanalei Taro 137
Honomu Goat Dairy 221
Kahuku Farms 110
Kahumana Organic Farms 91
Kona Coffee Living History Farm 225
Kona Sea Salt 228
Kula Country Farms 155
Kumu Farms 185
Lokoea Farms 110
Maui 154-5
Maui Bees 155
Moloka'i 184-5
Molokai Plumerias 185
Ocean Rider Seahorse Farm 228
OK Farms 225-6
Purdy's Macadamia Nut Farm 17, 185
Sweet Land Farm 110
festivals & events 22-9
Art + Flea 75
Chinese New Year 95
Hawai'i Walls 61
Hōlualoa Village Coffee & Art Stroll 212
Jaws Big Wave Championships 169
Ka Molokai Makahiki 180
Kamehameha Day 23, 55
Kona Coffee Cultural Festival 17, 24, 212
Korean Festival 95
Lei Day 29, 55
Merrie Monarch 28, 217
Molokai Ka Hula Piko Festival 180
Obon 22, 95
Okinawan Festival 95
Waimea Cherry Blossom Heritage Festival 26
Prince Kūhiō Festival 55
film locations
Jurassic Park 130-1
Lost World, The 191
Pirates of the Caribbean: On Stranger Tides 119
films 43
fish 138-9
fishing 196-7, 198

fishponds 107
He'eia Fishpond 107-8
Kālokō Honokōhau National Historical Park 216
Kaloko'eli Fishpond 198
Keāhole 33
Kīholo Preserve 223
Loko Ea Fishpond 109
flora 15, 88-9
food 13, 16-17, 96-7, *see also individual locations*
books 42
chocolate 16, 140, 226
festivals 24, 29
lū'au 54-5
seafood 228-9
Spam 29, 83, 96
taro 31, 78, 85, 117
taro patches 55, 108, 136-7, 185

G

galleries, *see* museums & galleries
games 85
gardens & parks, *see also* beach parks
Amy BH Greenwell Ethnobotanical Garden 216-17
Foster Botanical Garden 79
Hawai'i Tropical Botanical Garden 221
Ho'omaluhia Botanical Garden 87
Isaac Hale Park 209
Keahiakawelo 174-5
Koko Crater Botanical Garden 79
Lyon Arboretum 79
National Tropical Botanical Garden's Allerton Garden 131

000 Map pages

gay travelers 249
geography 210-11, 230-1
Glass Beach 140
golf 140

H

Hālawa Beach Park 189
Hālawa Valley 9, 181, 182-3, 185, 191-2
Haleakalā National Park 12, 37, 39, 149, 152-3, 162-3
Hale'iwa 34, 104
Halema'uma'u Crater 207
Hāmākua Coast 39, 220-1, **221**
Hāna 147
Hāna Coast 37, 164-5, **165**
Hānaiakāmalama 32, 53
Hanalei 31, 117
Hanapēpē 126
Hāpuna Beach 219
Hawai'i Island (The Big Island) 200-35, **202-3**
accommodations 205
costs 204
diving 214-15
drinking 205, 212-13, 235, **213**
farm tours 224-6
food 205, 221, 224-7, 228-9, 235
geography 230-1
helicopter tours 234
internet access 205
money 205
navigation 205
planning 202-3, 204-5
scenic drives 220-1, **221**
shopping 234
skydiving 234
snorkeling 219
surfing 218
swimming 219
travel seasons 204
travel to/from Hawai'i 204
travel within Hawai'i 204
volcanoes 206-9
volunteering 222-3
wi-fi 205
Hawai'i Ocean Science & Technology Park (HOST Park) 228-9
Hawai'i Volcanoes National Park 9, 39, 206-9, 216, 222
Hawaiian Kingdom 6, 40
monarchs 66-7
significant sites 32, 53, 63, 68-9, 174, 217
Hawaiian monk seals 41, 161, 223
Kaulakahi Channel 129
Kepuhi Beach 189
Nāpali 119
Pailolo Channel 187
Hawaiian Renaissance 7, 63
He'eia State Park 85
He'eia Wetlands 33, 108
heiau 230
Hālawa Valley 183
Halulu Heiau 175
Kūka'ō'ō Heiau 52
Pu'ukohola Heiau 32, 217
helicopter tours 19, 129, 131, 164, 170, 234
hiking 8-9, 242
Fagan's Cross 165
Hālawa Valley 9, 182-3
Haleakalā National Park 149, 152-3
Hawai'i Volcanoes National Park 9, 39, 207-8
Honolulu 79
Honolulu Mauka Trail System 8, 47, 64-5

Ho'opi'i Falls 141
Kahuku Unit 208
Kalalau Valley 8, 118, 125
Kalāwahine Trail 64
Kapa'a Bike Path 121
Keonehe'ehe'e Trail 9, 152
Lanikai Pillbox Hike 93
Māhā'ulepū Beach Heritage Trail 121
Makapu'u Lighthouse Trail 92
Nā Ala Hele 65
Nāpali Coast 8, 118-19
Nounou Mountain 121
Okolehau Trail 141
Pu'u Pehe 174
Shipwreck Beach 174
safety 242
Waihe'e Ridge Trail 152
Waimea Canyon 8, 30, 141
historic sites
Pā'ula'ula State Historic Site 125
Pearl Harbor 62-3
Pu'ukoholā Heiau National Historic Site 32, 217
history 6-7, 50-3, 62-3, 105, 125, 216-17, *see also* culture & heritage, Hawaiian Kingdom, plantations
books 42
festivals & events 22, 25
itineraries 32-3, **32-3**
homeless population 75, 249
Hōnaunau Bay 21, 33
Honolulu 35, 44-79, **46-7**
accommodations 49
architecture 76
breweries 61
Chinatown 31, 35, 53, 74-7, 95
costs 48, 49
culture 50-3, 54-5, 56-7
Downtown 74-7
drinking 49, 61, 77
food 49, 55, 59, 71, 77, 78-9
heiau 52
hiking 8, 47, 64-5, 79
history 50-3, 62-3
homeless population 75
internet access 49
Kaimukī 35, 58-9
Kaka'ako 30, 60-1
Lē'ahi 35, 70-1, **70**
money 49
museums & galleries 74-5
navigation 49
planning 46-7, 48-9
shopping 59, 61, 76-7, 78
surfing 68
travel seasons 48
travel to/from Honolulu 48, 238
travel within Honolulu 48, 239
volunteering 52
Waikīkī 20, 33, 35, 68-9, **68**
walking tours 68-9, 70-1, **69**, **71**
wetlands 63
wi-fi 49
Honolulu Mauka Trail System 8, 47, 64-5
honu 15, 21, 41, 103, 173
Ho'okena Beach Park 218
hula 25, 28, 55, 126, 204, 217
hurricanes 22, 242

I

insurance 240
internet resources 245, 247
'Iolani Palace 33, 63
itineraries 30-9, **30-1**, **32-3**, **34-5**, **36-7**, **38-9**, *see also individual locations*

J

jellyfish 242

K

Ka Lae 234
Kā'anapali 37
Ka'ena Point State Park 91
Kahekili's Leap 175
Kahuku 35
Kaka'ako 60-1
Kalalau Valley 8, 118, 125
Kalaupapa 36, 183
Kamakou Preserve 183, 191, 192
Kamehameha the Great 32, 66, 175, 217
Kāne'ohe Bay 84-5
Kapahulu 31
Kapuaiwa Coconut Grove 198
Kapukahehu Bay 198
Kapukahehu Beach 189
Kaua'i 112-41, **114-15**
accommodations 117
costs 116
drinking 117
food 117, 140-1
helicopter tours 19, 131
hiking 8, 118-19, 120-1, 141
kayaking 119, 140
money 117
navigation 117
planning 114-15, 116-17
plantations 122-3, **123**
scenic drives 122-3, **123**
shopping 141
travel seasons 116
travel to/from Kaua'i 116
travel within Kaua'i 116
weather 116, 117
wi-fi 117

Kaunakakai 36, 181, 185
Kaunolū 175
Kawai'ele State Waterbird Sanctuary 133
Kawaihae 32
kayaking, *see also* canoeing
'Anahulu River 104
Kāne'ohe Bay 84-5
Mākena Landing 159
Nāpali Coast 30, 119
Wailua River 140
Kazumura Cave 234-5
Keāhole 33
Keaīwa Heiau State Recreation Area 87
Keau'ohana Forest Reserve 223
Kepuhi Beach 189
Kīlauea Point 133
Ko Olina Lagoons 111
Kōke'e State Park 31, 126
Kona Coffee Belt 17, 212-13, **213**
Ko'olau Range 98-9, **99**
Kualoa Regional Park 87
Kula 149

L

Lahaina 40
Lāna'i 36-7, 172-5
Lāna'i Adventure Park 175
language 7, 40, 107
directional words 41
Hawaiian Pidgin 95
place names 72-3
Lapakahi State Historical Park 216
lava tubes 206, 234
legal matters 15, 41, 240, 248

000 Map pages

Lehua 129
lei 53, 88, 151, 170, 185
Lei Day 29, 55
shell 129, 149
leper colonies 36
leptospirosis 248
LGBTIQ+ travelers 249
Līhu'e-Kōloa Forest Reserve 131
literature 42
location tagging 51, 245
lo'i 231
loko i'a, *see* fishponds
lū'au 54-5
luxury estates 246

M

Mā'alaea Bay 21
Makawao 149
mālama 'āina 10-11, 222-3
malasadas 97
manta rays 161, 187, 214-15
Manini'ōwali Beach 219
markets
Hawai'i Island (The Big Island) 227
Kaua'i 140
Honolulu 61, 71
Maui 17, 155
Maui 142-71, **144-5**
accommodations 147
costs 146
drinking 147, 171
food 147, 154-5, 170-1
helicopter tours 164, 170
hiking 149, 152-3, 164
itineraries 36-7, **37**
kayaking 159
money 147
navigation 147
paragliding 170
planning 144-5, 146-7
Polynesian canoeing 21, 156-7
shopping 149, 150-1, 155, 166
snorkeling 158, 165, 170
stargazing 162-3
surfing 168-9, 170
travel seasons 146
travel to/from Maui 146
travel within Maui 146, 170
walking tours 166-7, **167**
whale-watching 158-9
wi-fi 147
Maui Nui 36-7, **36-7**
Maunakea 39, 223, 232-3
Maunaloa 181, 212
Moku'ae'ae Rock Islet Seabird Sanctuary 133
Moloka'i 176-99, **178-9**
accommodations 181, 185
costs 180
cycling 190-3, 198
diving 186-7
drinking 181
entertainment 198-9
farm tours 184-5
fishing 196-7, 198
food 181, 184-5, 192, 199
hiking 182-3
itineraries 36-7
money 181
navigation 181
planning 178-9, 180-1
safe travel 188
scenic drives 188-9, **189**
shopping 199
snorkeling 186-7, 189
travel seasons 180
travel to/from Moloka'i 180
travel within Moloka'i 180, 181
wi-fi 181

monarchy 66-7, *see also* Hawaiian Kingdom
money 238, 243
monk seals, *see* Hawaiian monk seals
mountain biking 19, 191, *see also* cycling
Mt Wai'ale'ale 130
murals 18, 26, 166-7, 208, **167**
museums & galleries 18
ARTS at Mark's Garage 75
Bishop Museum 51
Grove Farm Museum 123
Hawai'i State Art Museum 75
Hawaii's Plantation Village 94
Honolulu Museum of Art 75
Japanese Cultural Center of Hawai'i 63
Lāna'i Culture & Heritage Center 174
Molokai Museum & Cultural Center 199
Pāhoa Lava Zone Museum 208
Shangri La 71
music 42, 55

N

Nāpali Coast 20, 30, 118-19, 130
Nāhuku 208
national & state parks 205
'Akaka Falls State Park 221
Haleakalā National Park 12, 37, 39, 149, 152-3, 162-3
Hawai'i Volcanoes National Park 9, 39, 206-9, 216, 222
He'eia State Park 85
Ka'ena Point State Park 91
Kalaupapa National Historical Park 183
Kōke'e State Park 31, 126
Lapakahi State Historical Park 216
Pālā'au State Park 36, 198
Pu'uhonua o Hōnaunau National Historical Park 217
Wai'ānapanapa State Park 165
Ni'ihau 128-9
North Kohala 38
North Shore, O'ahu 20, 102-5
Nu'uanu Pali 32

O

O'ahu 80-111, **34-5**, **82**, *see also* Honolulu
accommodations 83
boating 84-5
camping 86-7
costs 83
culture 106-9
diving 104
drinking 83, 110-11
food 83, 85, 93, 94-5, 96-7, 104, 110-11
hiking 92-3
itineraries 34-5, 98-9, **34-5**
planning 82, 83
plantations 94-5
scenic drives 98-9, **99**
safety 103
snorkeling 84-5, 104, 111
stargazing 86-7
surfing 91, 103-4
travel to/from O'ahu 83
travel within O'ahu 83
viewpoints 92, 99
volunteering 106-9
weather 93
whale-watching 91
wi-fi 83
'ōhi'a lehua trees 207
'Ōlelo Hawai'i 7
One Ali'i Beach Park 189, 198

P

Pāhoa 208-9
Pailolo Channel 187
Pālā'au State Park 36, 198
Pā'ula'ula State Historic Site 125
palaces 33, 53, 76
Pāpōhaku Beach 189, 192
paragliding 170
parks, *see* gardens & parks
Pe'ahi 168-9
Pearl Harbor 62-3
petroglyphs 175, 216, 230
planning 22-43, 238-49, *see also individual locations*
plantations 13, 22, 32, 94-5, 122-3, **123**
plants 15, 88-9
plastic bags 41
Pohoiki Black Sand Beach 209
Polihale Beach 127
Polynesian canoeing 21, 24, 156-7
Polynesian Wayfinding 12, 163
public transportation 241
Punalu'u 218
Pu'u'ualaka'a State Wayside 65
Pu'uhonua o Hōnaunau National Historical Park 217
Pu'ukoholā Heiau National Historic Site 32, 217
Pu'uloa (Pearl Harbor) 62-3

Q

Queen Lili'uokalani 67

R

Rapid 'Ōhia Death (ROD) 244
rappelling 140
resorts 246, 247

responsible travel 10-11, 40-1, 52, 244-5, *see also* culture & heritage, volunteering
bike-share stations 240
carbon footprint calculators 241, 245
location tagging 51, 245
'talking story' 54
wildlife 14-15
rideshares 240
road trips, *see* scenic drives
rum tours 94

S

safe travel 87, 242, 248
Salt Pond Beach 140
Sandy Beach 92
scenic drives
Hāmākua Coast 220-1, **221**
Hāna Coast 164-5, **165**
Kaua'i 122-3, **123**
Kona Coffee Belt 212-13, **213**
Ko'olau Mountains 98-9, **99**
Moloka'i 188-9, **189**
seafood 228-9
shaka 13
sharks 187
shells 194-5
shopping 243, 249, *see also individual locations*
SIM cards 238
skydiving 234
snorkeling, *see also* diving
Hālawa Beach Park 189
Hamoa Beach 165
Hōnaunau Bay 21, 219
Kāne'ohe Bay 84-5
Kealakekua Bay 219
Mokuho'oniki 186
Moloka'i 186-7, 189
Molokini Crater 158
North Shore, O'ahu 104
Pūpūkea Beach Park 104
Waimea Bay 111
social media 43, 51, 245
sovereignty movement 7, 40
Spam 29, 83, 96
spas 170
stargazing 12, 86-7, 162-3, 232-3
sunscreen 10, 41
surfing 18, 27, 43, 116
'Anaeho'omalu Bay (A-Bay) 218
Kahalu'u Bay 218
Kohanaiki Beach Park (Pine Trees) 218
Maui 168-9, 170
North Shore 20, 103-4
Pe'ahi 168-9
Wai'anae Coast 91
Waikīkī 20, 68
swimming 219, 242

T

taro 31, 78, 85, 117
taro patches 55, 108, 136-7, 185
taxes 243
telephone services 238
television shows 43
theft 242
time 248
tipping 243
tours 19, *see also* ATV tours, farm tours, helicopter tours, scenic drives, rum tours, walking tours
travel seasons 22-9, 242, *see also individual locations*
travel to/from Hawai'i 238-9
travel within Hawai'i 40, 240-1
treaty, lack of 7
trekking, *see* hiking
tsunamis 242
tubing 13, 122-3
turtles 15, 21, 41, 103, 173

V

vegetarian & vegan travelers 111
viewpoints
Diamond Head Lookout 47, 71
'End of the Road' Lookout 209
Kalaeokauna'oa (Kahuku Point) 99
Lanikai Pillbox Hike 92
Nu'uanu Pali State Wayside 53
Pali Lookout 53
Pu'u'ualaka'a State Wayside 65
Waikolu Lookout 192
Waimea Canyon Lookout 127
visas 248
volcanoes 9, 39, 152, 206-9, 242
volunteering 106-9, 244
Hawai'i Island (The Big Island) 222-3
He'eia Fishpond 107-8
He'eia Wetlands 108-9
Honolulu 52
Loko Ea Fishpond 109
Hui O Ho'ohonua 63

W

Wai'anae Coast 34, 90-1
Wai'ānapanapa State Park 165
Waikapala'e 119
Waikīkī 20, 33, 35, 68-9, **68**
Waikōloa Dry Forest Preserve 223
Wailuku 166-7, **167**
Waimea Canyon 8, 30, 127, 141
Waimea Valley 105
Waipi'o Valley 220, 221

000 Map pages

walking, *see* hiking
walking tours
  Honolulu 70-1, **71**
  Maui 166-7, **167**
  Waikīkī 68-9, **68**
water sports 20-1, 242
waterfalls 248
  ʻAkaka Falls 221
  Hipuapua Falls 183
  Hoʻoipʻi Falls 131, 141
  Mānāwaiopuna Falls 130
  Mānoa Falls 79
  Moʻoula Falls 183
  Red Dirt Waterfall 127
  safety 248
  Twin Falls 165
  Waimoku 153
  Waipoʻo Falls 8, 127
Wāwāmalu 92
weather 22-9, 41, 248, *see also individual locations*
websites 245, 247
wetlands 63
whales 159, 160
whale-watching 15, 222
  Lānaʻi 37, 173
  Māʻalaea Bay 157
  Māhāʻulepū Beach Heritage Trail 121
  Maui 158-9
  Mokuhoʻoniki 186
  seasons 27, 116, 146, 204
  Waiʻanae Coast 91
wildlife 14-15, 38-9, 160-1, 215, 242, 249, *see also individual animals*
windsurfing 165
Windward Coast, Oʻahu 35

'During Kīlauea's eruptions I took a boat to watch lava hit the ocean and a doors-off helicopter to feel the heat from above. It's crazy to see the landscape literally transforming before your eyes.'

MEGHAN MINER MURRAY

'I'd been to the Bishop Museum several times as a kid, but I didn't realize how much more interesting it would be as an adult!'

JACKIE OSHIRO

'Nothing like watching a mama whale teach her baby to tail slap. Especially when you're nearby in an outrigger canoe.'

SARAH SEKULA

'The first time I tried shave ice was at Wailua Shave Ice on Kaua'i, and their pineapple strawberry creation atop vanilla ice cream is still my favorite.'

MEGHAN MINER MURRAY

'I was so stoked the first time I spotted a chameleon in the wild. As a photographer, I fully appreciate their slow movements.'

SARAH SEKULA

FROM LEFT: YVONNE BAUR/SHUTTERSTOCK, JUSTIN BERKEN/SHUTTERSTOCK

THIS BOOK

This 2nd edition of Lonely Planet's *Experience Hawai'i* guidebook was researched by Meghan Miner Murray, Amy C Balfour and Sarah Etinas. The previous edition was researched and written by Meghan Miner Murray, Jackie Oshiro and Sarah Sekula. This guidebook was produced by the following:

Destination editor
Melissa Yeager

Product editor
Katie Connolly

Cartographer
Hunor Csutoros

Assisting editor
Laura Crawford

Image researcher
Eoin T Loughney

Cover researcher
Matthew Dekneef

Thanks Ronan Abayawickrema, Kellie Langdon, Charlotte Orr